ROUTLEDGE LIBRARY EDITIONS:
POLITICAL PROTEST

Volume 17

POPULAR PROTEST AND PUBLIC ORDER

POPULAR PROTEST AND PUBLIC ORDER

Six Studies in British History, 1790–1920

Edited by
R. QUINAULT AND J. STEVENSON

Routledge
Taylor & Francis Group

LONDON AND NEW YORK

First published in 1974 by George Allen & Unwin Ltd.

This edition first published in 2022
by Routledge
2 Park Square, Milton Park, Abingdon, Oxon OX14 4RN

and by Routledge
605 Third Avenue, New York, NY 10158

Routledge is an imprint of the Taylor & Francis Group, an informa business

© 1974 George Allen & Unwin Ltd.

British Library Cataloguing in Publication Data
A catalogue record for this book is available from the British Library

ISBN: 978-1-03-203038-8 (Set)
ISBN: 978-1-00-319086-8 (Set) (ebk)
ISBN: 978-1-03-203358-7 (Volume 17) (hbk)
ISBN: 978-1-03-203359-4 (Volume 17) (pbk)
ISBN: 978-1-00-318689-2 (Volume 17) (ebk)

DOI: 10.4324/9781003186892

Publisher's Note
The publisher has gone to great lengths to ensure the quality of this reprint but points out that some imperfections in the original copies may be apparent.

Disclaimer
The publisher has made every effort to trace copyright holders and would welcome correspondence from those they have been unable to trace.

Popular Protest and Public Order

Six Studies in British History
1790–1920

Edited by
R. QUINAULT and J. STEVENSON

London   George Allen & Unwin Ltd
Ruskin House   Museum Street

Printed in Great Britain
in 11 point Baskerville type
by Alden & Mowbray Ltd
at the Alden Press, Oxford

To R. M. Hartwell
with appreciation

The Contributors

R. QUINAULT
Educated at Magdalen College and Nuffield College, Oxford, and spent a year studying at Columbia University. Now working on the landed interest and the decline of the aristocracy in Victorian Britain.

J. STEVENSON
Educated at Worcester College and Nuffield College, Oxford. Lecturer in Modern History at Oriel College from 1971.

E. RICHARDS
Author of *The Leviathan of Wealth* (1973) and several articles on Scottish economic and social history; now lectures at The Flinders University of South Australia.

D. PHILIPS
Born Johannesburg, South Africa; educated at Witwatersrand University and Nuffield College, Oxford. Now lectures at the University of Melbourne and is working on crime in mid-nineteenth century England.

F. C. MATHER
Author of *Public Order in the Age of the Chartists* (1959) and *After the Canal Duke* (1970). Senior Lecturer in History at the University of Southampton.

I. McLEAN
Born 1946; educated at Christ Church, Oxford; student and research fellow, Nuffield College, 1967–71. Lecturer in Politics at the University of Newcastle since 1971. Now working on a life of Keir Hardy.

Contents

Introduction   *page*   15

1   Food Riots in England, 1792–1818   33
    by J. STEVENSON

2   Patterns of Highland Discontent,
    1790–1860   75
    by E. RICHARDS

3   The General Strike of 1842: A Study
    in Leadership, Organisation and the
    Threat of Revolution during the Plug
    Plot Disturbances   115
    by F. C. MATHER

4   Riots and Public Order in the Black
    Country, 1835–1860   141
    by D. PHILIPS

5   The Warwickshire County Magistracy
    and Public Order, c. 1830–1870   181
    by R. QUINAULT

6   Popular Protest and Public Order:
    Red Clydeside, 1915–1919   215
    by IAIN MCLEAN

Maps

Food riots in South-eastern England in 1795–6 and
1800–1   44

Locations of Highland disorder, 1790–1860   79

Tables

1 Average price of wheat per quarter in England and
   Wales, 1792–1818   35

2 Burials per year in England and Wales, 1792–1818   38

3 Average price of wheat per quarter in England in
   1795–6 and the number of disturbances reported   52

4 Locations and kinds of Highland disorder in the
   first half of the nineteenth century   96

5 Number of sets of prosecutions, and individual
   indictments for riot and allied offences, in the
   Black Country, 1835–60   166

Introduction

During recent years no aspect of the social history of modern Britain has aroused more general interest and controversy than the study of popular protest and public order. This interest has been stimulated by the wave of riots and disturbance which swept over Europe and America in the 1960s. Yet it would be wrong to assume that academic historical studies in this field are merely a passing fashion. For in Britain at least the present interest in such questions is part of a much longer process: the gradual, but fundamental revision of the assumptions that underlie traditional accounts of the development of modern Britain. One of the principal canons of the orthodox version of our history is the belief that the peaceful evolution of our national institutions has been the hall-mark that has made Britain unique among the developed nations.

This emphasis on the peaceful character of modern Britain has, of course, some foundation in fact. But a variety of influences have tended to exaggerate the extent of such peaceful development and the reasons for such stability remain largely conjectural. Until recently, the Whig school of historiography was universally influential – indeed it still forms the foundations of many popular histories of Britain. This interpretation regarded the conflict between King and Parliament in the seventeenth century as the critical period in our national development. As apologists for the Revolution of 1688, the adherents of this school had little incentive to search for symptoms of protest and disorder in the subsequent history of Britain. Hence the view that the eighteenth century was merely a period of political stability and national expansion despite the existence of a virile radical tradition which helped to conceive both parliamentary reform and the American Revolution. Hence also the convenient exclusion of the disorders and coercion in Ireland and Scotland from the framework of English politics despite the Acts of Union.

The stress on the peaceful nature of British development has also reflected national insularity and chauvinism. In the nineteenth century the political *bouleversements* and excesses on the Continent were implicitly condemned by reference to the distaste for such proceedings in Britain. Such views were largely founded on emotive patriotism but were sometimes based on a misleading semblance of reason. To take one example, much of the strength of the British reaction to the French Revolution is to be ascribed to a traditional suspicion of French ambitions in a territorial rather than a constitutional context. Moreover, the worst excesses of the Revolution commenced only after Britain had joined in a coercive offensive alliance against France. What was true in 1794 was also true in 1870: the political system of France bent under the pressure of foreign invasion – with bloody consequences.

Such a conclusion is highly relevant in the context of the relative political stability of Britain. Between 1805 and 1914 Britain enjoyed a security from foreign invasion of a much higher order than the limited degree of protection which the continental powers erected against one another. In a real sense, it was the Royal Navy (and the national wealth that paid for it) rather than domestic reform which reduced the chances of political extremism. The security of the country and the empire also placated the army, which was socially too wedded to the governing establishment to feel excluded from power. The influential political career of the Duke of Wellington was not without significance in this context. Thus by retaining its military power and prestige untarnished the government ensured that political violence – save for assassination – was *hors de combat*.

It has to be recognised that the power and security of the governing establishment has played a major role in ensuring the peaceful evolution of British society. This is not to say that such power was in any way sufficient on its own to secure stability, but simply that it was one of the necessary prerequisites for such evolution. Yet the reality of this situation has only become apparent in historical accounts of temporary emergencies – such as the Chartist agitations in the North of England. For most of the time the truth has been obscured as much by liberal sensitivities as by the secretive policies of the authorities. Thus the Duke of Bedford, for example, confidentially admitted in 1914 that he was in favour of arming the 'classes' to protect them from the masses, but he was not prepared to say so in public.

At the other end of the spectrum we are becoming increasingly aware of the wide range of popular disturbances that have occurred in Britain since the beginning of the industrial revolution. Some of these disorders have been the focus of specialised historical investigation for many years but it is only more recently that attempts have been made to relate the findings to wider questions.

One of the earliest historians to draw attention to the incidence of popular protest in Britain was R. F. Wearmouth, who produced a useful chronicle of riots and disturbances for the eighteenth century. The Hammonds also dealt with some of the most important episodes of popular protest in their work on the social effects of industrial and agricultural change. But the first detailed study of a whole range of popular disturbances was that produced by Beloff for the period from 1660 to 1714. At about the same time, just before the Second World War, F. O. Darvall produced what is still the standard work on the Luddite disturbances and their suppression. Although in many ways Darvall's treatment of the causes of the Luddite outbreaks has been modified by later work, he gave much the most detailed and unbiased account to date of the workings of the authorities and the nature of the disturbances with which they were dealing. At a later date one of the present contributors produced a parallel and fascinating study of the organisation and mechanism of public order during the Chartist period.

However, although the studies of the apparatus of public order in England had progressed considerably, it was not until the pioneer work of G. Rudé that a new dimension was given to the study of popular protest. His work on the

Crowd in History, especially on the Parisian crowd in the French Revolution and the London 'mob' in the eighteenth century, opened several new lines of inquiry. In the first place the study of popular disturbances was rescued from relative obscurity by showing that crowd actions had an important influence upon the course of political events. In England Rudé's most important contribution in this direction was his classic work on the Wilkite movement, in which he showed the considerable involvement of the tradespeople and workmen of London. Further, his work on the composition and motivation of popular disturbances showed that the stereotypes commonly applied to the 'mob' by both contemporaries and later historians were highly misleading. Rudé preferred to use the less pejorative word 'crowd', for he considered 'mob' to contain overtones of irrationality and violence that were not borne out by a close study of crowd actions. He found that much popular action was a selective and disciplined form of protest, in which the populace acted in accordance with a coherent set of beliefs and values. His study of food rioting, both in England and France, suggested that they too were usually disciplined, rational, and often highly ritualised expressions of discontent. Rudé also found from an analysis of London sessions' papers and poll-books that most rioters were neither criminal nor unemployed, but were a fairly typical cross-section of the capital's population. In the systematic use of these sources to examine the composition of crowds, his work marked a major methodological advance in the study of popular disturbances. Most of the recent studies of popular protest owe a considerable debt to the work of Rudé, and his constructive achievement in social history can be seen to best advantage in the joint study that he has undertaken with E. J. Hobsbawm of the 'Captain Swing' disturbances. It is only necessary to compare this work with Darvall's study of the Luddites, thirty years earlier, to observe the advances which have been made in this field.

The work of Rudé and others has brought popular protest within the orbit of traditional politics, particularly for the

eighteenth century. Thus the London 'mob' has been put
within the context of the 'unofficial opposition' – that of the
'political nation without-doors'. Rudé has written that in
eighteenth-century London the opposition characteristically
took the form of a loose and temporary alliance between the
'middling elements' and the streets. Of the great agitations,
such as the Wilkite and Gordon episodes, he claims that:
'Anomic and associational movements, social protest and
political demands, well-organised and clear-sighted interest
groups and "direct-action" crowds, leaders and followers
came together in a chorus of united opposition . . .'[1]

The linking of popular disturbances with political action of
a formal kind has been taken further by Tilly, in a general
survey of collective violence in Europe, who argues that all
popular protest, especially violent protest, must be seen as
essentially 'political'. 'Instead of constituting a sharp break
from "normal" political life', he writes, 'violent protests tend
to accompany, complement, and extend organised, peaceful
attempts by the same people to accomplish their objectives.'
Similarly Hobsbawm has coined the convenient phrase
'collective bargaining by riot' for the extension of negotiation
through disorder by workmen in the early nineteenth
century. The problem with Tilly's view of popular protest is
that it stretches the definition of what is political so far as
almost to render it meaningless. The view that any violent
protest can be regarded as 'political' may be a convenient
one for political scientists, but for the historian it obscures
more than it reveals. More often historians are concerned
with the subjective perceptions of the participants in popular
protest, and whether they see themselves as acting against
the authority of the state or not. In this respect it is important
to make clear in what sense instances of popular protest are
being judged 'political', otherwise confusion can arise
between different levels of analysis.

Nonetheless, from the early forms of 'collective bargaining
by riot' there is a clear development of attempts to influence
the status quo by the use of protest. In the nineteenth and
twentieth centuries this has increasingly taken non-violent

forms, such as demonstrations and some kinds of strike. Tilly has characterised 'modern' disturbances as involving 'specialised associations with relatively well-defined objectives, organised for political or social action'. He has suggested that they tend 'to develop from collective actions that offer a show of force but are not intrinsically violent'. He argues that Britain was the first country to develop 'modern' forms of protest in the form of orderly demonstrations and strikes, from which violence only occasionally arose. He suggests that 'modern' protest is often expressed as an inter-action between the protesters and the authorities, claiming that in the twentieth century 'almost all collective violence on a significant scale involves the political authorities and their professional representatives: policemen, soldiers, and others'. A modern work on the police in contemporary Britain has suggested rather succinctly that recent demonstrations in London have essentially been 'a public relations contest, in which the demonstrators try to force the police to be seen as violent'. Thus where early 'collective bargaining by riot' attempted directly to influence employers or some section of the authorities, the development of demonstrations and strikes has given rise to a form of 'politics of protest', in which the demonstrators attempt to show their strength in numbers and determination whilst the authorities attempt to contain their protest within certain bounds. In Britain it can be seen that this type of 'political' protest developed at a relatively early date. Peterloo provided a classic example of a situation in which the government lost ground considerably because of their harsh treatment of an orderly and largely peaceful crowd, giving the radical press an enormous stick with which to belabour the government of the day. Here the crucial development was the early emergence of organised 'public opinion' in England, in the form of the popular press and political societies. From that time onwards, popular protest in England has usually been conducted in the full and conscious awareness that public opinion can be won or lost according to the behaviour of the participants, both authorities and protesters. It is in this context that most modern

popular protest should be seen, for it determines the character not only of the development of protest but also of the
actions taken by the authorities. As a result, the reactions of
the authorities and of protesters tend to show great regularity,
for example in the fear of the authorities that any large-scale
protest will be used by sinister forces for their own ends,
whilst protesters concentrate their attention upon charging
the army or the police with undue harshness. These elements
have been emerging in English popular protest from as early
as the post-Napoleonic period, and have been rehearsed as
recently as the anti-Vietnam demonstrations of 1968. They
reflect the extent to which popular protest in England has
increasingly become a sophisticated political game in which
two sides, the state and the protesters, battle for public
opinion, and in which points can be gained or lost at a
number of different stages in the exercise of the 'politics of
protest'.

Another feature of the contribution of popular protest to
political history is the way in which it can reveal the stage of
political development and the nature of political feelings
amongst otherwise inarticulate sections of the population.
Rudé's work on the London crowds in the eighteenth
century has shown that the primary political feelings there
were concepts of Englishmen's 'rights' and 'liberties',
mingled with a strong strain of anti-Popery and chauvinism.
Rudé has argued that these beliefs formed an early justification for the crowds' intervention in politics. He suggests
tentatively that in the semi-permanent and ritualised expressions of the mob can be found 'the first beginnings of the
mass Radical movement'. In a similar way E. P. Thompson
has suggested that English riots of the eighteenth century
showed a coherent set of assumptions about the world in
which the ordinary people lived and formed the basis for the
development of popular radicalism. Thompson has carried
the interpretation of popular protest even further, for in his
study of food riots he suggests that one can see in them the
resistance of eighteenth-century consumers to the adoption of
laissez-faire principles in the marketing of foodstuffs. Al-

though these conclusions are still under discussion and remain tentative, they illustrate the way in which popular protest can be used by historians to throw light upon the motives and beliefs of otherwise inaccessible groups of people. In one of the most detailed discussions of any outbreak of popular protest Hobsbawm and Rudé have carefully dissected the evidence for political involvement and motivation in the 'Captain Swing' disturbances, showing clearly that in the main the disturbances were motivated by economic and social factors rather than by politics. It is to further studies of popular protest in the nineteenth century that we can look for an appreciation of motives and attitudes behind many popular movements.

One of the most important ways in which historians touch upon popular protest is in relation to the growth of discontent within a society and the threat of revolution. It has been commonplace for British historians to regard periods of concentrated and violent protest as potentially revolutionary. It was this factor which made R. J. White regard the period following the Napoleonic Wars as the one in which England came closest to revolution. Other favourite candidates for near-revolutionary periods have been the 1840s and the periods both immediately before and after the First World War. There are two problems with this approach: the first is the difficult one of defining what is meant by a revolution, and the second is the nature of the relationship which popular protest has to revolution. There has been considerable discussion recently about the definition of revolution: interpretations vary between those who regard only certain 'great revolutions' as true candidates, whilst others are prepared to allow the much wider definition of any period of violent change. It is not our intention to enter this debate, but rather to raise the problem that faces British historians, with no recent 'model' of revolution to draw upon, of deciding whether a period is threatened with protest and discontent on a revolutionary scale. The conventional wisdom suggests that any period of protest, particularly violent protest, which is both sustained and directed at the political structure of the state, provides a crisis of near-revolutionary proportions. But even here it is important in any concrete discussion of the threat of revolution to make clear what conditions would give rise to an effective revolution in more precise terms than is usually done. Otherwise the description of situations by phrases such as 'near-revolutionary' do not add much to our understanding of their significance. Moreover, the way in which revolutions come about does not always conform to the conventional wisdom of historians. Those who regard a 'near-revolutionary' situation as one in which there is a swelling volume of protest conform to what has been called the 'natural history' view of revolutions. This has been summarised by C. Brinton who argues from a comparison of several revolutions that a revolutionary situation can be regarded as a 'fever' which infects the body politic, and of which the symptoms are increasing protest and discontent, eventually mounting to a revolutionary climax. Similarly the classic Marxist view expressed in the *Communist Manifesto* talks of the 'more or less veiled civil war, raging within existing society, up to the point where the war breaks out into open revolution, and where the violent overthrow of the bourgeoisie lays the foundation for the sway of the proletariat . . .'. Recently, however, this view has been challenged, for a careful quantitative study of the 1830 revolution in France has shown that far from there being a steady progression of disorder towards the overthrow of the government, most of the violent protest took place after it had been overthrown. Brinton himself has noted that many revolutions are accomplished with singularly little bloodshed in the period leading up to them and as they occur. Rather, experience of the Terror in France and the Civil War in Russia would suggest that the greater amount of violence often occurs after a revolution has taken place, when the new regime is defending itself and consolidating its position. Thus the easy equation of mounting popular protest and the threat of revolution is one which should be treated with great caution.

The presence of popular protest has also been seen as a

barometer of economic and social discontent. Rudé's work has shown that disturbances both in Paris and in London in the eighteenth century owed a great deal to movements of the price of bread. Several economic historians have drawn attention to the relationship between economic fluctuations and the incidence of popular disturbances. One of the earliest of these was W. W. Rostow who produced a 'social tension chart' constructed from the movement of the price of wheat and the fluctuations of the trade cycle. Similarly, T. S. Ashton highlighted the coincidence of popular disturbances and harvest failure in the course of the eighteenth century. More recently an attempt has been made by E. J. Hobsbawm to correlate economic fluctuations in the nineteenth century with a wide range of social movements, including not only food riots but the growth of trade unionism and political militancy. Some historians, however, have rejected the 'gross economic reductionism' of these explanations of popular protest. Certainly some of the most recent work on popular protest has shown that economic causes only operate as part of a complex process. Thus there is no direct relationship between absolute economic deprivation and popular protest, for if there were, popular protest would be much more common. Rather, it appears that popular protest is often motivated by 'relative deprivation' in which people perceive themselves to be underprivileged. It is this relationship between people's aspirations and their situation that is most crucial to the outbreak of popular protest. It is very close to the view of de Tocqueville that discontent within a society usually arises when the government is reforming itself and in so doing awakens new expectations and aspirations. Thus today one of the favourite 'models' of the cause of revolutions is a mathematical updating of de Tocqueville, which sees expectations raised by a period of reform or increasing prosperity, and then checked by a short-term crisis. A rather similar model might be suggested for popular protest, for there have been many periods of economic deprivation which have given rise to little popular protest, whilst it has often arisen from relatively privileged groups. This interpretation of popular protest offers a more complex view of the relationship between economic deprivation and popular protest, and it is one that would appear to be of relevance not only to modern forms of protest, such as strikes, but also to earlier incidents such as food riots.

It is also common to find popular protest, particularly violent protest, equated with periods of social and economic change, both as a symptom of discontent and as an instrument of change. Thus Marx wrote that violence 'is the midwife of every old society which is pregnant with a new one; it is the instrument with the aid of which social movement forces its way through and shatters the dead, fossilized political forms'. This was an early version of the theory that social unrest is caused by the lack of harmony between the social system and the political system. The extent of the upheaval that results from such a disequilibrium is partly determined by the stage of development of the society involved. In a medieval monarchy the discontent would usually take the form of a rebellion within the ranks of the governing elite, while in an underdeveloped country today it would take the form of a *coup d'état*, again within a restricted group of the most powerful forces within the country. But in societies that have undergone rapid economic development, population growth, or urbanisation, completely new groups and classes may begin to make demands and feel discontented. An example of this would be the rise of the bourgeoisie in eighteenth century France and another would be the growth of the demand for the vote in nineteenth-century England. Thus rapid and widespread changes in the social and economic structure can lead to popular protest on a wide scale, and movements such as early English radicalism and Chartism could be seen in this context. A characteristic of deep-seated protest movements of this type is that they often give rise to an ideology which legitimises and reinforces the demands of a particular group. Various ideologies have been considered to fulfil this function, and thus it has been argued that Calvinism in the sixteenth and seventeenth centuries formed an 'ideology of revolt' for a number of groups, as did the ideas of the Enlightenment in eighteenth-century Europe.

But though it can be argued that protest movements are generated by periods of rapid economic and social change, this is not to assume automatically that all protest is in any fundamental sense revolutionary. Both Rudé and Hobsbawm have shown that primitive rebellions were essentially concerned with manipulating the status quo, not with substituting something new. In that sense the political demands of the London 'mob' in the eighteenth century did not threaten the social order, for their demands for 'rights' and 'liberties' were essentially defensive and easily accommodated. Moreover, protest of a certain kind can strengthen the existing order by forcing it to incorporate demands from powerful vested interests. It is for this reason that protest should not always be seen as a weakness in society, but as a means by which demands are made and accommodated. This is particularly true of riots, which in recent times have frequently been interpreted as constituting some sort of 'crisis'. But if we take the example of food riots in eighteenth-century England or the interpretation of the Luddite outbreaks as given by Hobsbawm we can see that these outbreaks, far from threatening the social order, were an extended form of bargaining within the existing political structure. They were the means by which normally inarticulate sections of the population served notice of grievances to the authorities. It was this context which gave rise to the eighteenth-century view of the 'right to riot', which the authorities themselves were not above using for their own ends. Similarly, much modern violence, for example arising from strikes and demonstrations, can also be seen as a process of bargaining with the government for recognition of particular grievances. Such disturbances very rarely threaten the overthrow of the existing state, but rather operate within it to obtain their demands.

Moreover, many studies of popular protest, particularly of violent protest, have shown that violence is often the result of relatively fortuitous factors. Such conditions as the tradition of popular action in a particular town suggest that some places are more likely to have popular protest than others. On a more basic level outbreaks of violence have been specifically associated with the activities of the authorities. Particularly in the last century in this country violence has often occurred as a direct result of the actions of the authorities in attempting to check a demonstration or disperse a hostile crowd. Tilly has written that:

'As odd as it may seem, the authorities have far greater control over the short-run extent and timing of collective violence, especially damage to persons rather than property, than their challengers do. This is true for several reasons. The authorities usually have the technological and organisational advantage in the effective use of force, which gives them a fairly great choice among tactics of prevention, containment, and retaliation ... The authorities also have some choice of whether, and with how much muscle, to answer political challenges and illegal actions that are not intrinsically violent: banned assemblies, threats of vengeance, wildcat strikes. A large proportion of the European disturbances turned violent at exactly the moment when the authorities intervened to stop an illegal but non-violent action. This is typical of violent strikes and demonstrations.'[2]

Thus the actual incidence of violence has often been found to be bound up with the actions of the authorities in dealing with the challenges offered to them. One of the most recent and detailed discussions of the causes of popular protest, conducted to investigate the urban disturbances in the United States during the 1960s, suggests that their location and timing is often dictated by 'precipitating' factors of a largely fortuitous nature, little related to the underlying social and economic grievances. Such incidents are frequently decisive in determining whether a disturbance takes place at all, for there are many occasions when the pre-conditions for a disturbance are present without any further action taking place. For every riot that breaks out there are innumerable 'near riots' in which crowds disperse peacefully either under their own volition or through effective crowd control on the part of the authorities. Thus the incidence of disturbances is often only tenuously linked with the quality of the underlying social and economic grievances of the potential participants.

One difficulty in dealing with periods of popular protest is the natural tendency to group incidents under 'cover' labels, such as those applied to Luddism and Chartism. This is partly a question of convenience, but it is also a product of viewing movements from the centre, usually through government records. It is important to recognise in using, for example, the Home Office papers, that the sources bias our view of a movement like Luddism by giving it a coherence which it may not have possessed. Thus, to take the case of Luddism, we know from Darvall's study that this term is only a convenient short-hand for a movement which was both protracted and geographically diverse. In the same way it is important to dispense with the more emotive and usually confusing terms which are often applied to movements and episodes of popular protest, and to see them as they appeared to contemporaries. We should remember Darvall's caution-ary note about Luddism, that the whole of the disturbances created less stir in the press than a few murders in the East End of London. On other occasions it is necessary to treat critically central government sources which often reflect the fears of the authorities by seeing in episodes of popular protest an underlying coherence and organisation which they in fact lacked.

This brings us onto the methodological questions that are raised by a study of popular protest and public order. One of the most obvious of these is the vexed question of quantifica-tion. Some studies have gone a considerable way towards quantifying all popular protest in very precise terms. For some of his studies Tilly has used the concept of 'man-hours spent rioting' to bring some objectivity into discussions about the scale and scope of popular protest in France. This raises several problems, notably that by reducing events to statistics, the human and subjective dimension can be lost. A statistically 'large' disturbance can be of considerably less importance than a 'smaller' one in historical terms, depending upon its causes, object, and effect. Thus we are often forced to qualify purely quantitative statements with more subjective ones, by trying to discriminate between what can be considered as serious and important and what cannot. In that sense quantification can obscure more than it clarifies. The other problem is that of definition – what is being counted and how it is to be defined. The words 'protest', 'riot', and 'disturbance' are not always very easy to define precisely, but they must be defined if quantification is to be undertaken. Moreover, in attempting to quantify social phenomena like popular protest, historians are faced with a similar difficulty to that of criminologists, of assessing how much of the real level of events is being reported either through police and judicial records or through the press. This problem of the 'dark number' of unrecorded incidents presents an almost insuperable problem to reliable quantification of material of this kind. However, this does not mean that it is undesirable to try to be as precise and accurate as possible in measuring the number, scale, and severity of those disturbances for which information is available. It is only by doing this that it is possible to deal critically with episodes of popular protest.

Something also needs to be said about the role of the social sciences in investigating this field, for there is a considerable body of literature dealing with popular protest of various kinds. In fact, some of the earliest studies came from men such as Le Bon, whose classic study *The Crowd* marked a starting point for much research into the phenomenon of riots and crowd behaviour. Recently the wave of disturbances in the United States have given rise to a number of impressive studies which contain wide-ranging attempts to analyse popular disturbances.[3] Although the techniques employed and the nature of the quantification undertaken are sometimes open to question, they also offer many interesting new perspectives. Indeed, the most important contribution of the social sciences to the field of popular protest and public order seems to be less in providing a rigid 'model', than in adding to the range of perspectives that can be applied to their study. For example, in the cases of 'relative deprivation' and the role of rumour sociologists and psychologists have many important things to say, even if they cannot yet be very precisely handled by historians. A successful marriage of social science techniques and empirical historical research has so far eluded social history, but there is little doubt that in dealing with this area historians must increasingly recognise the contribution which the social sciences have to make.

Despite much recent interest, many aspects of the history of protest and order in modern Britain still await proper investigation. We know little of disturbances in enclosed institutions – such as colleges, prisons and barracks – for obvious reasons. Not all popular protest was also public protest. Fear of reprisals often drove protesters to seek relatively discreet ways of voicing their complaints. Thus much agrarian protest was manifested anonymously by rick-burning or cattle-maiming. More attention should also be paid to protests that were essentially reactionary. Too often it is mistakenly assumed that disorder emanates only from those anxious to change society. But the history of religious riots in England from the 'Church and King' protests of the early eighteenth century to the Hyde Park Riot of 1896 shows how strong and how popular was the resistance to concessions to religious minorities. Other essentially reactionary disorders were directed against the introduction of enclosed fields, machinery, tollgates and workhouses.

What needs to be stressed is the very diverse nature of popular protest in modern Britain. Movements varied immensely from one another in their objectives, their social composition, their tactics and their geographical milieu. The life-cycle of particular protests or old traditions of participation in them presents many unresolved problems for the historian. Why, for example, did London play an increasingly less important role in national protest after the 1820s? In most other respects the power of the capital in relation to the provinces continued to grow throughout the nineteenth century. Why had election riots largely disappeared by 1880? Why were there so few genuine Socialist disorders? The list of unresolved problems is endless.

In this collection of essays we have tried to bring together works that reflect both the diversity of the subject matter and the different methodology by which it is studied. Considerations both of length and of the ongoing nature of much of the work in this field precluded any attempt at a comprehensive coverage of protest and order from 1790 to 1920. Although Ireland was part of the United Kingdom it presents such special problems in this field that it has been deliberately excluded from this collection. The exclusion of a contribution on Wales was largely fortuitous, although a study has recently appeared of popular protest in the principality.[4] The contributions which are included all consider in detail a specific local situation, but also raise questions of much wider relevance. Some of the studies are principally concerned with popular protest, while others are mainly related to the agencies for maintaining order. But all the contributions are self-contained and must speak for themselves.

Notes

1. G. Rudé, *Paris and London in the Eighteenth Century* (London, 1970), p. 319.
2. C. Tilly, 'Collective Violence in European Perspective' in H. D. Graham and T. R. Gurr, *Violence in America* (New York, 1969), p. 10.
3. See the *Report of the National Advisory Commission on Civil Disorders* (New York, 1968) and H. D. Graham and T. R. Gurr (eds), *Violence in America, op. cit.*
4. D. J. V. Jones, *Before Rebecca* (London, 1973).

I

Food Riots in England, 1792–1818

J. STEVENSON

In eighteenth-century England the most characteristic form of popular protest was riot, and riots occurred on a wide range of issues, including elections, religion, politics, recruiting, and enclosures. However, the most persistent and widespread riots were those associated with food, for it has been calculated that two out of every three disturbances in the eighteenth century were of this type.[1] Food riots covered a wide range of activities, such as stopping the movement of grain, forcible seizure and resale of food, and various types of tumultuous assembly to force dealers or local authorities to reduce prices. On other occasions disturbances took the form of attacks upon mills, or the shops, warehouses, and houses of prominent dealers. In its classic form the food riot could be found in many parts of western Europe. It was usually marked by a high degree of discipline amongst the rioters, concentration upon those specifically concerned with the trade in foodstuffs, and by the resale of food at 'fair' prices.[2]

Recent work has shown that food riots became common in England in the latter part of the seventeenth century, occurred with increasing frequency during the eighteenth century, and began to die out in the first decades of the nineteenth century. A number of the major waves of eighteenth-century food riots have been identified and related to periods of serious harvest failure or trade depression, for example the disturbances of 1727, 1756–7, 1766–8, and

1773–4.[3] The aim here is to examine the major food disturbances of the late eighteenth and early nineteenth centuries in an attempt to discover their incidence, location, and causes. From these findings it should be possible to discover whether disturbances tended to be concentrated in particular areas or towns, why some towns were affected and others were not, and finally how food rioting related to other forms of popular protest that were emerging in the first decades of the nineteenth century.

The pre-conditions for the frequent appearance of food rioting in this period were the dependence of the majority of the population upon a limited range of staple foods, of which the most important was bread. The budgets for this period make it plain that bread formed the most important part of the budget and diet of ordinary people.[4] The amount of bread consumed varied between different areas and income groups, but at least a pound of bread per day appears to have been the average per capita consumption by the 1790s.[5] Even though other foods were important, particularly in urban areas, such as meat, dairy products, and vegetables, bread remained the staple foodstuff in the absence of a cheap and filling alternative. The bread consumed was largely wheaten bread by the opening of this period, and only in poorer areas, such as the Pennines or south-west, were other cereals important, principally barley and oats. Potatoes were only coming into common use as a staple food at the beginning of this period, and this was largely restricted to northern England.[6]

As well as forming the staple part of the diet in this period, a considerable degree of status value had become attached to bread by the end of the eighteenth century, particularly to white bread. There had been continuous pressure throughout the eighteenth century for both finer and whiter bread, a demand which had been met by developments within the milling and baking industries.[7] Paradoxically the whitest bread was eaten in the poorest areas, such as the 'rookeries' of London, where it was often adulterated with alum to whiten it.[8] Even for the prosperous artisan or town worker, periods of high prices tended to increase dependence upon bread by forcing other items out of the budget in order to procure the customary quantity of bread.[9] The result was to heighten sensitivity to the price of bread, not only among the poorest sections of the community, but also among quite prosperous artisans.

TABLE I

Average price of wheat per quarter in England and Wales, 1792–1818

1792	43s 0d	1801	119s 6d	1810	106s 5d
1793	49s 3d	1802	69s 10d	1811	95s 3d
1794	52s 3d	1803	58s 10d	1812	126s 6d
1795	75s 2d	1804	62s 3d	1813	109s 9d
1796	78s 7d	1805	89s 9d	1814	74s 4d
1797	53s 9d	1806	79s 1d	1815	65s 7d
1798	51s 10d	1807	75s 4d	1816	78s 6d
1799	69s 0d	1808	81s 4d	1817	96s 11d
1800	113s 10d	1809	97s 4d	1818	86s 3d

Source: Mitchell and Deane

There were four major outbreaks of food disturbances in this period, and they all occurred in periods of harvest failure and high prices. These were 1795–6, 1800–1, 1810–13, and 1816–18 (see Table 1). The shortage of 1795–6 started with the harvest of 1794 which was about 25 per cent below average. As a result of this prices began to rise sharply in the pre-harvest months of 1795. By July wheat had reached an average of 108 shillings per quarter. The harvest of 1795 was also deficient, with the result that high prices were maintained through the winter of 1795–6, reaching a peak in the spring of 1796, when heavy imports of foreign grain broke the price spiral.[10] It is this crisis which Professor Williams has called the 'English *crise des subsistances*'; and E. P. Thompson has described 1795 as the 'climactic' year for food riots in England.[11] In the face of such claims it is necessary to obtain a clear view of the number and distribution of food riots in these years. I have found evidence of seventy-four food disturbances in England in these two years; these were distributed geographically as shown in List 1.[12]

Geographical distribution of food disturbances, 1792–1818

LIST 1: FOOD DISTURBANCES IN 1795–6

South-West: Bristol, Bath, Chudleigh, Bideford, Frome, Honiton, Topsham, Exeter, Ashburton, Totnes, Dartmouth, Plymouth, Launceston, Callington, Okehampton, Truro, Penryn, Penzance.

South-East and East Anglia: London, Portsmouth, Chichester, Southampton, Seaford, Lewes, Newhaven, Canterbury, Hastings, Rye, Chatham, Croydon, Guildford, Windsor, Potters Bar, Aylesbury, Gosfield, Buntingford, Halstead, Hitchin, Bedford, Cambridge, Sudbury, Norwich, Yarmouth, Ely, Wisbech, Wells, Blakeney, Ipswich.

Midlands: Oxford, Deddington, Handborough, Burford, Witney, Tewkesbury, Mitcheldean, Ross-on-Wye, Ludlow, Coalbrookdale, Dudley, Coventry, Birmingham, Shackerstone, Nottingham.

North: Liverpool, Sheffield, Heath, Pontefract, Brough, Carlisle, Manchester, Hull.

LIST 2: FOOD DISTURBANCES IN 1800–1

South-West: Bristol, Bath, Honiton, Blandford, Wimborne, Plymouth.

South-East and East Anglia: London, Southampton, Alresford, Midhurst, New Romney, Tunbridge Wells, Great Marlow, Sheerness, Chatham, Rochester, Luton, Gosfield, Attleborough, Norwich, St. Ives, Huntingdon.

Midlands: Abingdon, Oxford, Witney, Banbury, Stony Stratford, Leicester, Hinckley, Nuneaton, Coventry, Worcester, Kidderminster, Derby, Birmingham, Somerford, Bilston, Stafford, Longton, Nottingham.

North: Wigan, Blackburn, Leeds, Mansfield, Chesterfield, Sheffield, Chester-le-Street, Knottingly, Castleford, Methley.

LIST 3: FOOD DISTURBANCES IN 1810–13

South-West: Falmouth, Barnstaple, Plymouth, Frome, Truro, Bristol, Sampford Peverell.

South-East: Romford.

Midlands: Birmingham (2), Wolverhampton, Worcester, Nottingham.

North: Liverpool, Barnsley, Chester, Leeds, Carlisle (2), Sheffield, Stockport, Royton, Macclesfield, Wakefield (2), Oldham, Heywood, Rochdale, Manchester.

LIST 4: FOOD DISTURBANCES IN 1816–18

South-West: Bideford, Frome, Bridport, Radstock.

South-East and East Anglia: London, Brandon, Norwich, Littleport, Downham, Cambridge.

Midlands: Towcester, Birmingham, Walsall, Coventry, Hinckley, Woodthorpe.

North: Sheffield, Newcastle, Preston, Stockport, Bolton, Maryport.

Three years of ordinary harvests and moderate prices were ended by the harvest of 1799, which was between 25 and 40 per cent below average. By December 1799 the average price of wheat was almost 94s per quarter; by May 1800 it had reached 120s. A further poor harvest in 1800 pushed prices still higher, reaching 140s per quarter in January 1801. Before foreign imports could have their effect, the price of wheat reached its highest level for the whole period, 156s per quarter in March 1801.[13] This period of shortage has received less attention than the earlier one, but contemporary evidence suggests that it was severely felt. Pellew in his *Life of Lord Sidmouth* wrote that 'a few days of rain in September 1800 produced consequences for which Pitt confessed he could see no adequate remedy and compared with which, he considered the great question of peace or war was not half so formidable'.[14] Similarly, Archibald Prentice wrote of Manchester that 'old inhabitants of the industrial classes shudder at the recollection of the sufferings endured in 1800 and 1801'.[15] Rudé, quoting Wearmouth, suggests that there were about a dozen disturbances during this period of shortage,[16] in fact there were at least fifty food disturbances in England, distributed as shown in List 2.

Wheat prices remained moderate until 1809. However, the crop failed in that year and in the three subsequent years. Wheat prices exceeded 100s per quarter every week from October 1811 until the scarcity ended in 1813. By August 1812 wheat had reached 155s per quarter.[17] It was also a period of acute commercial distress and disturbances broke out against machinery as well as against the price of food. During this period of shortage there were at least twenty-nine food disturbances, distributed as shown in List 3. There was a further outbreak of disturbances in 1816–18. Prices had fallen almost to pre-war levels in 1815, but in the spring of 1816 they began to rise again, leading to a number of disturbances. The harvest of 1816 was also poor and as prices rose in the winter of 1816–17 there were more disturbances.[18] During this period there were at least twenty-two food riots, distributed as shown in List 4.

Before these disturbances are examined it is important to put them into perspective by attempting a more precise evaluation of these four periods of scarcity, in particular to try to assess their demographic impact. For mortality data in this period we are dependent upon the parochial burial registers, a source that has been much criticised for un-reliability by demographic historians.[19] Nonetheless, they do provide a general indication of the broad movement of mortality each year, and from Table 2 we can assess the relationship between mortality movement and high prices. It is clear from this that the first year of high prices in each of these periods of shortage saw a significant, though relatively small, increase in burials. Certainly there appears to be

TABLE 2

Burials per year in England and Wales, 1792–1818 (in 'ooos)

1792	189	1801	204	1810	208
1793	204	1802	200	1811	189
1794	198	1803	204	1812	190
1795	210	1804	181	1813	186
1796	191	1805	181	1814	206
1797	191	1806	183	1815	197
1798	188	1807	196	1816	206
1799	190	1808	201	1817	199
1800	208	1809	191	1818	214

Source: Mitchell and Deane

nothing here approaching a major subsistence crisis, unless we can assume heavy under-registration of deaths specifically in the years of shortage. On the face of it, this appears un-likely. Moreover, other factors need to be borne in mind before the excess mortality of these years is attributed directly to food shortage. We must be careful not to mistake a simple correlation for a causal relationship, for the climatic con-ditions which contributed to a poor harvest, could *per se* lead to a rise in mortality. The winter of 1794–5 was one of the worst of the eighteenth century, and an investigation of London monthly burial totals suggests that most of the excess mortality in 1795 was in the winter months of 1794–5, *before* high prices could begin to have an effect.[20] Disease too should not be left out of the account, for both the summer of 1795 and 1800 were marked by epidemic disease.[21] It does not appear then that there was a catastrophic rise in mortality in any of these periods of shortage. The disturbances that occurred must therefore be placed in the context of shortage and hardship rather than of real famine and starvation.

Having established these parameters of the problem, it is necessary to investigate the nature of the trade in food-stuffs in this period, principally the grain trade. Essentially we are concerned with internal trade for by the end of the eighteenth century England had ceased to export grain other than in exceptional conditions. In normal years the total wheat consumption of the country was about one quarter per head per year, which could be accommodated by domestic output, aided by a marginal amount of imports.[22] Between 1775 and 1786 the annual average quantity of wheat imported was about 180,000 quarters, representing two and a half per cent of total requirements. Population growth, however, was steadily eroding the margin of supply, so that even with increased grain production the annual average of grain imports continued to increase. Thus in the next decade, 1787–98, the annual average of imports of wheat was 325,000 quarters; and in 1799–1810 almost 700,000 quarters per year.[23] As well as population increase, which made an insufficient harvest more likely, there were a large number of poor harvests for purely climatic factors. Olson has suggested that at least fourteen of the twenty-two war-time harvests, from 1793–1814, were below the pre-war average.[24] Unfortunately in the absence of precise production figures it is impossible to determine exactly how these two factors inter-related.[25] Nonetheless, the result was an increasing dependence on foreign imports, though in normal years to a marginal extent. Only in the periods of major harvest failure did imports become important. In 1801, 1810, and 1818 imports of wheat reached about one and a half million quarters, representing about 15 per cent of total consumption.[26]

Moreover, the problem was not simply one of increasing

population and periodic harvest failure, but also of an increasing urban population which was dependent upon transport and marketing arrangements for its food supply. In the House of Commons in 1795, Fox observed that:

'It is indeed a melancholy and alarming fact, that the great majority of the people of England – an enormous and dreadful majority – are no longer in a situation in which they can boast that they live by the produce of their labour; and that it does regularly happen, during the pressure of every inclement season, that the industrious poor are obliged to depend for subsistance on the supplies afforded by the charity of the rich'.[27]

The nature of the internal trade and marketing of foodstuffs has been little studied in this period, but its major features can be sketched out from the available evidence.[28] The most important commodity was grain, and it is clear that by this period there was a well-developed corn trade in England. Prices throughout the country moved in a similar way and stayed within reasonable proximity of each other. Within the national market there survived a number of regional markets: the most important of these was the one which supplied London with grain.[29] With a consumption of almost a million quarters of wheat per year, London drew its grain from a wide area of south-eastern England. Grain was brought by river, road, canal, and coastal shipping to the capital from a large number of small market towns and ports. The largest traffic came by coastal shipping from the ports of East Anglia, such as Wells, Blakeney, Lynn, Ipswich, and Yarmouth, for the farmlands of this area were the single most important producing area for the supply of the capital.[30] Other population centres had their own catchment areas for agricultural produce, for example, dealers from Lancashire were often active in North Wales and Cumberland to supply the growing manufacturing towns.

It is also important to an understanding of the context in which the disturbances of this period occurred to look at the government's actions and attitude towards the trade in foodstuffs, particularly the grain trade. In the shortage of 1795-6 the complicating factor was the virtual absence of any large-scale foreign supplies of grain to make up the deficiency in the domestic harvest. The government felt that the foreign grain trade was so speculative that it could not be left to private merchants. The government therefore entered the trade and chartered ships to scour foreign markets for grain.[31] These efforts were only partly successful with the result that the internal corn trade became distorted as the large urban centres expanded their catchment areas for agricultural produce. London, which according to the Privy Council normally drew its grain from East Anglia and the Home Counties, was by the early summer of 1795 drawing supplies from as far away as Hampshire and Lincolnshire. As a result there were a number of protests from local authorities about grain being shipped out of their area to the large urban centres, especially London. The Mayor of Winchester claimed that a much greater quantity of grain had been shipped out of the area than was usual, 'from which cause the neighbourhood has been drained to an alarming degree and a great scarcity is much feared before the harvest'![32] Similarly, the bakers of Essex complained to the government that the shipments of grain to the capital had exhausted the locality of supplies, and asked the government to interfere.[33]

The government, however, was determined to keep out of the internal corn trade and attempted to keep up the normal circulation of grain, so that the large urban centres would be supplied. On these grounds the government refused to yield to the pleas of local authorities and interfere with the normal movement of grain. The Mayor of Winchester received the reply that the government had no power to prevent the movement of corn, 'and if their Lordships were vested with such power, they should not think it prudent or wise to exercise the same'.[34] Similarly, the Essex bakers were told that the government could do nothing to help them.[35] The government was then faced with a local reaction against the movement of grain; many local authorities attempted to restrict operation of the market. At Witney the local magistrates prevented corn agents from outside the area from buying grain, and went so far as to stop a consignment of wheat from being taken to Woodstock.[36] At Burford the magistrates called a meeting with the local farmers at which it was decided that grain would only be sold to local dealers.[37] It was reported to the Home Office that stopping the movement of grain had become so widespread that country millers were said to be frightened to send grain to the capital except by night.[38] In an attempt to free the circulation of grain from these checks the government passed an act to prevent the stopping of grain by making the whole hundred liable to fine and individuals liable to fine and imprisonment.[39] By emphasising the communal responsibility for such actions the government was giving a clear warning to local authorities as much as to the common people.

In the shortage of 1800–1 the authorities did not enter the external corn trade for there were plentiful supplies of foreign grain available. Moreover, a parliamentary committee which reported in the last months of the shortage of 1795–6 had advised against it as a policy on any subsequent occasion, on the grounds that it discouraged private merchants from entering the trade.[40] In spite of repeated requests from local authorities for emergency supplies or interference in the circulation of grain, the government stood by the principles of the free market. The Mayor of Portsmouth was informed that the government had 'given notice to all merchants and dealers in corn that government would not be concerned in procuring grain in order that the markets might be left entirely open to those who are concerned in that branch of commerce'.[41] Similarly, the Home Office explained to a Devonshire correspondent that any interference by the government would 'prevent competition' and 'annihilate speculation', therefore its sole concern was to provide security for free trade.[42] In the subsequent shortages the policy of the government remained the same, for it refused to interfere in the internal trade in food-stuffs. Prices had to find their own level by allowing trade to flow freely.

Something needs to be said here about the communications network and the movement of food. Water transport provided the only means of moving a bulky commodity such as grain over long distances at bearable cost. It has often been assumed that coastal shipping relieved the most acute problems of shortage and disturbance in England.[43] But the ease of transport was a mixed blessing in a period of scarcity, for it meant that grain could be taken out of an area, as easily as it could be brought in. In the shortage of 1795–6 canals were blamed by one correspondent for opening up the inland counties to the market, so that 'the whole Kingdom is become for the purpose of exportation, a seaport'.[44] This seems to have been at least partly recognised by the government itself in 1795, when it decided to send relief supplies of grain to the coastal districts in an attempt to keep grain in the inland counties. The standard government letter on this subject was revealing, for it explained that it was impossible to move grain into the internal parts of the country either sufficiently cheaply or quickly to affect the situation.[45] Indeed the communications system was still only partially effective in moving bulk commodities inland. Several towns were informed that there was no easy means of sending them grain, such as Northampton and Kettering.[46]

It is against this background that we can examine the distribution of food disturbances in this period. The incidence of disorder shows a striking relationship to the communications network, particularly in 1795–6 and 1800–1. The map shows the extremely close relationship of disturbances to the communications network in the production areas around London in these two shortages. The most striking pattern overall is that of 1795–6 when at least fifty food disturbances took place at communication centres, either coastal ports, canal or river ports, or towns within easy carting distance of major population centres. In 1795 many of the disturbances took place at small ports such as Seaford, Chichester, Wells, Boston, and Wisbech. Others took place inland at canal or river termini, such as Bedford, Ipswich, Winchester, and Lewes.[47] Disturbances also broke out at small market towns

FOOD RIOTS IN SOUTH–EASTERN ENGLAND IN 1795–6 AND 1800–1

~~~ Navigable rivers and canals   • Disturbances

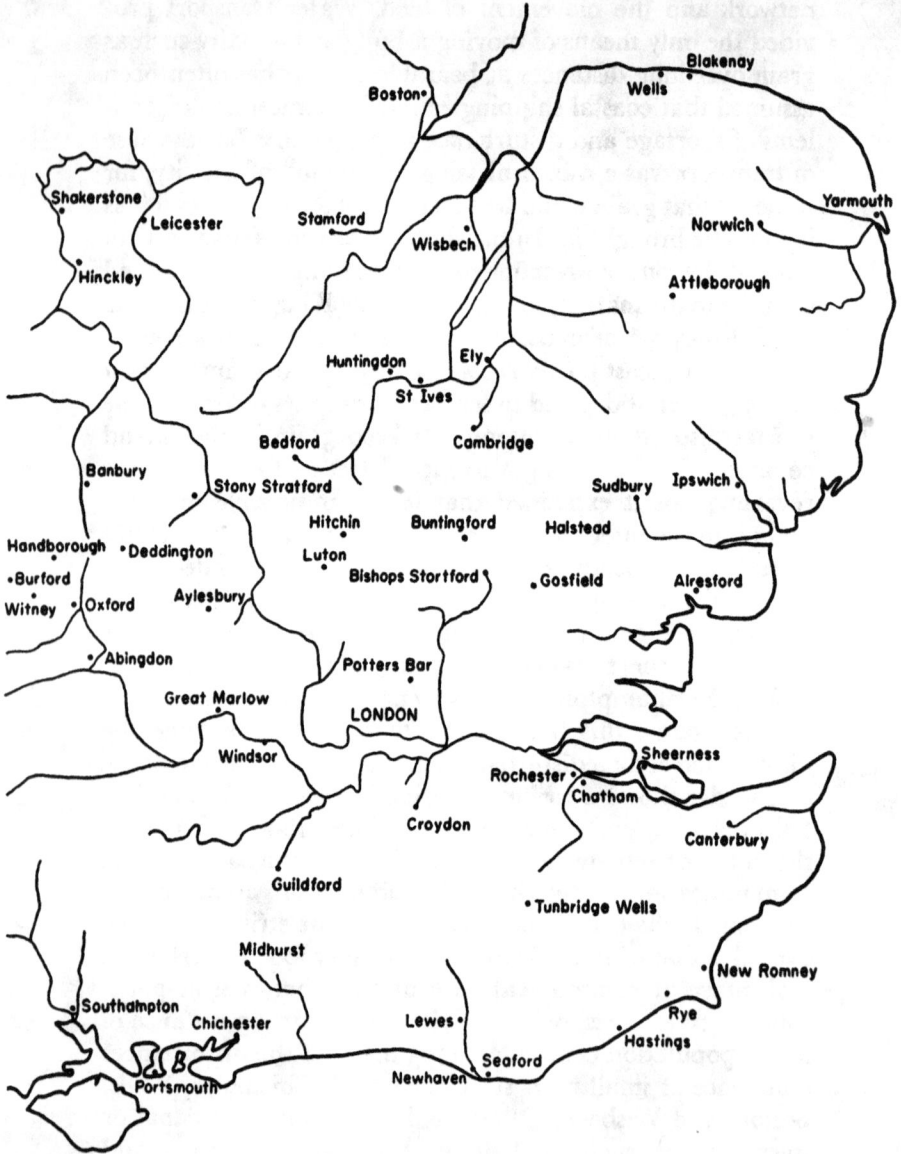

Blakenay

Wells

Boston

Yarmouth

Shakerstone

Leicester

Stamford

Norwich

Wisbech

Hinckley

Attleborough

Huntingdon

Ely

St Ives

Bedford

Cambridge

Banbury

Stony Stratford

Sudbury

Ipswich

Hitchin

Buntingford

Halstead

Handborough

Deddington

Luton

•Burford

Bishops Stortford

Gosfield

Alresford

Witney

Oxford

Aylesbury

Abingdon

Potters Bar

Great Marlow

LONDON

Windsor

Sheerness

Rochester

Chatham

Croydon

Canterbury

Guildford

Tunbridge Wells

Midhurst

New Romney

Southampton

Chichester

Lewes

Rye

Seaford

Hastings

Portsmouth

Newhaven

from which grain was normally carted to London, such as Hitchin, Halstead, Potters Bar, and Buntingford. In the Midlands a similar pattern emerged, for there were disturbances in the towns from which grain was being sent to Birmingham; at Tewkesbury a mob of women unloaded barges bound there, and in Burford carts bound for the same destination were forcibly unloaded.[48] In the north the catchment area for south Lancashire was much disturbed, with riots in many of the small ports and market towns of North Wales, such as Abergele, Conway, Mold, and Denbigh. Most of these were explicitly against the activities of dealers from Lancashire.[49] In Carlisle there were disturbances about the export of grain by dealers from Liverpool.[50]

Similarly, in the shortage of 1800–1 a number of disturbances occurred at transhipment points, such as the disturbance at Midhurst at the end of the navigable section of the River Arun, and at ports such as Southampton, Plymouth, and Bristol. Through the subsequent shortages of 1810–13 and 1816–18 the communications factor continued to play a part. In 1816 the most serious disturbances took place around Ely, in an area which was one of the richest grain-producing areas in the country, but where grain was being taken out of the area in the pre-harvest months.[51] Some small ports were perennially disturbed in periods of shortage, places such as Carlisle and Bideford.

But it is also clear that the incidence of riots was shifting during this period to the manufacturing towns of the Midlands and the north. In 1795–6 only a minority of disturbances took place in what could be described as manufacturing towns. By 1800–1, however, the majority of disturbances were taking place in the manufacturing areas, particularly those at a considerable distance from the coast, such as Nottingham, Sheffield, and Manchester.[52] This pattern was confirmed in 1810–12, when the food riots again took place predominantly in the Midlands and north. The centres of disturbance were the manufacturing towns of the Midlands, mainly Birmingham and Nottingham; the cotton towns of Lancashire around Manchester, with another grouping on

the Yorkshire coalfield.[53] The disturbances of 1816 occurred
in several parts of the country, but the majority again
occurred in the Midlands and north, although the centres of
production and transportation in East Anglia and the small
ports were also disturbed.[54]

An increasingly important influence upon the distribution
of disturbances was the presence of a large non-agricultural
population, vulnerable to rapid fluctuations in the price of
provisions at the local market. In 1795–6 many of the disturbances were composed of local workmen, often in a semi-
rural situation. The Cornish tinners were active throughout
1795–6. For example, on 30th March, 1796 500 tinners
assembled in Penryn to force a reduction in the price of
provisions.[55] In April 1796 3,000 tinners were reported to
have assembled in Truro, demanding a reduction in the
price of food, before they were dispersed by the military.[56] In
the Midlands, colliers were active in the disturbances at
Shackerstone, Dudley, the Forest of Dean, Bristol, and Coalbrookdale.[57] Even in East Anglia in 1795 many of the disturbances were not the work of the local population but of
the canal 'bankers' who were employed in building and
repairing the dykes and canals of the Fens. These were
reported to have been responsible for the disturbances at
Ely, Boston, and Wisbech.[58]

In the disturbances from 1800–1, there was an increasing
degree of participation by the manufacturing population.
As in 1795–6, groups such as the colliers were important in
the disturbances in the Midland towns. At Witney the
blanket weavers led the disturbances and at Banbury a mob
of stocking-weavers and canal boatmen forced a reduction of
the price of provisions.[59] At Stony Stratford the 'navigators'
building the Grand Junction Canal rioted over the price of
bread and meat.[60] These disturbances again illustrated the
precarious situation of groups of workmen in semi-rural
situations, where provisioning was often difficult, particularly in competition with the larger urban centres. In 1800–1
disturbances also involved the population of the large
manufacturing towns, such as Leeds, Sheffield, Nottingham,

and Birmingham. Similarly, in the later disturbances in the north and Midlands between 1810–13 and 1816–17 the local manufacturing population took an important part in the food disturbances which occurred.[61]

Soldiers in particular played a large part in the riots of 1795–6. Barracked and encamped all along the east and south coast to meet the invasion threat, they seriously distorted the local corn trade as well as the price of other provisions. From Weymouth in 1795 a correspondent wrote that the area was accustomed to importing grain from the Isle of Wight, but that the soldiers encamped there had used up the surplus.[62] On the east coast at King's Lynn the local authorities complained that 700 soldiers and their families were exhausting the town of supplies.[63] The most spectacular evidence of the effect of the soldiers on local price levels was in south Devon in spring 1795; the outward-bound fleet was held up off shore for a number of weeks with around 25,000 men on board. A local correspondent pointed out that this was a number equal to the resident population of the towns and villages of that area.[64] The result was a rapid increase in the price of grain and other provisions in Devon; by March 14th the average price for a quarter of wheat in Devon was five shillings above the national average. Between April 11th and 18th the average price soared to seventy shillings, eight shillings above the national average. The result was a wave of rioting in the towns of South Devon and the Tamar valley in which it was reported that the soldiers had taken an active part.

The militia in particular proved extremely riot-prone; newly raised, poorly disciplined, and often with their officers billeted far from the rank and file, they instigated a whole series of riots along the south and east coast in April 1795. Because their food allowance was fixed at fivepence a day they were vulnerable to the high level of prices which their presence aggravated. At Wells the 122nd Regiment marched into the market place with bayonets fixed and compelled the market men to sell their provisions at lower prices.[65] At Portsmouth the Gloucestershire militia forced a reduction in the price of provisions.[66] The most serious of these riots occurred at Lewes where the Oxfordshire militia was in barracks. There had been a stream of letters from the area to the Home Office, complaining that the exportation of grain and the presence of the soldiers was exhausting the neighbourhood of grain. Eventually on April 16th 400 men from the barracks on Bletchingdon Down fixed bayonets and entered Seaford and Newhaven, seized provisions and sold them at reduced prices. The townspeople did not join in and the militia eventually returned to barracks.[67] As a result of their action two of the militia were shot, two hanged and several flogged and the Cinque Port Volunteers had to take over the convoying of wheat out of the area.[68] At Canterbury the South Hampshire militia went into the town and forced the butchers and bakers to reduce the price of food. The Mayor called out the Volunteers to deal with them, but they returned to barracks before any clash could take place.[69] As a result the Home Office took steps to ensure that the forces of order were supplied with grain. Emergency supplies were diverted to the soldiers and the army victuallers were allowed to borrow from the supplies allocated to the capital.[70] On a local level the militia had messes set up and the men were assured a supply of bread at a fixed rate, the difference to be made up by the army paymasters.[71] As the militia became better-organised and its supply position became regularised the threat of it taking part in riots diminished; in 1800 the militia played virtually no part in the disturbances.

One of the most striking features of the disturbances is the relative lack of participation by agricultural workers. Two reasons can be suggested for this, one is that the Speenhamland system introduced in April 1795 tended to cushion agricultural workers from changes in the prices of food, by fixing the rate of poor relief in relation to the price of bread.[72] Agricultural workers probably also had easier access to grain in times of shortage; there were several reports in 1795–6 from harassed urban magistrates, that what little grain was available for sale was being sold off at artificially low prices by the farmers to their labourers.[73] The major exception to this pattern is the outbreak of disturbances in East Anglia in the spring of 1816, where agricultural labourers played the predominant part in the disturbances centred upon Ely, Littleport, and Downham. In this area, however, agricultural change had created a large population of wage-labourers, living in populous 'open' parishes.[74] In East Anglia the position of agricultural labourers most closely resembled that of those engaged in manufacturing, and it was significant that in 1816 they combined demands for a reduction in food prices with one for higher wages.[75]

The participants in disturbances were often drawn from clearly identifiable groups in the community, particularly women, youths or the 'poor'. At Tewkesbury in 1795 the wheat was taken from barges at the quayside by the women.[76] At Honiton in May 1800 it was 'the wives, widows and daughters of the poor' who assembled, demanding food.[77] At Nathan Crompton in July 1795 'women and children' threw provisions into the street off the carts in the market.[78] At Blandford Forum in September 1800 the Mayor wrote to the Home Office, complaining that his house was surrounded by the local women demanding food at reasonable prices.[79] References like these abound for the reports in both 1795 and 1800, as well as references to the urban poor; at Chesterfield in 1800 we hear of 200 'of the dirtiest men' or simply the 'poor' as at Brough and Bristol in 1795. Their participation was regarded as normal, for example, the *Leicester Journal* in 1800 commented that 'all public disturbances generally commence with the clamour of women and the folly of boys'.[80] During the food disturbances in Lancashire in 1812 women and boys were again prominent in the disturbances at the market places in Manchester and Macclesfield.[81]

The nature of the communications network and the presence of a large non-agricultural population therefore had an important influence upon the distribution of disturbances, and this was reflected in the two areas that were most prone to food disturbances, the south-west and the Midlands. The south-west in particular was an area of marginal subsistence, where a poor harvest could soon push up prices in the local market towns. The tin miners and quarrymen of the area were a poor but homogeneous group of workmen with a strong tradition of riot and disorder. The poverty of internal transport and the unproductive nature of the agriculture inland made these workmen vulnerable to shortages; frequently their food supply seems to have broken down so that they were forced to march upon the local market towns or ports in order to obtain food.[82] The poverty of internal communications, however, contrasted with the small ports of the coast, so that at the same time as it might be difficult to obtain food inland, grain could be exported from the coastal towns, or from the towns with access to navigable rivers.[83] It was this complex of factors that made the south-east a perennial area of food disturbances into the nineteenth century.

The other area of frequent disturbances was the Midlands. Here again the problem in the eighteenth century was one of poor communications, aggravated by the presence of considerable and growing bodies of colliers and other manufacturers.[84] Long-established manufacturing centres such as Witney and Kidderminster were frequently disturbed in the eighteenth century by food rioting, and continued to be so. By this period the growth of the canal network was beginning to have an effect on these areas, but in times of shortage they still had to bring imported grain from a considerable distance. For example in 1800 the magistrates of Nottingham were told that they would have to look for grain at Hull, in spite of the considerable cost of transporting it by river and canal.[85] Here again was an area which suffered from several factors, including its large non-agricultural population and its relative inaccessibility.

As well as places that were prone to food disturbances, there were others that had very few. The north-east, for example, in spite of its large body of manufacturers had only two food disturbances in this period. Here the communications network seems to have helped food supply, because the industrial towns were close to the coast and were often ports.[86] But during these shortages the most important example of effective food supply was the capital. London was the largest city in Western Europe, with a population of almost one million people by the end of this period. It posed acutely the problem of feeding a large urban population at prices that would not excite serious commotion. The authorities were alive to the threat which food shortages could raise. In 1795 the Board of Agriculture warned that 'if London were but ill-supplied with food for a single day the consequences might be extremely serious'.[87] London's basic advantage was its well-developed supply system and its dominant position as a market for much of south-eastern England. As a result it could be supplied, providing its normal channels of trade remained undisturbed. Thus the government's emphasis upon preserving the normal circulation of grain effectively discriminated in favour of the capital, for it was able to continue to draw upon its normal area of supply and expand its catchment area without serious interference. In the capital itself the local authorities devoted considerable attention to the state of prices in the capital by watching the principal markets and fixing the Assize of Bread.[88] Relief activities were also taken up on an extensive scale to provide cheap substitute foods in times of high prices.[89]

On the whole these measures worked, though there were some food disturbances in the capital, principally in 1795 when the crowd which mobbed the King's coach cried out 'Bread, Bread'.[90] In September 1800 there were disturbances which lasted for almost a week, although they did little serious damage.[91] Again in 1816 there were minor demonstrations about the price of food.[92] None of these disturbances, however, were very serious, nor were they the most serious food riots to break out during the periods of shortage. In numbers of participants, damage inflicted, and casualties, they fell below several of the disturbances in the country. London could have been most vulnerable to scarcity, but its well-developed food trade and its maintenance by the government through the shortages, combined with relief operations, helped to see the capital through without serious difficulties.

The timing of disturbances also shows some interesting features. Table 3 shows that the largest number of disturbances in 1795–6 occurred in months of relatively low prices compared with 1796. For the population as a whole the important factor was less the absolute level of prices than the rate and direction of price movements. The large number of riots or disturbances in April represents the effect of a local increase in prices in Devon and Cornwall where the average

TABLE 3

Average price of wheat per quarter in England in 1795–6 and the number of disturbances reported[93]

| | *1795* | | | *1796* | |
	Price of wheat	*Disturbances*		*Price of wheat*	*Disturbances*
Jan.	42s 0d	—		92s 0d	—
Feb.	44s 0d	—		93s 6d	—
Mar.	45s 4d	5		104s 2d	2
Apr.	62s 0d	14		84s 0d	1
May	64s 8d	2		76s 0d	—
Jun.	78s 0d	3		80s 8d	—
Jul.	84s 0d	20		80s 8d	—
Aug.	108s 0d	7		75s 4d	—
Sep.	79s 8d	6		64s 0d	—
Oct.	76s 8d	1		60s 1d	—
Nov.	83s 4d	—		59s 4d	—
Dec.	87s 8d	—		58s 8d	—

price and the rate of increase was much higher in April than in the country as a whole. July was the month when prices increased most rapidly in the country as a whole and it was then that the bulk of the riots occurred. The disturbances carried on through the harvest months before petering out in late autumn and winter. In the period of highest prices in early 1796 there were very few riots.

Similarly in 1800–1 the majority of the riots occurred not in the months of highest prices, but when the rate of increase in prices was most rapid. The pre-harvest months of 1800 and early 1801 were relatively undisturbed, although prices

were very high. In fact two-thirds of the riots occurred in
September 1800 which had the second lowest monthly
average price for wheat, but when prices had begun to rise
sharply after a fall with the harvest. In spring 1812 there
were a number of riots in the north against a rapid rise in the
price of potatoes and meal.[94] In East Anglia in 1816 the price
of grain leapt by almost sixteen shillings per quarter in the
month of the disturbances, one of the most rapid rises in the
whole period.[95]

The short-term movement in prices was the most important factor in precipitating disturbances. For example, a
correspondent to the Home Office in mid-September 1800
explained that in Nuneaton the poor had been patient in the
hope of relief from the harvest, 'a hope that two or three
weeks since appeared to be realised, the price of wheat
having fallen to nine shillings and some I believe to eight
shillings, but upon the first shower of rain . . . the farmers
made it a pretence to increase the price even to its former
amount'. He claimed that this disappointment had been the
direct cause of the riot in Nuneaton.[96] This view seems borne
out in the case of the London riot of 15th September, 1800. In
the capital the price of grain was translated each week into
an Assize price for the quartern loaf. The price had risen
steadily to late July, but dropped to 1s 0½d in mid-August.
Instead of further falls in September, however, the price
rose in larger increments. The largest weekly increase at the
Assize in the year had been no more than ½d, but on September 2nd the quartern loaf went up by 1½d and on the 9th
by 1¾d. It was in anticipation of another such rise on the
16th that a crowd assembled in the Mark Lane market,
demanding bread at sixpence for the quartern loaf.[97]

As well as reacting to the movement of prices, the populace
also had to feel that direct action could be effective in some
way, either in reducing prices by a forced sale or by forcing
the local authorities to intervene. The source of the discontents had to be felt as within the immediate scope of
direct action and this involved finding scapegoats. In these
disturbances the obvious targets were the middlemen who

were accused, often with some justice, of exploiting the condition of the people. In 1795 they were accused of sending grain out of the country or out of the localities. A correspondent wrote from Gloucestershire in August 1795 that previously in bad times the people had been open to reason, but that popular anger was now inflamed by the thought that grain was being sent out of the country.[98] Naturally the feeling that the shortage was artificial created great bitterness; the Duke of Portland received an anonymous letter in July which ran: 'You find My Lord Duke how serious the times grow and how serious the times are and how discontented the lower orders of people are. Governments should not think it below their notice to take every method of informing their minors what occasions the present scarcity and that it is really not artificial.'[99] The result in 1795 was widespread popular interference with the movement of grain and price-fixing riots against the dealers.

In 1800–1 the situation was even more hostile to the middlemen, who had something of a press campaign directed against them in the spring and summer of 1800; Sir Samuel Romilly commented that 'great pains have been taken by persons in high authority to persuade them [the people] that what they suffer is not to be ascribed to those natural causes which were obvious to their senses, but to the frauds and rapaciousness of the dealers in provisions'.[100] As a result considerable hostility focused upon the middlemen, as shown in some of the hand-bills and posters displayed in many places. A paper put up in Portsmouth signed by 'Old England' ran:

> 'To the Farmer, Miller and Baker,
> These three you see,
> Each of you take your choice,
> The greatest Rogue shall have the greatest hoist'.[101]

In Wigan a handbill declared 'Do for God's sake stop the business of monopoly and forestalling otherwise the consequences will be dreadful', while in Oxford a paper was put up on Carfax Church asking for some journeyman carpenters to come forward to make a guillotine for the mealmen and farmers.[102] The dealers were accused of monopoly and the crimes of forestalling, regrating and engrossing, all of which were crimes against the free market.[103] The local authorities themselves seized on this explanation; as one magistrate put it: '. . . we are starving in the midst of plenty, by a combination of the opulent farmers and millers'.[104] Another recognised that in 1799 the poor had never clamoured against the scarcity of that year as being artificial, but that now 'the greater number of rich and poor impute the present high price of corn to the speculation of farmers'.[105] The middlemen, according to yet another middle-class correspondent, were 'unfeeling wretches who, by the arts and practices of forestalling and monopoly, keep back from market and enhance the prices of the most essential necessaries of life.'[106]

The focusing of grievances upon an immediately accessible group played an important part in the disturbances of 1800–1, for the climate of opinion amongst the natural leaders of the community seemed to justify popular action. Earl Fitzwilliam in Sheffield wrote that the complaint of high prices was one which 'every man's feelings admit as a sufficient cause for assembling to state it'.[107] Lord Kenyon, the Lord Chief Justice, proclaimed that: 'Private individuals are plundering at the expense of public happiness . . . when the sword of justice is drawn, it shall not be sheathed until the full vengeance of the law is inflicted on them; neither purse not person shall prevent it.'[108] The sympathy shown by the authorities can have done little other than reinforce the strong popular feeling that action against the food-dealers was legitimate.

The role of political agitation in these disturbances is not easy to evaluate, although the government continued to fear that political capital might be made out of scarcity. Anxious magistrates and other observers watched the price of grain with an acute awareness of the ease with which discontent could be exploited. A correspondent to the Home Office in August 1795 believed that 'a want of food must and will keep the popular mind in such a state of irritability as to be easily worked upon by mischievous men'.[109] An anonymous correspondent in the same month warned that 'the democrats are taking every pains to persuade them [the people] that this scarcity is occasioned by the bad management of ministers'.[110] Agitation was present on several occasions. At Lewes in June 1795 there was a call to arms which obviously came from radical sources. It ran: 'Soldiers to arms, arise and avenge your cause on those bloody numskulls, Pitt and George . . . Let prudence guide and patriotic valour give the blow and whelm in ruin the aristocratic foe . . .'[111] At Richmond in 1800 the magistrates found 'seditious' tickets posted about the time and which ran: 'We are oppressed people who cry for help, but vengeance is mine and I will repay you saith the Lord.'[112] At Wigan in 1800 hand-bills were put about during food riots which proclaimed: 'When we erect the Tree of Liberty then you the magistrates like others will wish you had acted otherwise.'[113] At Walsall in October 1816 it was reported that the riots there had started after the circulation of a petition to the Prince Regent, while in Radstock in March 1817, the riots were blamed upon the circulation of 'seditious and blasphemous' pamphlets.[114]

On the whole, however, the element of 'sedition' was smaller than the authorities thought, though it was by no means insignificant. Probably the most effective piece of agitation was that which focused the attention of the London crowd on the Mark Lane cornmarket on 15th September, 1800 with placards and posters, proclaiming Liberty and a sixpenny loaf if the people assembled at the cornmarket. One ran:

'Fellow Countrymen, how long will ye quietly and cowardly suffer yourselves to be thus imposed upon and half-starved by a set of mercenary slaves and government hirelings? Can you still suffer them to proceed in their extensive monopolies, and your families are crying for food? No! Let them not exist a day longer. Ye are the Sovreignty. Rouse then from your lethargy and meet at the Corn Market on Monday'.[115]

The result was a protracted riot in the capital and the only pure price-fixing riot to occur there in the eighteenth century. Agitation of this type, however, was exceptional and most riots broke out without it. Such coincidence as there was between the outbreak of rioting in one part of the country and another, owed less to the operation of 'seditious' societies than to the relative uniformity of price movements and the reaction to them. Normal processes of circulating news and rumour served to communicate the events of one neighbourhood to another.

In many ways the disturbances conformed to the classic pattern of eighteenth-century food riots as described by Rudé, Thompson, and others. The transportation or storage of food in times of scarcity was often prevented by the populace, and the food re-sold at 'fair' prices. On other occasions the disturbances could take the form of assemblies in the market place to compel the dealers to reduce their prices to a just level; sometimes the intimidation was directed at the local authorities to compel them to intervene in the marketing of provisions.[116] Stopping the movement of grain was particularly prevalent in 1795–6, when vessels, barges, and carts were frequently seized and unloaded, sometimes having their contents sold at a just price. For example at Bath a group of women boarded a vessel laden with grain and refused to let it sail.[117] At Deddington a group of women seized flour from barges and re-sold it at a fair price.[118] Again in 1800 there were frequent attempts to stop food moving out of particular areas, at Lane End, a mob of people headed by a woman ringing a bell forcibly unloaded a group of carts on their way to Newcastle-under-Lyme.[119] There were a number of incidents of barges being stopped on the Aire and Calder from taking grain to Leeds and Bradford.[120] This type of disturbance continued in the later shortages, for example in 1812 carts passing through Manchester had their contents seized and re-sold at a 'fair' price.[121] In 1816 a cargo of potatoes was prevented from being shipped from Bideford by a body of men armed with bludgeons and other weapons.[122]

On other occasions the dealers had their goods seized in the market place and forcibly re-sold. Along the south and east coasts in 1795 the soldiers usually went straight to market where they enforced a fair price for provisions. Similarly at Aylesbury a mob, largely composed of women, seized upon the wheat in market and sold it at their own price.[123] In 1800 dealers were commonly intimidated to reduce prices; at Oxford, for example, a large crowd assembled and compelled the food dealers to reduce their prices; those who refused to comply had their stalls or carts overturned.[124] At Manchester in 1812 it was reported that a 'sort of maximum' price for potatoes had been forced on the dealers by women at the market.[125] At Oldham and Sheffield shop-keepers were presented with price lists and threatened with attack if they refused to comply.[126] At Macclesfield a mob entered the town and interrogated the dealers, who giving unsatisfactory answers, had their goods spoiled.[127]

In a rare example of an account of a food riot from 'below', a letter found upon a weaver from Middleton Cheney described events in Nottingham in September 1800 and showed the influence of the populace upon the dealers.

'... the Bakers and flour sellers had had a private meeting on Sunday and had agreed to raise the price of flour up to six shillings a stone on Monday and there having been But a Very Scanty Supply all the Week Before exasperated the inhabitants to that degree that they Begun with them on the Sunday night. Breaking their windows and doing all the damage it was in their power to do them continuing it all night long and having done with them proceeded the next morning to the new canal and begun with unwarehousing the corn and flour they could find there together with two boats loaded with corn . . . on Tuesday a loaded waggon appearing with rioters from Arnold escorted by the Yeomanry they [the mob] attacked both Yeomanry and infantry with such fury . . . that they was their masters tho' armed with nothing but stones . . . Wednesday a deal of fighting and tumult Thursday beginning to subside and selling of flour at 3/6 the stone at the Malt Cross the corporation having purchased 130 quarters of wheat for the use of the poor. Your hearts would have ached to have seen the women Calling for Bread and Declaring they would fight till they died Before they would be used so any longer however the Gentlemen Began to be frightened and a meeting of the Sheriff and County Gentlemen has been held at the County Hall and they have agreed to compel their tenants to bring corn to market and to sell it in small quantities to the poor thus has the price been lowered almost 4 pounds a quarter by nothing but the courage of the people in declaring against oppression . . . All seems now to wear the appearance of tranquillity But the people swear that it shall not continue so long unless the price of provisions is brought to its proper height.'[128]

Other disturbances took the form of attacks upon corn mills. In June 1795 a body of Dudley colliers attacked a mill and were only driven off after a party of dragoons opened fire upon them, killing one and wounding two others; in 1800 a local corn mill was attacked at Blandford.[129] In October 1816 men from Walsall marched a mile out of the town to destroy some new mills in the area, which were gutted and their contents carried away.[130] Other disturbances took the form of attacks upon the property of dealers and food-sellers. In September 1800 a mob at Banbury set fire to an inn belonging to a local farmer and corn-dealer.[131] At Nottingham a millers house was attacked.[132] In London a whole series of attacks took place from September 13th, lasting almost a week, in which the shops of bakers, food wholesalers, and the houses of men convicted of monopolistic offences were attacked.[133] Similarly in Carlisle in 1812 a mob of '300 men and women' plundered a warehouse containing food; and in 1816 the disturbances in the Midlands, East Anglia, and London followed a similar pattern.[134]

Another dimension to the disturbances was given by the

latent conflict between town and country. In some cases
market towns felt threatened or were actually invaded by
groups of workmen from isolated country areas. In the south-
west in 1795 the tinners entered several towns to demand
provisions at a reasonable price.[135] In Bristol the magistrates
were intimidated by groups of colliers who demanded a
meeting with the food dealers.[136] In 1800 the stocking-
weavers from the Banbury area played a leading part in the
disturbances in the town.[137] The actual instances of such
invasions quickly became compounded by alarmist rumours.
Thus at Banbury in 1800 it began to be feared that the
Warwickshire colliers as a body would come to the town
seeking provisions.[138] In a similar way, in 1795, Gloucester
felt itself threatened by the colliers from the Forest of Dean,
although this threat never materialised.[139] Again in the later
shortages similar movements took place. In Macclesfield in
1812 a mob assembled outside the town before entering it to
interrogate the dealers on the price of provisions.[140] At Truro
in 1812 the tinners came into the town from the Redruth-
Camborne area on a similar errand.[141] In May 1816 the
East Anglian rioters descended upon the market towns of
Downham and Ely.[142]

Elsewhere the movement was reversed with mobs marching from the towns into the surrounding countryside to force
millers and farmers to bring grain and other food-stuffs to
market. This occurred in September 1800 at Oxford when a
number of forays were made into the surrounding countryside to compel farmers to bring grain to market at reasonable
prices.[143] At Sheffield in the same year, a mob went out of the
town to the nearby collieries to recruit more forces.[144] In
Cornwall in 1812 it was reported that the tinners were scour-
ing the countryside with empty sacks which they hoped to
fill with grain.[145] Because of the large groups of workmen
living in a semi-rural environment, the conflict between
town and country in England was never so clear-cut as it was
in France in the same period. Although a common enemy
might be found in time of shortage in the dealer and farmer,
this antagonism could take equally the form of a descent

upon the local market town or a *journée* into the country-side.[146]

Scarcity sometimes revealed a conflict between the local authorities and the central government. As shown earlier, in these shortages the central government was often acting against the natural inclination of local magistrates in emphasising the free circulation of grain. The local authorities could be prevented by legislation from interfering with the movement of grain about the country, but little could be done to prevent local magistrates from intervening in the marketing of food in their area. Thus in many towns the local magistrates took the initiative in arranging a reduction of prices with the food dealers, as for example at Banbury in 1800.[147] In the same year at Nottingham it was reported that the J.Ps were considering taking over the corn trade from the dealers.[148] At Brandon in 1816 the magistrates agreed to press the corn dealers for a reduction in prices.[149] In other places the authorities revived the medieval instrument of the Assize of Bread, which fixed bread prices in relation to the cost of grain.[150] In places where it had ceased to be observed, a number of exemplary prosecutions were made.[151] Similarly, the legislation against monopolistic market practices was revived and prosecutions undertaken. In 1800 the most important trial was that of John Rusby, a London corn dealer before Lord Kenyon, for regrating. At Oxford the city council started actions against a number of dealers, although they were discontinued as the crisis passed.[152] These actions by the local authorities often showed them acting in sympathy with the local inhabitants against the spirit of the central governments.

Many of the food riots of this period continued to exhibit the ritual elements associated with earlier food disturbances. These were to be found in abundance in 1795, for example at Seaford the Oxfordshire militia took meat from the market stalls and re-sold it in a churchyard at reduced prices.[153] In 1800 carts were stopped at Lane End on their way to New-castle-under-Lyme by a mob wearing blue ribbons and headed by a woman ringing a bell.[154] In Bridport in 1816 rioters paraded the streets of the town bearing a quartern loaf stuck on the end of a pole.[155] The East Anglian rioters in May 1816 exhibited several ritual elements, displaying banners inscribed 'Bread or Blood' and marching upon the local market towns headed by musical instruments, such as 'fife and horn', or simply by a man carrying a horn.[156] These ritualised elements even survived in highly urbanised environments, such as London, where many protests about food prices were accompanied by people carrying loaves draped in black crepe on top of poles.[157]

The survival of the characteristic forms of food rioting and their accompanying ritual should not, however, obscure the most important feature of this period, which is the declining importance of food rioting as a means of popular protest. Not only were food riots declining in number, but they were being replaced by other forms of protest more suited to an industrial environment. Even in the shortages of 1795–6 and 1800–1 there was some overlap of forms. Strikes were common in both years, and occasionally they merged with attempts to reduce the price of provisions. Thus in 1795 when the Chatham shipwrights struck work on some naval vessels, they assembled that evening in the market to reduce the price of provisions.[158] In September 1800 the cloth-workers of Wotton-under-Edge were reported to have struck work to reduce the price of bread.[159] By the end of this period food rioting overlapped with other forms of disturbances and activity. In the period 1811–13, food riots and frame-breaking took place side by side in south Lancashire and north-east Cheshire.[160] During that period of shortage, however, food rioting was completely overshadowed in the Midlands and Yorkshire by the Luddite outbreaks.[161] In 1816–18 a similar transitional situation can be seen. In some of the small ports and market towns, traditional food riots survived. In other areas, however, such as the East Anglia riots, demands for reductions in the price of food were accompanied by demands for higher wages.[162] In the Midland manufacturing towns in 1816–17 'collective bargaining by riot' overlapped with food rioting, for the disturbances in the area (as in South Wales) frequently saw strikers moving about the area, demanding a stoppage of work and supplies of provisions.[163]

In this way the traditional forms of food rioting were giving way to other forms of protest. In some cases it was merely the targets that changed, so that food riots merged into 'collective bargaining by riot'. Thus, at Radstock in March 1817, 3,000 miners assembled to resist a cut in wages; they forced the men working underground to come to the surface and join them and march to the neighbouring mines to spread the stoppage. They then assembled at Radstock armed with bludgeons and refused to disperse even though surrounded by the local Yeomanry Cavalry. They are reported to have cried out 'Bread or Blood' and that they were starving. Eventually the Riot Act was read and the miners dispersed.[164] Elsewhere rioting had already been overtaken by trade union activity and strikes, even under the combination laws.[165] Thus the post-war period saw widespread strike activity amongst many different types of workers.[166] Protest also took other forms, some of them quite new; for example in 1816 groups of colliers from the Midlands dragged carts full of coal as far as London in an attempt to draw attention to their distress and obtain relief.[167] Although other forms of riot continued well into the nineteenth century, food rioting was overtaken by other forms of protest in urban and industrial contexts.

In rural areas a similar transition was taking place during this period. Agricultural labourers played little part in food disturbances during the eighteenth century and in the first shortages of this period. By 1816, however, in the most advanced agricultural areas, such as East Anglia, where extensive arable farming by wage-labour had become the norm, the agricultural labourers began to take part in popular protest of various types. In 1816 these included food rioting, 'collective bargaining by riot' for higher wages or relief, incendiarism, and machine-breaking.[168] It was these forms of protest that dominated agricultural disturbances between 1816 and the 'Captain Swing' outbreaks of

1830–2.[169] By the time of the 'Captain Swing' disturbances
of 1830–2, food rioting was a very minor part of the wave of
protest which swept over southern England; only three food
riots have been found in the area affected by the disturbances.[170]

The last bastion in England of the traditional food riot was
Cornwall. In the winter of 1830–1 there were food riots at
Mevagissey, Fowey, Penzance, and Helston.[171] The last
major outbreak of food disturbances occurred in spring 1847,
again in Cornwall, when poor harvests and trade depression
led to disturbances in Callington, Launceston, and Penzance.
In the usual manner the miners and quarrymen invaded
markets and fixed prices for wheat, barley, and butter.[172]
This survival can be related to the relative backwardness of
the economy in the south-west, which remained little
changed by industrialisation and urbanisation. The Cornish
tinners remained a group with difficulties of food supply in a
poor and infertile part of the country. In the British Isles as a
whole, areas similar to Cornwall provided the last strongholds of food rioting, which occurred in the remoter parts of
Wales and Scotland until the middle of the nineteenth
century.[173]

As shown earlier the food riots of this period rarely
denoted a real subsistence crisis, but rather a consumer
reaction to prices that were considered to be 'unfair'.
Unfortunately evidence of the prices at which food was re-
sold or to which it was reduced is only available in a small
number of detailed reports of food disturbances. From these,
however, it appears that the 'fair' price for food was by no
means constant. In 1795 the lowest price at which wheat was
re-sold was 42s per quarter (Seaford), which corresponded to
the lowest average for the past decade, that of the immediate
pre-war year, 1792.[174] By 1800, however, wheat was being
re-sold and reduced to prices of between 80s per quarter
(Oxford) and 100s per quarter (Leicester). Here even the
'fair' prices were higher than anything previously experienced. The prices at which bread was demanded also
show an increase – in 1795 the quartern loaf was demanded

at 9d (Hadstock), but for a 1s in 1800 (Banbury). Similarly meat, which was re-sold at 4d per pound in 1795 (Guildford, Seaford, and Handborough) was fixed in 1800 from 5d per pound (Oxford) to 7d per pound (Nuneaton). Butter too showed an increase in the 'fair' price, from 8d per pound in 1795 (Wells) to 1s per pound in 1800 (Oxford). From this evidence, albeit fragmentary, it appears that the 'fair' price was not a fixed one, deriving from some standard in the past, but one that was dictated by local circumstances and the conditions of the market in each year.

The interpretation of these disturbances as manifestations of general 'consumer consciousness' is borne out by considering how many of them, even in 1795–6, were 'grocery' riots, concerned not only with the price of wheat or bread, but with other foodstuffs that were not essential to subsistence. The commodities involved included meat (Wisbech, Coventry, Portsea: 1795; Oxford, Nuneaton: 1800; Brandon: 1816), cheese (Seaford: 1795; Nuneaton; London: 1800), butter (Wells, Aylesbury, Deddington: 1795; Oxford, Banbury: 1800; Carlisle: 1812), potatoes (Hull: 1795; Manchester, Carlisle: 1812; Bideford: 1816). These were usually treated in the same way as grain or bread, with attempts to regulate the price, and spoiling the food if this was not complied with.

The war-time food shortages of this period saw the last major waves of food rioting in England, certainly the last in which food rioting predominated as a form of discontent with economic and social conditions. As we have seen the disturbances of the years 1795–6 were the most widespread, and they have some claim to be regarded as the largest outbreak of food disturbances to occur in England at any period. The largest group of disturbances before them had been the food riots of 1766, of which Rudé suggests there were at least sixty within three months. Over a longer period, about twelve months from spring 1795 to spring 1796, there were over seventy food disturbances.[175] In this sense they formed a peak in the outbreak of disturbances of this type between the end of the seventeenth century and the early decades of the nineteenth century. However, there is no evidence to suggest that the disturbances of 1795–6 denoted a crisis of revolutionary proportions. The disturbances themselves were not markedly dissimilar from earlier food disturbances and on the whole showed little political involvement or motivation. The disturbances do not seem, in the light of present evidence, to have been born out of a real subsistence crisis, for the behaviour of the rioters and their choice of targets does not suggest an exceptionally desperate situation. Although more work needs to be done on the mortality data for the period, particularly on a regional basis, before conclusive evidence is forthcoming, it appears unlikely that these years saw a major demographic catastrophe.[176] Equally, none of the later waves of food rioting seem to have offered a major crisis–rather they were increasingly overshadowed by other forms of protest.

The distribution and incidence of the food disturbances in this period lead to a number of important conclusions about their nature and origins. It is clear that the incidence of food disturbances owed a great deal to the operation of the market in foodstuffs. Thus certain towns and villages were more likely to have food disturbances because they were transshipment points or market towns. Another important factor was the distribution of particularly vulnerable sectors of the population, such as manufacturing workers. In the earlier waves of food riots it was workmen in isolated or marginal areas of subsistence who were most likely to be involved in food disturbances, but in the later food disturbances there was a marked shift in their incidence to the larger manufacturing towns of the north and Midlands. These two factors – communications and composition of the population –were crucial in deciding whether particular towns or villages were disturbed. As in the timing of disturbances, fairly precise reasons can be given for the occurrence of food disturbances in particular areas and towns, and it is to these factors, rather than to more general interpretations that we should look for the outbreak of disorder. Too often in the past general explanations have been regarded as sufficient for outbreaks of food rioting: where earlier economic historians looked to the incidence of harvest failure to explain them, recent writers, notably E. P. Thompson, have turned to generalised social explanations – that food riots were the outcome of the 'moral economy' of the eighteenth-century crowd, who operated 'within a popular consensus as to what were legitimate and what were illegitimate practices in marketing, milling, baking, etc.', and who reacted to any 'outrage to these moral assumptions'.[177] Perceptive as these comments might be about the motivation and significance of food disturbances, they tell us virtually nothing about why some places were almost perennially subject to disturbances, whilst others remained almost completely undisturbed. General economic and social interpretations do not provide an explanation on this level, otherwise food disturbances would have been universal phenomena, which clearly they were not. It is necessary to examine the precise economic and social context, often on a regional level, before the critical causes become apparent in the outbreak of disturbances of this type. In this study food disturbances have been found to be the result of a highly complex interaction of factors, some of which have been stressed as the most important, but still only part of a complex process.

After a short period in which food rioting existed side by side with other forms of popular protest, it quickly gave way to other forms of popular protest. In this sense there was a 'modernisation of protest' as the patterns of protest appropriate to the 'face to face' society of the small market town gave way to the more permanent and larger-scale organisations of urban and industrial life.[178] It was not a simple process, for there were many overlaps between one form of protest and another. Nonetheless the direction of change was clear. Essentially then this was a period of transition in which one tradition of popular protest reached its peak and began to be replaced by another which drew its strength from the changes in the social and economic structure of the country.

Notes

1. G. Rudé, *The Crowd in History* (New York, 1964), pp. 33–8.
2. *Ibid.*; see also R. B. Rose, 'Eighteenth Century Price Riots and Public Policy in England', *International Review of Social History*, vol. VI (1961), pp. 277–82; C. Tilly, 'Collective Violence in European Perspective', pp. 16–19 in H. D. Graham and T. R. Gurr (eds), *Violence in America* (New York, 1969).
3. G. Rudé, *op. cit.*, pp. 37–8; R. B. Rose, *op. cit.*, pp. 283–4.
4. See F. M. Eden, *The State of the Poor* (ed. A. L. Rogers, London, 1928), pp. 100–1; W. Ashley, *The Bread of Our Forefathers* (Oxford, 1928), pp. 22–5).
5. See J. Middleton, *View of the Agriculture of Middlesex* (London, 1798), p. 389.
6. See R. N. Salaman, *The History and Social Influence of the Potato* (Cambridge, 1947), p. 493; J. C. Drummond and A. Wilbraham, *The Englishman's Food* (2nd edn, London, 1957), p. 181; Eden *op. cit.*, pp. 100–4.
7. T. C. Barker, J. C. McKenzie and J. Yudkin, *Our Changing Fare* (London, 1966), pp. 61–2.
8. See *Hansard*, 1795, vol. XXXII, 698; *The Times*, 15th December, 1795.
9. Barker, McKenzie, and Yudkin, *op. cit.*, p. 69.
10. W. M. Stern, 'The Bread Crisis in Britain, 1795–6', *Economica*, vol. XXXI (1964); M. Olson, *The Economics of the Wartime Shortage* (Durham, NC, 1963), pp. 49–51.
11. G. A. Williams, *Artisans and Sans-Culottes* (London, 1968), p. 101; E. P. Thompson, *The Making of the English Working Class* (2nd edn, London, 1968), p. 73.
12. I have counted as a 'disturbance' any tumultuous assembly which was serious enough to be reported by the press or by the authorities. These have been compiled from the Home Office papers in the Public Record Office, series 42 and 43 and from the national and local press.
13. M. Olson, *op. cit.*, pp. 52–3; *Gentleman's Magazine*, 1800–1.
14. G. Pellew, *Life and Correspondence of First Viscount Sidmouth* (London, 1847), vol. I, p. 270.
15. A. Prentice, *Historical Sketches and Personal Recollections of Manchester* (3rd edn, London, 1970), p. 26.
16. G. Rudé, *op. cit.*, p. 37.
17. M. Olson, *op. cit.*, p. 63; monthly averages from *Gentleman's Magazine*, 1810–13.
18. From an average price of 55s per quarter in March 1816, the average price of wheat moved to 90s in November and 105s in December.
19. For a discussion of this problem see J. T. Krause, 'English Population Movements between 1700 and 1850', *International Population Conference, New York 1961*, vol. I (1963).
20. See the monthly mortality returns in the *Gentleman's Magazine*, 1794–5. In 1795 the three winter months, January, February and March accounted for 35 per cent of total deaths. The average for the 1790s was only 30 per cent.

21. E. P. Thompson, 'The Moral Economy of the English Crowd in the Eighteenth Century', *Past and Present*, vol. L (1971), p. 134.

22. M. Olson, *op. cit.*, pp. 69–70.

23. British Museum, Place newspaper cuttings, Vol. 12.

24. M. Olson, *op. cit.*, pp. 62–3.

25. For the weakness of agricultural returns see W. E. Minchington, 'Agricultural Returns and the Government during the Napoleonic Wars', *Agricultural History Review*, vol. I (1953); see also Olson, pp. 68–71.

26. *Mitchell and Deane*, pp. 94–5.

27. *Hansard*, 1814, vol. 235–41.

28. See G. E. Fussell and C. Goodman, 'The Eighteenth Century Traffic in Farm Produce', *Agricultural History* (1938) and 'The Eighteenth Century Traffic in Livestock', *Economic History*, vol. III (1934–7); see also W. Freeman Galpin, *The Grain Supply of England during the Napoleonic Wars* (New York, 1925).

29. For the existence of a national market see A. Young, *Tours in England and Wales* (reprint, London, 1932), p. 258 and E. W. Gilboy, *Wages in Eighteenth Century England* (Harvard, 1935), p. 219. Within short fluctuations, however, prices have been found to be less connected over the country as a whole, see C. W. J. Grainger and C. M. Elliot, 'A Fresh Look at Wheat Prices and Markets in the Eighteenth Century', *Economic History Review*, vol. XX (1967), p. 261.

30. See O. A. K. Spate, 'The Growth of London, A.D. 1660–1800', in H. C. Darby, *An Historical Geography of England Before A.D. 1800* (Cambridge, 1936), pp. 541–2; W. Marshall, *The Rural Economy of the Southern Counties* (London, 1798) vol. I, 122–3; BT 6/139, p. 17; An Account of the Wheat and Wheaten flour brought coastwise to London, 31st October, 1800.

31. See W. M. Stern, 'The Bread Crisis in Britain, 1795–96', *Economica*, new series, vol. XXXI (1964), pp. 176–8; Olson, *op. cit.*, pp. 50–1.

32. Public Record Office, Privy Council papers, PC 1/27, A.54: Mayor of Winchester to Privy Council, 8th August, 1795.

33. PC 1/29, A.57, Petition of Essex bakers, 16th July, 1795.

34. PC 1/27, A.54, Privy Council to Mayor of Winchester, 9th July, 1795.

35. PC 1/29, A.57, reply to Essex bakers, 16th July, 1795.

36. HO 42/35, Charlwood to Portland, 30th June, 1795.

37. M. S. Gretton, *Burford* (London, 1944), p. 90.

38. HO 42/35, Atkinson to Portland, 2nd July, 1795.

39. 36 Geo. III cap. 9. The act received its third reading on 18th December, 1795.

40. *British Parliamentary Papers, Reports*, 1774–1802: First Report of the Parliamentary Committee on the High Price of Provisions, November 1795.

41. HO 43/7, Portland to Mayor of Portsmouth, 10th June, 1800.

42. HO 40/3, Portland to Bastard, 13th April, 1801.

43. See for example, R. Cobb, *The Police and the People* (2nd edn, Oxford, 1972), p. 262.

44. PC 4/6, Sockett to Dundas, 26th October, 1795.

45. PC 1/26, A.54, draft letter of Duke of Portland, 2nd July, 1795.

46. HO 43/7, Portland to Grafton, 1st August, 1795.

47. HO 43/7 and HO 42/35.

48. HO 42/35, Fowks to Portland, 24th June, 1795.
49. HO 42/34, reports to Home Office, April 1795.
50. HO 42/35, Mayor of Carlisle to Home Office, 28th July, 1795.
51. *London Chronicle*, 10th May, 1816; A. J. Peacock, *Bread or Blood* (London, 1965).
52. HO 42/51, September 1800.
53. F. O. Darvall, *Popular Disturbances and Public Order in Regency England* (2nd edn, London, 1969), pp. 90–105; *London Chronicle*, 20th July, 1810 (Wolverhampton); 17th April, 1812 (Sheffield and Stockport); 21st April, 1812 (Macclesfield and Barnsley); 23rd April, 1812 (Carlisle); 27th August, 1812 (Wakefield).
54. F. O. Darvall, *op. cit.*, Ch. vii; A. J. Peacock, *op. cit.*
55. HO 42/34, report to Home Office, 30th March, 1795.
56. HO 43/7, Report to Home Office, 11th April, 1796.
57. See for example HO 42/34, report to Home Office, 6th April, 1795; and HO 42/35, 29th July, 1795.
58. HO 42/35, Clayton to Portland, 11th August, 1795; letter from Wisbech, 25th July, 1795 and 1st August, 1795.
59. HO 42/51, report from Witney, 22nd September, 1800; Hughes to Portland, 15th September, 1800.
60. HO 42/50, Buckingham to Portland, 6th May, 1800.
61. See F. O. Darvall, *op. cit.*
62. PC 1/27, A.54, Mayor of Weymouth to Privy Council, 7th July, 1795.
63. *Ibid.*, Mayor of King's Lynn to Privy Council, 7th July, 1795.
64. HO 42/34, Elford to Home Office, 6th April, 1795.
65. *Ibid.*, Turner to Portland, 28th April, 1795.
66. *Ibid.*, Mayor of Portsmouth to Portland, 12th April, 1795.
67. War Office papers 1/1088, ff. 117, 133; *Annual Register*, 1795, Chronicle, p. 23.
68. *Annual Register*, 1795, Chronicle, p. 328; WO 1/1088, f. 125.
69. *Kentish Register*, 1795, p. 153.
70. PC 4/7, Minutes of Privy Council, 25th January, 1796.
71. See for example the action taken with the South Hampshire Militia at Canterbury in April 1795; *Kentish Register*, 1795, p. 153.
72. For confirmation of this point see D. J. V. Jones, *Before Rebecca* (London, 1973), pp. 31–2; see also S. G. E. Lythe, 'The Tayside meal mobs 1772–3', *Scottish History Review*, vol. XLVI (1967), p. 35; G. Rudé, *The Crowd in History*, *op. cit.*, p. 45; E. P. Thompson, *op. cit.*, p. 119.
73. See PC 1/26, A.51, Willoughby to Carter, 28th June, 1795; PC 1/27, A.54, Mayor of Weymouth to Privy Council, 7th July, 1795.
74. See A. J. Peacock, *Bread or Blood*, Chs 1–3.
75. See E. J. Hobsbawm and G. Rudé, *Captain Swing* (London, 1969), Ch. 4.
76. HO 42/35; Foulks to Portland, 24th June, 1795.
77. HO 42/50, Mayor of Honiton to Home Office, 10th May, 1800
78. HO 42/35, report to Home Office, 30th July, 1795.
79. HO 42/51, Mayor of Blandford to Home Office, 9th September, 1800.
80. *Leicester Journal*, 12th September, 1800.
81. See A. Prentice, *op. cit.*, pp. 52–5; F. O. Darvall, pp. 93–8.
82. J. W. Rowe, *Cornwall in the Age of the Industrial Revolution* (Liverpool, 1953), pp. 160–1; see also W. Marshall; *The Rural Economy of the South-West*

(London, 1796); Marshall commented upon the backwardness of agriculture inland from the coast which he blamed upon the poverty of communications, he urged the construction of a canal across the peninsula from Exeter to the north coast, pp. 36–7.

83. See S. G. E. Lythe, 'The Tayside Meal Mobs 1772–3', *op. cit.*, p. 31 for similar conditions on Tayside.

84. See G. Rudé, *The Crowd in History, op. cit.*, pp. 41–5 for riots in 1766 in the Midlands; and R. B. Rose, 'Eighteenth Century Price Riots and Public Policy in England', *op. cit.*, p. 285.

85. HO 43/7, Portland to Sheriff of Nottingham, 24th July, 1795.

86. It is possible that the widespread use of potatoes in the north also eased the situation.

87. PC 1/26, A.55, J. Sinclair to Home Office, 12th July 1795.

88. See P. Colquhoun's report on prices in the capital, PC 1/27, A.54, Colquhoun to Portland, 9th July, 1795; for the Assize of Bread see S. and B. Webb, 'The Assize of Bread', *Economic Journal*, vol. XIV (1904), pp. 211–16.

89. There was, for example, an extensive development of soup-kitchens in the capital from the winter of 1795–6. They provided a large number of cheap meals in the poorer parishes. See HO 42/66, An account of the public services of Patrick Colquhoun (undated), 1804 and Society for Bettering the Conditions of the poor, *The Economy of an Institution* (London, 1799).

90. *Gentleman's Magazine*, vol. LXV (1795), pp. 965–6.

91. See Home Office 42/51 for reports on the disturbances; see also Corporation of London Record Office, Repertory of Court of Aldermen, 204, ff. 420–22; *Gentleman's Magazine*, vol. LXX (1800), pp. 894–5.

92. Following the Spa Fields meeting on 15th November, 1816 'a considerable body' of young men and boys paraded about the West End and attacked a number of bakers' shops, *London Chronicle*, 16th–18th November, 1816.

93. Monthly averages from the *Gentleman's Magazine*.

94. See. F. O. Darvall, *op. cit.*, pp. 96–7; Prentice, *op. cit.*, p. 53.

95. Average prices of wheat per quarter from the *Gentleman's Magazine*.

	Cambridge	Norfolk
February	52s 11d	54s 8d
March	50s 3d	52s 9d
April	62s 11d	61s 1d
May	77s 1d	77s 5d

96. HO 42/51, Bracebridge to Home Office, 19th September, 1800.

97. Place Newspaper cuttings, Vol. 12: a return of prices of the quartern loaf in London, 1799–1801, 22nd February, 1815.

98. PC 1/29, A.64, Pane to Portland, 7th August, 1795.

99. HO 42/35, Anonymous letter to Portland, 15th July, 1795.

100. S. Romilly, *Memoirs of Sir Samuel Romilly* (London, 1840), vol. I, pp. 73–5. Hostility particularly focused upon the Quakers who were prominent in the corn trade, see I. Grub, *Quakerism and Industry before 1800* (London, 1930), pp. 124–7. In the London area they were accused of hoarding grain in a Quaker meeting house at Uxbridge. See also F. H. Allport and M. Lepkin, 'Wartime Rumours of Waste and Special Privilege', *Journal of Abnormal and Social Psychology*, vol. XL, pp. 3–36.

101. HO 42/51, Enclosure sent into Home Office, 18th September, 1800.
102. *Ibid.*, Enclosure to Portland, 20th September, 1800; Hughes to Portland. 7th September, 1800.
103. Forestalling was buying food coming to market; regrating was the resale of food immediately after a market; engrossing was buying growing crops. See D. G. Barnes, *A History of the English Corn Laws* (London, 1930), p. 2.
104. HO 42/51, Bracebridge to Portland, 19th September, 1800.
105. HO 42/52, Rauby to Portland, 24th October, 1800.
106. HO 42/51, Mitchell to Portland, 23rd September, 1800.
107. *Ibid.*, FitzWilliam to Portland, 2nd September, 1800.
108. Quoted Olson, *op. cit.*, p. 54. See *Annals of Agriculture*, 1795, p. 3.
109. PC 1/29, A.64, Pane to Privy Council, 7th August, 1795.
110. HO 42/35, Anonymous information to Portland, 6th July, 1795.
111. *Ibid.*, Enclosure sent into the Home Office, June 1795; see also the report of 'inflammatory papers' at the Birmingham riots, *Annual Register*, 1795, Chronicle, pp. 25–7.
112. HO 42/51, Enclosure sent into the Home Office, Sep. 1800.
113. *Ibid.*, Enclosure sent into the Home Office, 20th September, 1800.
114. *Annual Register*, 1816, Chronicle, p. 174 and 1817, Chronicle, pp. 15–16.
115. *London Chronicle*, 13th–16th September, 1800.
116. See for example the report from Banbury, HO 42/51: Walford to Portland, 11th September, 1800.
117. J. L. and B. Hammond, *The Village Labourer* (5th edn, London, 1966), p. 117.
118. *Ibid.*, p. 118.
119. HO 42/50, Turner to Portland, 29th April, 1800.
120. HO 42/51, Willoughby to Portland, 5th August, 1800.
121. Prentice, *op. cit.*, p. 52.
122. *Annual Register*, 1816, Chronicle, pp. 68–9.
123. J. L. and B. Hammond, *op. cit.*, p. 117.
124. HO 42/51, Hughes to Portland, 7th September, 1800.
125. Prentice, *op. cit.*, p. 52.
126. F. O. Darvall, *op. cit.*, p. 99; Annual Register, 1812, Chronicle, p. 104.
127. Darvall, *op. cit.*, pp. 96–7.
128. HO 42/51, Whitmore to Portland (letter enclosed), 17th September, 1800.
129. HO 42/35, report from Dudley, 23rd June, 1795; HO 42/51: Mayor of Blandford to Home Office, 9th September, 1800.
130. *Annual Register*, 1816, Chronicle, p. 174.
131. HO 42/51, Hughes to Portland, 16th September, 1800.
132. *Ibid.*, Smith to King, 13th September, 1800.
133. *Gentleman's Magazine*, vol. LXX (1800), pp. 894–5.
134. *Annual Register*, 1812, Chronicle, pp. 46–7.
135. See the reports from Cornwall in HO 42/34.
136. HO 43/6, report from Bristol, May 1795.
137. HO 42/51, Walford to Portland, 11th September, 1800.
138. *Ibid.*
139. HO 42/34, report from Gloucester, 11th May, 1795.
140. F. O. Darvall, *op cit.*, pp. 96–7.
141. *Annual Register*, 1812, Chronicle, p. 52.

142. A. J. Peacock, *Bread or Blood, op. cit.*; at Cambridge there were reports of 'strange countrymen, coming in with large sticks, for two or three days past': *Annual Register*, 1816, Chronicle, pp. 70–1.

143. HO 42/51, Willoughby to Portland, 21st September, 1800.

144. *Ibid.*, FitzWilliam to Portland, 2nd September, 1800.

145. *Annual Register*, 1812, Chronicle, p. 52.

146. For urban and rural conflict in France during the scarcities of this period, see R. Cobb, *op. cit.*, pp. 215–45.

147. HO 42/51, Walford to Portland, 11th September 1800.

148. *Ibid.*, Smith to King, 13th September, 1800.

149. A. J. Peacock, *op. cit.*, pp. 77–81.

150. See for example HO 42/51: Bracebridge to Portland, 19th September, 1800 (Nuneaton); S. and B. Webb, *op. cit.*, pp. 209, 213–4.

151. S. and B. Webb, *op. cit.*, p. 209.

152. *Jackson's Oxford Journal*, 6th September, 1800.

153. WO 1/1088, f. 117, Harbin to War Office, 16th April, 1795.

154. HO 42/50, Turner to Portland, 29th April, 1800.

155. *Annual Register*, 1812, Chronicle, pp. 60–1.

156. A. J. Peacock, *op. cit.*, pp. 79, 87–9.

157. See *London Chronicle*, 16th–18th November, 1816.

158. *Kentish Register*, 1795, p. 115.

159. HO 42/51, report to Home Office, 16th September, 1800.

160. See F. O. Darvall, *op. cit.*, Ch. 5; Prentice, *op. cit.*, pp. 52–7.

161. See Darvall, *op. cit.*

162. See Peacock, *op. cit.*, pp. 81, 89, 102.

163. See Darvall, *op. cit.*, pp. 154–5; for the disturbance in Wales see *London Chronicle*, 12th February, 4th March, 12th March, 1817; see also the strikes and riots near Bath and Maryport, *London Chronicle*, 4th, 12th March, 1817.

164. *Annual Register*, 1817, Chronicle, pp. 15–16.

165. M. D. George, 'The Combination Laws Reconsidered', *Economic History*, vol. II (1927); S. and B. Webb, *The History of Trade Unionism* (3rd edn, London, 1907), pp. 65–75. For example in London in 1795–6 there were strikes amongst the shipwrights, coal-heavers, paper-makers and rope-makers.

166. S. and B. Webb, *op. cit.*, pp. 75–85; in 1816–18 there were strikes amongst the Midlands colliers and metal-workers; the keel-men of the north-east, the cotton spinners of Lancashire and Cheshire, as well as several London trades.

167. See *Annual Register*, 1816, Chronicle, pp. 95–7, 98–100.

168. A. J. Peacock, *op. cit.*; Hobsbawm and Rudé, *Captain Swing*, Ch. 4.

169. Hobsbawm and Rudé, *op. cit.* For reports of incendiarism in 1816 see *London Chronicle*, 10th May, 1816; *Annual Register*, 1816, Chronicle, pp. 61–2.

170. Hobsbawm and Rudé, *op. cit.*, Appendix I.

171. Hobsbawm and Rudé, *Captain Swing, op. cit.*, pp. 102–3.

172. J. Rowe, *op. cit.*, pp. 160–1; A. Rowe, 'The Food Riots of the Forties in Cornwall', *Report of Royal Cornwall Polytechnic Society, 1942*. Individual food riots were recorded as late as the 1860s in the south-west.

173. See E. P. Thompson, 'The Moral Economy of the English Crowd in the Eighteenth Century', p. 129; R. B. Rose, *op. cit.*, pp. 282–3.

174. Averages from *Mitchell and Deane*.
175. G. Rudé, *The Crowd in History*, *op. cit.*, p. 44; *Annual Register*, 1766, Chronicle, pp. 137–40.
176. Areas of marginal subsistence, such as the extreme north and south-west, would especially reward further study from this viewpoint. New techniques of measuring the incidence of malnutrition, through a fall in the number of conceptions due to the phenomenon of 'amenorrhea' might have something to contribute in this area. See A. B. Appleby, 'Disease or Famine? Mortality in Cumberland and Westmorland, 1580–1640', *Economic History Review* vol. XXVI (1973), p. 414.
177. E. P. Thompson, 'The Moral Economy of the English Crowd.', *op. cit.*, pp. 78–9.
178. See C. Tilly, *op. cit.*, for further discussion of this point.

2

Patterns of Highland Discontent, 1790–1860[1]

E. RICHARDS

The voice of the poor themselves does not come to our ears . . .'
J. L. and Barbara Hammond[2]

The origins of popular disorder in traditional societies are often sought in the social turmoil that attends sudden economic change: in 'the dissolution of norms, controls and social attachments by large-scale structural change'.[3] No part of Britain experienced a more dramatic series of structural upheavals in the framework of life than the Scottish Highlands in the early nineteenth century. The old patriarchal system had been in decline for a century. To this was added the devastating psychological shocks of the Jacobite rebellions and then the overwhelming impact of the industrial revolution.[4] The latter accelerated the commercialisation of land-use and further loosened social relations on the *latifundia* of the great landed proprietors. Upon these complex economic changes were superimposed the consequences of a rising peasant population. For some time, perhaps until 1815, the demographic pressure was largely accommodated within the old structure. But after Waterloo many of the basic sources of subsistence declined, and the economic possibilities for labour-intensive activities narrowed. In effect the Highland economy was caught in the economists' scissor blades of rising population and diminishing employment opportunities.

These larger forces and pressures set the limits within which social relationships were moulded and directed. In retrospect it is clear that the landlords, who possessed virtual monopolies of land, capital and political power, were able to quicken or retard the transformation of Highland society in their own localities. By Scottish law they could enclose, evict and resettle on their estates with the widest freedom. The popular restraints on landlord autonomy is a central theme of this paper.

'Sheep clearances' is too simple a term[5] for landlord policy in these years. Some proprietors switched land-use from arable to cattle in the mid-eighteenth century. Some sponsored semi-industrial activity on their estates. Some encouraged population growth and the subdivision of holdings; others forced their unwanted tenants to emigrate, and discouraged marriages among the poor. Some evicted their tenants without either compunction or alternative accommodation, while some created elaborate re-settlement areas for the cleared people of the hills. The introduction of commercial sheep farming is a unifying theme in the Highlands: but the diversity of landlord response cuts against generalisation. Nevertheless the exercise of arbitrary landlord power was undeniable – as was the loud antipathy of the common people of the Highlands to the great changes subsumed in the phrase 'the clearances'.

The Highlanders have not lacked eloquent spokesmen. 'In the sixty years before 1850 one of the most despicable chapters in British history was written in the Highlands of Scotland, a chapter in which a society was destroyed and a race driven from the lands it had held since the depths of time,' – such is a typical modern condemnation. William Cobbett used similar language: '. . . the inhabitants of an almost entire country had had their houses burnt down, and themselves driven at the point of a bayonet from the land upon which they were born'.[6] The collective memory of the clearances – often in highly coloured form – has kept alive the old hatreds into the present.

The methods of eviction were, on occasion, extremely

crude. There is conclusive evidence that, on a number of occasions, the dwellings were set on fire, but it is far less clear that murder was perpetrated. In addition to the physical act of dispersion, the landlord policies undermined the notion, popularly held, that the land was a communal property vested in the tribe. In violating this tradition, said some, Highland landlords departed to the opposite extreme – and employed 'a more despotic power than even the most absolute monarchs of the continent possess'.[7] There is no doubt that, to the common people, almost all shades of landlord policy were totally unpalatable, complete anathema. Yet there is general agreement that the passionate literature of protest was unmatched by any equivalent physical resistance on the part of the common people.

One of the most perplexing paradoxes of modern Highland history relates to the apparently passive social response to the radical policies of the clearing landlords. The standard view is that the violent traditions of the Highlands, popularly associated with cattle-thieving, internecine factiousness, and the Jacobite rebellions, had petered out by the nineteenth century. Apart from occasional eruptions, the Highlands became a pacific fringe contrasting with the social turmoil of the new industrial order to the south, or even the troubles of peasant Ireland. *Prima facie* the distance from centres of military force, the difficulty of the Highland terrain, and the derisory local sources of law and order, all favoured communal resistance to the hated landlord policies. It is not unreasonable for D. G. Macrae to ask: 'Why didn't the Scots peasant shoot his landlord?'[8]

This survey of the Highland experience reconsiders some of the actual cases of opposition to established authority and the pattern of disturbance that characterised the social response. It entails the relationship between radical agrarian change initiated from above, and the peasant reaction to these changes.

I

Sporadic acts of popular resistance to the clearances erupted
in every decade. The first major outburst was in 1792, but
there had already been a record of disorder and breakdown
of co-operation – for instance, there was widespread disaffection in the mid-eighteenth century on the Argyll estates
where ambitious landlord plans were often frustrated by a
spirit of resistance which acted as a powerful restraint on
landlord policy.[9] The outbreak of disorder in July 1792
on the Ross-shire estate of Sir Hector Munro of Novar is
regarded as one of the most dangerous of the anti-clearance
riots.[10] The people appear to have resisted the entry of sheep
farmers and then scouted support from neighbouring estates.
The noteworthy feature of the Ross-shire trouble was the
reported possession of arms and the co-ordination of several
parts of the Highlands to resist landlord policy. Apparently
an attempt was made to rid the northern Highlands of the
cheviot sheep – it was believed that a 'mob' of 400 men was
gathered to drive the sheep out of Ross and Sutherland.
Munro wrote to neighbouring proprietors that they should
co-ordinate to resist 'the very dangerous tendency of the
associations', that 'we are at present so completely under the
heel of the Populace that should they come to burn our houses
or destroy our Property in any way their caprice may lead
them to, we are incapable of resistance'. The sheriff-
substitute believed that '200 men would not suppress the
Insurrection'. The fear of an armed uprising, inflated by an
allegation of radicalism, induced a substantial military
intervention – in the face of which the revolt against landlord
policy evaporated. Five supposed ringleaders were taken but
they escaped from custody. The incident was notable for its
timing (which inevitably, but wrongly, suggested a Jacobin
involvement), its collective action, its armed threat, and its
failure. No armed confrontation actually occurred. The
defeat, at least one writer believes, broke the back of anti-
clearance resistance.

In comparison with the 1792 disturbances many clear-

LOCATIONS OF HIGHLAND DISORDER 1790–1860

ances passed with little or no opposition: for large areas the record is quiet. But in Sutherland, where the clearances were the most extensive, the most dramatic, and probably the best documented, the tactics of popular challenge to authority were diverse and the consequences were varied. On the great estate of Sutherland – a territory of some 1¼ million acres owned by the Countess of Sutherland and her husband, the Marquis of Stafford (first Duke of Sutherland in

1833) – there were special circumstances. The estate planners had conceived the most elaborate re-settlement schemes for the tenants to be displaced by the incoming sheep. With major capital expenditures a new diversified economy was established along the coasts. The plan implied an unprecedented degree of co-operation from the common people at a time when public opinion was becoming increasingly sensitive to eviction stories from the north of Scotland. The first clearances on the Sutherland estate were in 1806, and the factor specifically complained about the common people – of 'a sort of discontent among them, and also a stirring up by some disaffected persons' which had led some to emigrate rather than to re-settle on the estate. He was especially keen to 'shut their mouths against clamours and prevent a plea of hardship'.[11]

By 1811 a schedule of clearances had been drawn up by the Stafford family which, within a decade, was to re-settle a large proportion of the population of 15,000 along the coastal fringes of the estate. Sullen discontent had been simmering for some time but it was not until February 1813 that direct physical resistance developed. The landlord's agent, William Young, had sent valuers into Clyne and Kildonan to prepare arrangements for the removal of more than sixty families. 'I had determined to set off this part of the property to shepherds', he wrote. 'The natives rose in a body and chased the valuers off the ground and now threaten the lives of every man who dares dispossess them.' Moreover, he added, 'their conduct is not much disapproved of by many who ought to know better'. Young observed that the eyes of the Highlands were on the contest to see 'how *the war will end*'. He felt isolated: '. . . all our movements are watched and everything we do is improperly construed'. The re-settlement plans had been expressly designed to avoid 'harassing the people' – but, if he did not get 'power to quell this banditti, we may bid adieu to all improvement'. He got moral support from his superiors in London where James Loch, a commissioner for the far-flung Stafford estates, was mobilising legal action (he was a kinsman of Lord Advocate Adam). Loch pointed out the implication of the Kildonan Rebellion (as it became known) to the sheriff: the people had 'openly resisted the law and refused obedience to your substitute and peace officers. The effect of this resistance has been such that the same spirit of insubordination appears to have extended itself all over the Country, and the whole people are anxiously watching the issue of this contest, for so it is now called, some to resume farms they have formerly possessed, others to follow the same plan of resistance in other projected arrangements.' Loch's two great anxieties were that the contagion would spread across the estate, and that, without prompt action, the disorder would jeopardise the elaborate plans of the Stafford family.[12] The Kildonan episode demonstrated both the weakness of local sources of law and order,[13] and the problems of communication between London, Edinburgh and the Highlands.

The response of authority was twofold. Cranstoun, sheriff of Sutherland, was in central Scotland and necessarily left the affair in the hands of his Depute, Mackid. The estate administrators were also separated by distance–Lord Stafford was in London. There was already friction because Mackid's precognition had not been transmitted to London with sufficient dispatch to satisfy the landlord's agents. Eventually authority was at last obtained to request Major-General Leslie in Aberdeen to furnish troops from Fort George and Inverness. The troops were dispatched in fishing boats. Meanwhile William Young had arranged informal meetings with the ringleaders of the Kildonan disturbances whom, he claimed, he had admonished and told that troops were *en route*. He told them that, as far as Lord Stafford's policy was concerned, 'there was no law to prevent him turning them out of the Estate', without re-settlement provision at all. According to Young it was the impending arrival of the troops that broke the resistance – as soon as the news was heard the people began to repent their action, 'and signed a petition to Lord and Lady Stafford begging forgiveness'.[14] But Young had also negotiated directly with the people – indeed, according to a later

critic, he had entertained them in style, and promised that
no harshness would be used in the clearance arrangements.[15]
For their part, the protesting people of Kildonan used
several methods of drawing attention to their plight which
caused embarrassment to the landlord.[16] The physical
resistance was enough to draw the attention of newspapers
in Inverness and Edinburgh; in addition reports were sent –
very probably by the people's representatives – to the London
newspapers, notably *The Star*. This was bad enough publicity
for the Stafford family, but its effect was compounded by a
Petition sent to the Prince Regent and to Lord Sidmouth.[17]
It requested intervention against the landlord or, failing that,
assistance for emigration to Canada. A representative, a half-
pay soldier, went to London to press the case. In the upshot
these public demonstrations forced the Stafford family to
negotiate with the people, even to the point of making
promises concerning future action. Thus, although the
concessions were small, and the threat of military intervention was crucial (Young remarked: 'We shall never again
have . . . occasion to bring Military into the Country and
our plans called into question'), some of the people's
objectives were met, merely by the attraction of public
attention. The rebellion collapsed, but the estate administrators were left regretting that 'the disturbances had . . .
become in some degree of a public nature'. Action against
the leaders could not be contemplated. The landlord's camp
was expressly afraid that a further sanction might apply –
that the subject would come before the House of Commons.
As one agent wrote, regretfully, 'we have a publick here to
regard whose opinion on the subject is very material; to
stand right in their eyes is of much consequence – even if it
should most unfortunately delay your final settlement [i.e.
the clearance programme] for a few weeks'.[18]

The Kildonan Rebellion was undoubtedly a challenge to
landlord authority. As James Loch noted: 'The measure
must be persevered in or the improvement of this Country
must forever be abandoned and the Proprietors must resign
their property to their Tenants and Dependents.'[19] He was

confident that the common people of Sutherland had been brought to their senses. The irony of the affair was that the ambitious plans of the Stafford family required the full co-operation of the people to be re-settled. Co-operation was never achieved, and the years that followed demonstrated the depth of the planning failure in Sutherland.

Clearances were not the sole source of Highland discontent. In July 1813 an incident, equally as violent as the Kildonan rebellion, erupted in Assynt on the north-west coast. It concerned the installation of a new minister whose place was in the gift of the Countess of Sutherland. The induction of unpopular ministers provoked innumerable cases of parochial resistance in the Highlands, often bursting into violence. Only two years previously, at Creich, a new minister had required military protection for his introduction, and even this failed to prevent a riot.[20] The Assynt trouble took on more serious proportions, following closely on the heels of the Kildonan skirmishes. William Young accompanied the minister to Assynt where the common people had their own preferred candidate, and they resisted fiercely. Young reported, 'We cannot even place a pious Clergyman but some of these mountain savages contend with us and it was ten to one that our lives were not lost . . . the Clergy and myself were all driven home, and the people had a quarrel among themselves because those who were sent after me had failed in bringing me back handcuffed and to be sent in that state to sea in an open boat.' Sheriff-Substitute Mackid began a precognition, and Young remarked that 'if such lawless proceedings are not effectively stopt [it] must end in the loss of all authority – the Kildonan riots were a mere nothing as to this and the people [then] had some shadow of excuse'. The Sheriff Cranstoun called in a King's Cutter with 150 men of the Norfolk Militia from Leith Roads. In fact he had over-reacted (to the irritation of the Stafford family) since the disturbances had subsided completely before the troops arrived – and Cranstoun hurriedly ordered them not to land. Mackid arranged for five ringleaders to appear at the Inverness Assizes; the settlement of the minister proceeded.[21] Donald Sage later commented of the new minister that 'his appointment to Assynt was a personal arrangement between himself and Lady Stafford. *The people of Assynt were not consulted in the matter.* They however, took the liberty of thinking for themselves in the case'.[22] The new man never gained the co-operation of the people, and was transferred in 1817. One rioter taken to Inverness received nine months imprisonment.

The double intervention of military force in Sutherland in 1813 did not put an end to all resistance. As the great clearances proceeded it became clear that there was widespread disaffection among the people. Opposition was mainly non-violent in the phase between 1813 and 1820: delaying tactics were employed, petitions written and publicity sought. But the most elaborate and sophisticated opposition came in the form of a campaign against one man, Patrick Sellar: probably the most provocative of the landlord agents, and pre-eminently the man with whom the policies became identified.[23] It is unnecessary to speculate on the perplexing details of the Sellar affair: the challenge was evident. In the winter of 1813–14 Sellar, in his role as factor and prospective sheep farmer of large tracts of the Sutherland estate, had toured the area, pursuing recalcitrant rent arrears and making preparation for the forthcoming removals from Strathnaver. At Whitsunday 1814 Sellar and the removal party set about the business of clearance. Although the numbers of people were very large, and although some had to be physically ejected from their homes, there was no reported resistance on the part of the people. Six weeks elapsed before complaints were raised – specifically against Sellar and his men, that the muirs had been set afire, and that the people had been given insufficient notice of removal. Eventually, after the passage of ten months, the Stafford family received a petition of complaint about the conduct of the removal party. This led to a precognition by Mackid and then the arrest of Sellar, now charged with several atrocities including the culpable homicide of an infirm elderly woman whose house Sellar was alleged to have set alight. Sellar was deposited in Dornock Gaol by Makid (an acknowledged personal enemy) and was refused bail for several days. The entire proceedings had thus been promoted by Mackid and the numerous witnesses he had precognosed. Another ten months passed before Sellar's trial at Inverness.

The Sutherland estate regime saw the affair as the climax of a wide-ranging conspiracy of resistance to the clearances – the people of the interior had been roused and skilfully co-ordinated into an attack not merely on Sellar, but on the entire exercise of landlord authority. Unless the clamour were dealt with, said fellow estate agent Young, 'it will be a death blow to the improvement of this princely property and ruinous to the people'. Young believed that the policies were likely to be 'unhinged' since 'the people suppose they have got a complete victory and I sincerely believe that these proceedings of Mackid's have done more to strike at the root of improvement than years can remedy'.[24]

Sellar was able to illustrate his conspiracy theory by reference to various acts of the people in the area. He recalled that, when his shepherds attempted to serve notices of removal, they were told 'that I never should possess that farm. That I should be a ruined man before they would permit me to enjoy it.' While James Loch observed that the previous dispute with the Kildonan people (in 1813) had 'made a much deeper impression on the public mind in Scotland that well could have been conceived', Sellar contended that the general amnesty given by the landlord to the rebels had been a grave mistake, too much like Napoleon at Elba. Sellar identified other acts of resistance – the intimidation of shepherds and the general belief that 'the day was appointed for driving every South Country man out of the country'. Similar antagonism was found in the threats (unfulfilled) on the life of the unborn child of Mrs Reid, the Highland wife of an English sheep farmer. The riots of Kildonan and Assynt, he noted, were now to be followed by a different strategy – not the defiance of the law, for now 'they conspired by *Law* . . . to take the life of the Agent'.[25]

The 'conspiracy's' leaders were also singled out. Mackid,

according to Loch, possessed 'local prejudices in favour of the people and against the system of improvement . . . [which] quite unfit him to be a judge where the agent and the people were parties'. Sellar asserted that Mackid was the instigator of the plot, and had raised the expectations of the people and coerced those who would not co-operate. Mackid was not alone. Loch in particular was convinced that the leaders were from the class of middlemen, half-pay captains and tacksmen who had most to lose in the re-settlement plans. Suspicion fell especially on the two Sutherland brothers, one in the county, the other in London. Both were half-pay Lieutenants and provided a line of communication with the London press to the intense embarrassment of the Stafford family. 'They have formed a plan to do all the mischief they can,' it was claimed, and they had been involved in the Kildonan Rebellion. It is likely that they were the effective means by which national attention was focused on Sutherland – initially through articles in *The Star* and *The Military Register*, and then more widely. This was not underestimated by Sellar who regarded public opinion 'as being the most powerful engine in the world'. *The Military Register* was especially envenomed: it spoke of the Highland discontent that had been smouldering for eighteen months . . . 'those like the latent fires of a volcano, the longer they have been stifled by a gigantic system of terror and oppression, the more formidably will they explode'. If successful, the campaign against Sellar would, it contended, lead to the re-instatement of the people in their lands, then to the effective collapse of landlord policy.[26] Sellar himself fulminated against 'the abominable conspiracy organised for years among all classes. Like a College of *Jesuits* they have slipped no opportunity. They act in concert . . . in a word to thwart and overturn the system of police and improvement'.[27] One great anxiety in the landlord camp was that the affair would draw the attention of Parliament – which indeed was an object of the resistance. As Young remarked, 'their plan seems to be to raise a Hue and Cry in favour of the Highlanders and set the nation by the Ears' – with the prospect of Parliamentary interference in the issue.[28]

In the outcome, at Inverness, April 1816, despite genuine forbodings on the landlord side, Sellar was acquitted.[29] At the trial, it is evident that many witnesses failed to come forward and others reduced their accusations. It is not possible to determine whether the trial was fair or the verdict correct. The aftermath was clearer. The triumphant Sellar set out (with partial success) to wage retribution on his erstwhile opponents. For the landlord the result was the greatest relief. Young was told: '. . . it puts you in a situation of comfort now in carrying on the arrangements'. For the common people it was defeat. Mackid, the man 'who opposed the factor and defended their rights' (as Loch put it), had been humiliated. The clearances continued, albeit with greater caution. Just two acts of protest – trivial but symbolic – were perpetrated. The throats of twenty of Sellar's sheep were slit, as also that of Lady Stafford's prize Tibetan goat.[30]

The Sellar affair was a dramatic and, in a minor way, a most ineffective act of peasant resistance to landlord authority. It drew national attention to the circumstances in the Highlands; it embarrassed the landlord; it temporarily halted the Sutherland clearances; and it forced a new degree of caution in the implementation of the clearances. Thereafter – in Sutherland – the landlord leant over backwards to avoid provocation, unsuccessfully in the event (see below). The Sellar affair represented a relatively elaborate challenge to authority without recourse to violence; it involved a collective (although not sustained) response by the Strathnaver people; it required an unusual degree of leadership (not always steadfast) and the use of the radical press to generate wide support. Had the assault on Sellar succeeded it would have been a decisive moment in Highland history.

II

It was inevitable that events in Sutherland should dominate
the Highland story of the 1810s. Again, between 1819 and
1821, the Sutherland estate pursued wholesale clearances,
involving several thousand people. Landlords in adjacent
counties followed similar policies. Mostly the evictions
passed with little notice. But in 1819–20 discontent erupted
sufficiently to alarm the established authorities and, as
previously, the forces of order were, for a short time, stretched
full length.

In the early summer of 1819 the Sutherland agent, in the
midst of the clearances, reported that the people were
'inoffensive and timidly pliant'. He had found it necessary
to burn the roofs of some houses to prevent re-occupation;
the ministers had assisted the removal party – accompanying
them 'to several towns and used their influence and arguments with the people to submit with cheerfulness to the will
of the proprietors'. Nevertheless, despite the passivity,
'clamour' was rising on the fringe of the estate. It took an
unusual form. Among the displaced persons of the clearances
Thomas Dudgeon, a farmer and former factor, had formed
the so-called Sutherlandshire Transatlantic Emigration
Society, ostensibly as a friendly society and based at Meikle
Ferry. With the help of a Tain teacher, a half-pay captain
and a publican, Dudgeon had begun a subscription to assist
the emigration of dispossessed Sutherland tenants. Their
activity coincided with an outburst of public criticism in
The Scotsman where the Sutherland removals were described
as 'more barbarous than anything I ever heard of in Ireland
or anywhere else'.[31] Dudgeon held several meetings at
Meikle Ferry, including one gathering with an attendance
estimated at over 1,000 which produced a petition to the
Regent and both Houses of Parliament pleading for a grant
of land or aid for emigration. Critics claimed that he had
promised the people money, but instead had extracted
subscriptions from them – 6d or 1s from 672 persons with
2,367 children. Dudgeon's campaign effectively spotlighted

attention on the Sutherland situation, gave a focus for concerted action, and excited the authorities into an advanced state of anxiety.[32] Mounting abuse, and renewed allegations of atrocity, filled the Scottish newspapers.[33] Moreover, Dudgeon's association was sending emissaries over the entire Highlands. The less sanguine of the estate officials were beginning to panic in the face of collective action. One prospecting sheep farmer reported the mood of the people in October 1819: 'It is impossible for me to tell you here what he [Sergeant Mackay of the Association] revealed of the intentions of the people – not only against myself as an expectant of succeeding to their land [in the forthcoming 1820 clearances] – but against all law and authority. They declared they intended to resist being moved . . . that they were determined to have blood for blood in the struggle for keeping possession.'[34]

The greatest fear of authority in the north was the suspected danger that Dudgeon's Association was connected with the rising tide of radicalism in the south. Informers' reports were mixed. One described Dudgeon as 'a thorough *Radical* and he is perhaps endeavouring to create a diversion by an appearance of a rising in the North', i.e. as part of a national conspiracy. Others denied any political connection. But landlords had to consider 'how far the police of the Country should permit a set of individuals, unconnected with it, to travel up and down and make the people dissatisfied with their condition so as to interfere even with the management of private property'. They were in the grip of demogogues.[35]

The Emigration Association countered the charges of radicalism in a manner potentially even more dangerous. At the end of 1819 Henry Brougham was told reassuringly from the Highlands that '*our Rebellion* wants one most important feature of such a proceeding, namely it wants actors'. At that moment Dudgeon was organising another public meeting with the avowed object of refuting the aspersions that the Association was composed of thieves and rebels. To prove their point the Association offered its

'services in a military capacity' to the government.[36] This
doubled the anxiety of the authorities. Dudgeon's men were
reported touring the north, 'using the most inflammatory
language and infamous falsehoods' to raise support. The
Magistrates acted promptly: they declared Dudgeon's
forthcoming meeting illegal under the Seditious Meetings
Act. The meeting failed, Dudgeon did not appear and the
leadership disintegrated. He was declared an imposter. But
the authorities maintained vigil – especially on Dudgeon's
influence by way of 'his intercourse with the people through
the pensioners' – i.e. the half-pay captains who were seen as
a constant source of discontent in the post-war Highlands.[37]

Major clearances were in preparation for 1820 – hundreds
of families were to be cleared on various estates, although
Sutherland again predominated. The people of Ascoil were
described as 'a turbulent set – complete Dudgeonites' and an
order went out to evict all known Dudgeonite agents in
Assynt where continued activity was reportedly designed to
make the people 'lose confidence in the Minister, the
Tacksmen' and especially the factors.[38] In March 1820
violence erupted on the Culrain estate of Munro of Novar in
Ross. The pattern was familiar. A populous Highland area
had been marked out for a clearance; the officer sent to
deliver the first notice of removal had been 'frightened back'
and threatened with 'the severest corporal punishment'. On
the second attempt a party of constables 'were seized by men
in women's cloths – beat – and the summons burnt in their
presence'. The Sheriff then mustered a party of about forty
constables as well as armed militia – 'he went in person . . .
supposing such a force more than sufficient for his purposes –
but he had no sooner entered upon the grounds than he was
attacked by columns of women and young men – and pelted
with stones – as if forces from Hell had come forth. The men
– I mean the Country people . . . organised in the rear of the
women – with firearms to give battle in case the latter were
not successful – it is calculated about five hundred of them –
upon the blowing of horns they advanced to their station
from all quarters – and it is confidently believed there were a

great number from Sutherland.' Two women and a boy were shot when a *mêlée* occurred and shots were fired without orders; but the official force was driven back with its own lesser casualties. The common people apparently used only stones, the armed men (one report said there were 200) keeping their distance. They had commanded a narrow pass into the estate. The officials were 'obliged to retire and leave the field to these amazons, some of whom were supposed to be *gentlemen* in female attire'. One report said of the women: '. . . they did not regard the soldiers daring them to shoot as they would sooner suffer in that manner than remove'.[39]

In alarmist quarters it was believed that the Highland disturbances were part of a national radical conspiracy and the authorities maintained the closest vigilance. In the north the fear was that 'the evil may spread', and the influence of Dudgeon was widely suspected.[40] A regiment and three pieces of cannon were sent for from Aberdeen. Meanwhile a heated public discussion ensued. *The Scotsman* insisted that it was essential 'to separate this unfortunate [Culrain] business from the political discussions of the day and . . . to speak for a body, of illiterate people' who had never heard of 'radicalism'. No provision had been made by the landlord for the 600 cleared people; they felt there had been a breach of promise by the landlord who, they maintained, had nothing to gain by the clearances in any case. Their desperate resistance lasted a fortnight and then was pacified largely by the intervention of the minister. The latter publicly condemned the landlord's action, denied any connection with radicalism, with Sutherland,[41] or that arms were in the hands of the rebels. The people, he said, had been goaded to distraction. He calmed them to an acceptance of their fate.[42]

The Culrain episode was one of several in 1820. The Sutherland estate – close to the last of its great clearances – was especially nervous. 'In these times', wrote the chief agent to his man in the north, 'depend upon it every motion is watched and if you do anything at all which will occasion public observation it will be brought before the house of commons.' The use of fire in the ejection was forbidden. Local officials were instructed to use better informants in their surveillance of Dudgeonites. It was reported that the Culrain rebels had told the Assynt people (at Unapool) that 'if they had the spirit to resist they would come in a body to their assistance'. The estate official tried to scotch Dudgeonism at Unapool by ejecting one of the adherents – but the Sheriff's men were 'opposed by a party of women who rushed on us like furies, and told us they were determined to resist the man's being turned out'. The officers persisted and the incident collapsed. Meanwhile the clearances passed without resistance, although often the people had to be physically dislodged from their homes in the interior.[43]

At much the same time, however, violence occurred on a small neighbouring estate, Gruids. Once more a Sheriff's party serving notice of removal was deforced. It was reported that 'a great number of Women (or I should rather imagine men in female attire) attacked the party and stripped the clothes off them and sent them home *stark naked* and tore all their papers'. Not amused, the authorities gathered a force of sixty constables, but the Gruids people were also 'mustering and preparing all sorts of weapons', and 'prepared to oppose whatever species of force may be brought against them'. Rather than force the issue a delay was called.[44]

But, while the Gruids' resistance continued, another spasm of violence occurred – at Achness on the Sutherland estate. This was taken very seriously for it seemed that the contagion of revolt was spreading. A precognition was taken and a hundred fusiliers with artillery were put at the ready for service in Sutherland. Any delay, it was said, would keep 'Sutherland in a flame'. Additionally, it was believed that the Achness people were expecting 'their friends in Caithness, the heights, and Ross-shire . . . to join them there', while other disturbances were developing in Caithness estates. At Gruids, in March 1821, another Sheriff's officer was deforced – again stripped naked. The situation led one landlord's agent to complain that 'the Civil Power of this country is inadequate to eject them'–and that the constables were 'lukewarm' in their task of ejecting the people since they partook of 'the general feeling of the natives in their cause'. James Loch opined that there was 'a regular organised system of resistance to civil power' throughout the north, and that it had been allowed to go too far. 'We shall be put into a state that will require all the energy of Government and its disposals force to put down.'[45]

In April 1821 troops arrived, seventy men of the 21st Regiment under Major Tallon. They toured the trouble spots. 'Their presence seems to have operated like magic,' reported one observer, 'and proves the importance of a distinct demonstration that the civil authority is to be supported by the government.' At Achness the men 'took off up the hillside like mountain deer'. Letters of removal were planted on the deserted houses and the roofs of the huts were pulled down. Three prisoners were eventually taken. The number of troops was then increased to 200 at Bonar Bridge whence they travelled to Gruids. But no opposition was offered. Prisoners were taken. The Achness people, it was reported, 'skulk from one place to another' trying to get help to emigrate. The local factor remarked that: 'All the people are now convinced that they will not be supported by government – the appearance of the soldiers put an end to all their hopes. I never saw people who boasted as they did so crestfallen, they are completely cowed and I am certain we shall have no more trouble.'[46]

'You must not . . . in your future transactions', the Sutherland agent was told, 'cast them [the Achness people] on the wide world, ill as they have behaved – let the less guilty have lots on their signing that they are sorry for their conduct and that they acknowledge the kindness of Lord and Lady Stafford. It would produce a great sensation here [in London] that any set of people were wandering about without habitations.' The weight of public opinion rested heavily on the Stafford family. They specifically requested Major Tallon to stay in the country for the few remaining clearances. In the event there was virtually no resistance. 'We are extremely busy just now with our removings', said a factor, 'which God be praised will be completed effectively and without a whisper on Wednesday.' Thenceforward only minor clearances were undertaken in Sutherland. The management expressly acknowledged that the pressure of publicity had checked the full exercise of the policy of clearance. Nonetheless they had executed the greatest of all the Highland clearances with only minor resistance.[47]

III

After 1821 the clearances never again matched the scale of the Sutherland case: never again were several thousand people uprooted and re-settled within a few weeks. But, despite recurrent protests of public opinion, lesser clearances continued in the following decades. Significant for the future was the growing volume of critical writing and thinking on the problem of landlordism in the Highlands – a literature that prepared the way for the first tentative legislative acts curbing landlord power in the 1880s. The rise of literate criticism ran parallel with the desperate run-down of the Highland economy in mid-century which was associated with the drain of population, and with repeated outbursts of popular discontent. The established pattern of Highland disorder was repeated many times before the best-known case of, and climax of, resistance with the 'Crofters' War' in Skye in 1882.[48]

Radical critics of landlord authority were surprisingly slow in coming forth. On occasion newspapers took up the Highlanders' cause in political terms, but the common people threw up few spokesmen of their own. William Cobbett was one who publicly questioned the legal framework that permitted the clearances. At Paisley in 1832 he addressed a public audience: ' "What", exclaimed I, "have we not the right to be upon the land of our birth? Are we to be told, that we are bound in duty to come out and venture our lives in defence of that land against a foreign enemy, and yet that we can be swept off from it when the landowner pleases?" '[49] Both the Swiss economist Sismondi and Marx found the Highland clearances a splendid example of the abuse of landlord power,[50] and their work was greeted warmly by some Scots critics. But, for the most part, local writers held back from any direct challenge to 'the land monopoly' until the 1840s when, with the writings of Donald Macleod, Hugh Miller, and Donald Ross, a radical current in the Highlands began to flow.

The upsurge of the literary protest coincided with re-newed eruptions of resistance to clearances. In July 1839 a disturbance occurred on Lord Dunmore's estate in Harris where fifty families were to be removed. The landlord had offered financial help for their emigration. Unimpressed, the people put up a determined resistance and troops from Glasgow were called in–at which point the resistance collapsed. No legal action was taken against the Harris people, which, it was alleged, 'encouraged resistance to the Law in the Northern Countries'.[51] In the following year trouble flared up at Culrain – twice before the scene of anti-landlord violence. This time, according to one incensed landlord spokesman, 'A strong body of civil officers em-ployed to execute warrants of Removing by a principal Tacksman against his sub-tenants was deforced. The farm-stead of the Tacksman was set on fire and twenty cattle consumed. Yet no criminal trial followed.'[52] This was further evidence, not only of the total popular abhorrence of the clearance policy, but also of the dissolution of all vestige of cohesion in Highland society. The tacksman, so far from being the leader of popular feeling, had become the enemy of the people.

The sub-letting middleman in the Highlands was often the cause of the most insensitive of the clearances. In 1841, at Durness (near Cape Wrath), James Anderson–fish curer and tenant of Lord Reay and then of the 2nd Duke of Sutherland – decided to cease fishing and convert his lands to sheep pasture. Anderson–as ruthless an entrepreneur as the Highlands had seen–had encouraged sub-tenants to

TABLE 4

Locations and kinds of Highland disorder in the first half of the nineteenth century

Place and Year of Disturbance	Type of Disturbance	Officers deforced	Stoning	Police or troops called	Women prominent	Prisoners taken	Minister involved	Arms reported
CLYNE 1777	(I)		X		X			
ROSS-SHIRE 1782	(C)			X		X		X
CREICH 1811	(I)				X			
KILDONAN 1813	(C)	X	X	X				
ASSYNT 1813	(I)	X		X		X		
CULRAIN 1820–1	(C)	X	X	X	X	X	X	
GRUIDS 1820–1	(C)	X	X	X	X	X		X
ACHNESS 1820–1	(C)	X	X	X	X			
UNAPOOL 1820	(C)	X			X			
CROY 1823	(I)				X	X		
KINLOCHBERVIE 1834	(I)	X						
HARRIS 1839	(C)	X	X	X				
DURNESS 1840–1	(C)	X	X	X	X		X	
CULRAIN 1840	(C)	X						
LOCHSHIEL 1842	(C)	X			X			
LOGIE and RESOLIS 1843	(I)		X	X	X	X		
GLENCALVIE 1842–5	(C)	X			X		X	
BALLINDALLOCH 1843	(C)	X			X	X		
WICK 1847	(FR)			X		X		
CASTLETOWN 1847	(FR)			X		X		
AVOCH 1847	(FR)			X				
BEULY 1847	(FR)					X		
THURSO 1847	(FR)		X	X				
INVERGORDON 1847	(FR)			X				
BLACK ISLE 1847	(FR)							
SOLLAS 1849	(C)	X	X	X	X	X		
STRATHCONAN 1850	(C)							
STRATHAIRD 1850	(C)	X						
COIGEACH 1852	(C)	X		X	X			
STRATHCARRON 1853	(C)	X	X	X	X	X		
KNOYDART 1853	(C)							
GREENYARDS 1854	(C)		X	X	X	X		
BORERAIG and SUISHNISH 1854	(C)					X		

(I) Induction   (C) Clearance   (FR) Food riot

It is unlikely that this analysis is either comprehensive or fully accurate. It attempts to summarise presently available evidence on Highland disorder in the first half of the nineteenth century.

settle on the smallest patches of land; subdivision went unchecked and the fishermen sank into his debt.[53] By 1840 Anderson decided that fishing no longer repaid his capital. He thus embarked on a programme of eviction quite independently and beyond the control of the landlord. He gave no alternative accommodation, no amelioration. He simply evicted on the shortest notice. He cleared Shegra in 1840. In August 1841 the officer delivering summonses to the Durness people was opposed by 'a large body of men and women' who took his papers and burnt them. The people addressed a petition to the Duke of Sutherland for 'shelter against the threatened and expected storm of tyrany'. Thirty-one families, 163 people, had been summoned to remove at forty-eight hours notice. While the Duke dallied, awaiting the appointment of a new district factor, Anderson arranged for a party of special constables to force through the eviction on Saturday, September 18th. The people said they would depart on the Monday. The officials declined the offer and, in the course of the attempted eviction, were successfully resisted, and eventually put to flight – the people saying that they would rather break the law on a Saturday than on the Sabbath. The Minister explained that 'the serving officers were resisted by almost all the females of the district . . . when no prospective opening was provided for so many destitute people, public sympathy could not possibly be suppressed'. The Sheriff's party retreated to Durnine Inn but were there attacked, manhandled and set to flight. The next inn was twenty miles away and some of the officers hid among the corn and rocks till daylight. It was reported that the people threatened to throw Sheriff Lumsden into Smoo Cave and the Sheriff himself recorded that his party had 'been deforced, assaulted, threatened with instant death, and expelled at midnight . . . by a ferocious mob'. He believed that the Minister had fomented the insurrection, and had sat quietly by his fireside while the mob did its worst. Moreover, reported Lumsden, 'no consideration will induce any of these officers to go back on such a mission to Durness without the aid of military force'.[54]

The Durness incident was a sensation in the Highlands and was widely reported in the newspapers. The landlord's agent observed that 'it will leave an unpleasant feeling throughout the country'. Many connected the eruption with the recent Culrain resistance and there was rumour of 'a Tongue uprising'. Lumsden, in a state of continuing panic, sent alarmist letters to Sir William Rae, the lord advocate, insisting that he could not return to the scene and that Infantry should be sent by sea to catch the ringleaders. There was considerable criticism of Lumsden's personal timidity and alarmism – and Rae described him as 'the fool of a sheriff'. Calm was required, the people should be talked to, and Rae was keen to know 'the real causes which led to this outbreak and all the alleviating circumstances which have attended it'. The rumour of military intervention had an effect in Durness – the women were reported to have dispersed to neighbouring Edderachilles. The Sutherland factor reported significantly: 'I have not of late dreaded any other measures for defence but I was always afraid of this passive sort of resistance, and, if resorted to it will no doubt create a vast deal of difficulty and trouble to all concerned.' With the help of arbitration by both the local minister as well as the landlord the dispute was eventually settled in mid-October. Findlater, the minister, met the assembled people and was able to say that they repented and that the military would not be required. The people apparently apologised to Anderson and petitioned for a delay of clearance. This was granted – until May 1842, and no criminal prosecutions followed. Findlater blamed Anderson for his lack of prudence, while Rae complacently observed that the Sutherland rebellion was over. Anderson received the castigation of the Duke of Sutherland. For the latter the lesson was clear – even small clearances could provoke outrages which were probably not worth the candle – indeed, the memory of Durness was used as counsel against further clearances as late as the mid-1850s.[55]

While most of the currents of national life – including Chartism – left the Highlands unmoved, repeated outbursts of anti-clearance discontent broke surface. In June 1842 at Lochshiel an eviction party was resisted and driven off by 'a party of women' defending a proposed sheep farm then occupied by 300 people. In April of the same year the Glencalvie people successfully held out against Sheriff's officers, seizing and burning papers on two occasions. Another attempt was made in 1843 – when 'the women met the constables beyond the boundaries, over the river, and seized the hand of the one who held the notices, whilst some held it out by the wrist others held a live coal to the papers and set fire to them'. The Glencalvie people were again warned out in May 1844 to remove in 1845 – by which time the correspondent of *The Times* was on the spot to give national publicity to prevailing conditions and to the treatment of ordinary people in the Highlands. Further resistance occurred and the clearance was not implemented until 1846 when, with the advice of the Free Church minister, the people removed peacefully.[56] In August 1843 Hugh Lumsden's authority was once more resisted on the west coast while attempting to eject one man at Balcladdich. He was told that '*the whole people of Assynt*' would rise, and they might gain the support of the returning herring fishermen. The incident however petered out and four prisoners were taken.[57]

Alexander Mackenzie wrote of the Sollas eviction, in North Uist in 1849, as the almost solitary case in the history of the clearances 'where the people made anything like real resistance'.[58] It was one incident among several during the post-famine clearances: a time when landlords concurred in the view that the only solution to the general subsistence problem was wholesale emigration. At Sollas there were about 400 people involved. The landlord, Lord MacDonald, had offered to assist them to Canada. When the officer tried to serve notice he was deforced and, as *The Inverness Courier* recorded, the people 'threatened with instant death any officer who should attempt to eject them'. Refusing to compromise MacDonald pressed the constables forward in full view of an accompanying journalist. No opposition had

been prepared but the atmosphere became highly charged
and a full confrontation occurred. Despite volleys of stones
the police persevered with the clearances to the accompani-
ment of the harrowing pleas of the womenfolk. Eventually the
factor accepted signed promises from the people that they
would emigrate in the following year, and four prisoners
were taken. They were tried at Inverness. The presiding
judge, Cockburn, recollected that 'The popular feeling is so
strong against these (as I think necessary, but) odious
operations, that I was afraid of an acquittal.' Sympathetic
to the people, the jury gave the barest minimum sentence
and noted that, although legal, the eviction was cruel and
unworthy. 'That statement will ring all over the Country,'
wrote Cockburn, 'the slightness of the punishment will
probably abate the public fury.' In 1850 the Sollas eviction
was carried through. The evicted people gained some public
assistance, but eventually found themselves adrift in an
alien world.[59]

As the pace of clearance accelerated in the early 1850s most
cases went unrecorded and probably unresisted. The island
of Skye was more turbulent. On the Strathaird estate in 1850
the threatened evictions (of 620 souls) was opposed regardless
of the offer of assisted emigration.[60] On the mainland, particularly at Wick, the elections of 1852 produced an opportunity for political comment on landlordism in the Highlands. In particular James Loch, the sitting member and the
man who had been closely identified with the Sutherland
policies for forty years, was subjected to a barrage of public
abuse which drew on the accumulated hatred of the clearances. Loch's political agents described Wick as 'a den of
radicalism' under the 'misrule of demagogues'.[61] Given a
political focus, with local newspaper support, the successful
rival candidate demonstrated the possibilities of political
opposition to Highland landlordism. Loch was defeated.
Some landlords clearly jibbed at the prospect of such
public emnity. At Coigeach on the dour west coast of Ross,
for instance, stout resistance to a tentative effort to re-settle
the people was sufficient to reverse landlord policy, despite

mounting arrears. The Sheriff-officers had been deforced by the women of Coigeach: 'The men formed the second line of defence in case the women should receive any ill treatment.'

Non-violent resistance occurred also on the MacDonald estates in Skye in 1853. At Suishnish and Boreraig thirty-two families were being cleared for a sheep farm. The estates' trustees were ineffectually opposed and three men were taken. No resettlement provision had been made. At the subsequent trial, with the assistance of a good solicitor paid by charitable donations in Inverness, the Skyemen were acquitted 'to the cheers of an Inverness crowd'.[62] *The Inverness Courier* commented that 'the sympathies of the public were strongly with the Skyemen, and there was a general impression that the proprietor himself sympathised with them'.[63] It did not prevent the subsequent eviction of the same people. Adverse publicity also attended clearances on the MacDonell of Glengarry estate at Knoydart in the same year. Four hundred souls were evicted, most of them directly on to the emigration ships. Indignation ran high but no resistance was offered. The newspapers, although active, had only publicity to offer.[64] Many clearances passed without even this, for example the Strathconan clearances, over a decade, dispersed several hundred peasants, and the process was repeated in the Islands and on the mainland.

A more dramatic response occurred at Greenyards near Bonar Bridge on the same estate that witnessed the Glencalvie incidents. On their first attempt to serve notices of removal the sheriff-officers were assaulted by a crowd, stripped naked, and their papers burnt. *The Northern Ensign* noted that the officers were deposited 'at the braes of Dounie where the great Culrain riot took place thirty years before' – a symbolic but pathetic act. He returned at the end of March 1854 with thirty constables. They were received, it was reported, by a crowd of 300, two thirds being women. The women were lined in front, the men behind, and the only arms mentioned were sticks and stones. The constables apparently wielded their batons freely and, while sustaining no injuries themselves, managed to produce between ten and fifteen serious wounds among the women. Donald Ross wrote of the pools of blood and the butchery at the hands of the police: 'The Ross-shire Haynaus have shown themselves more cruel and more blood-thirsty than the Austrian women-floggers.' *The Inverness Courier* considered that the police had over-reacted and criticised their failure to induce a compromise. At the Inverness trial one man received eighteen months hard labour and a woman was imprisoned for a year.[65]

In the 1850s a great deal of attention was paid both to the harrowing drama of the clearances, and to the underlying political issues. Writers as various as Karl Marx, Mrs Stowe, Donald Ross and Leone de Lavergne wrote on the question.[66] The current of radicalism ran strongly. Public criticism in the Highlands was more audacious, bringing the land question into focus – *The Elgin Courier* was widely read and the tone of criticism was increasingly threatening. Landlords were anxious. In 1855 the Duke of Sutherland was reliably told that there had 'arisen a feeling among the people that they would soon resume possession of what they conceived to be the possessions of their fathers. Some strong influence had been used to inculcate the feeling. A radical feeling is abroad propagated from Wick – that most radical of the radical towns of Scotland.'[67]

Yet the social discontent, evident in the literature as well as the acts of protest during the 1850s – did not yield positive political results until the 1880s. The Battle of the Braes in Skye in 1882[68] stands out as the prelude to a climax of sustained agitation which exhibited an unprecedented cohesion in Highland discontent. It generated incongruous spectacles such as the march of 1,400 men up Strathnaver in 1884.– ostensibly supported by their landlord – chanting: 'Give us back our Bonnie Strathnaver', and 'Highlands for the Highlanders'.[69] It also produced the pressure that paved the way for the Crofter Commission Inquiry of 1884. Nevertheless, seen in larger perspective, the Crofter's War in Skye in 1882 was merely one act, not clearly atypical, in a century of sporadic popular resistance in the Highlands. Indeed, it followed faithfully the well-established pattern of Highland disorder. It was unique perhaps only in its aftermath – the co-ordination of opinion to exert pressure at the political centre.

IV

Clearances were not, of course, the exclusive occasion for the expression of social discontent in the Highlands. Some of the most disorderly of incidents were connected with religious disputes. Most frequently they were associated with the induction of a new minister against the choice of the people.[70] Many cases of violence are documented: an unpopular minister at Clyne in 1777 is said to have been in danger of his life;[71] outbursts occurred in Creich in 1881 and in Assynt in 1813; also at Croy in 1823 when four men and a woman were incarcerated for asserting violently their feelings about a new minister. At Kinlochbervie in 1834 the local congregation believed their feelings paramount in a similar dispute which was marked also by considerable intimidation. At Logie and Resolis in 1843 a 'serious disturbance' over an induction led to violence, to the rescue of a woman prisoner and to the intervention of troops.[72] But even more important than such sporadic outbursts was the phenomenon of the Disruption which was perhaps the most novel and effective challenge to authority – a challenge in which popular support and leadership were for once joined.[73]

Physical confrontation between authority and the people came also in the classic form of the food riot – notably in the famine year of 1847. Appalling distress was found in much of the peasant Highlands, but especially along the west coast. There was, however, little violence or even protest in these areas: pathetic petitions reached landlords and emigration/relief committees, but there was little strife. Disorder was limited to points at which food was being transported. At Wick and Thurso, for instance, soldiers used bayonets and bullets to keep at bay crowds demonstrating against the loading of meal on to ships. Similarly, at Invergordon and

Dingwall the people tried to prevent the movement of grain, and troops were required to guard convoys of carts. 'It is mentioned that country people had recently begun to break into granaries and mix the different kinds to make them unmarketable', was one report. Similar opposition occurred at Beauly and, on the Black Isle, one exporter desisted in order to prevent bloodshed. At no time did such disorders threaten the foundations of authority in the Highlands in the way that anti-clearance agitation might have: had the Highlanders been less passive.[74]

V

From the record of Highland discontent and its containment emerges the spectacle of a peasantry on the retreat in the face of alienating landlord policies. How far the landlords had real alternatives to their policies is a separate question. The common people, with so much in common, subject to an apparently unifying experience, had relatively little resort to co-ordinated resistance: they had greater recourse to submission and to emigration[75] than to violence.

The forms of resistance were fragile and sporadic but it would be a mistake to dismiss the record as totally ephemeral. There were moments when authority reached a high state of alarm, as in 1814–16 and 1819–21. In retrospect the forces of order appear to have consistently over-reacted to popular disturbances: although this itself may have been a factor checking the cumulative rise of disaffection. The pattern of anti-clearance revolt, where it is known, is surprisingly consistent. In virtually all cases the officer delivering summonses of removal was set upon and humiliated. Very often a petition was dispatched to some distant figure. The second confrontation would involve a much larger body of constables whose approach was never secret. They would be met at some strategic point by a body of women who would attempt to intimidate the party with abuse and stones. At the rear would be the men, armed with sticks and stones. In several cases this was enough to deter the constables. Sometimes the resistance fed on the belief that the government would recognise the justice of the case; the recruiting of newspaper publicity was another vain hope in the direction of outside intervention against landlord power. The entry of the military effectively shattered such illusions. Resistance might last for several weeks but military power was never challenged: it was usual at this point for the minister to intercede with some face-saving compromise. The net result, almost invariably was the continued progress of the clearance. Most of the incidents show the marks of spontaneous desperation – unpreparedness, absence of arms, lack of co-ordination, isolation, no clear leadership, and collapse in the face of military intervention.

Almost certainly the people believed that they had traditional rights to their lands, and that the landlords were acting against real justice. Inchoate, dispersed, apolitical and rural-based, Highland discontent until the 1870s lacked political focus for this doctrine. Much of the thinking and motivation was essentially backward-looking – there was much discussion of lost rights, but little radical thought was devoted to any consideration of the future of the Highlands, or even of any notion of an alternative to landlordism. The evidence before the Napier Commission in the 1880s demonstrated the tenacity of this conservative frame of mind. Sismondi was the first effective voice questioning the political and legal bases of landlordism, and it was not until the rise of a much more vigorous Irish agitation that the Highlanders made much headway. In part it reflected the curious neglect of the land issue by British radicals in the first half of the nineteenth century.

The Highland discontents lacked also leaders: the terrain was ostensibly ideal for Hobsbawmian rebels and myths. The poverty of leadership may be related to the polarisation of Highland society and the demise of the tacksman – many had emigrated,[76] many had thrown in their lot with the landlords. Fragmentary evidence suggests that returned army captains often led the discontented, but never openly. Thomas Dudgeon and Robert Mackid were the only men

who stood out as co-ordinators, but both lacked the resources and charisma of leadership. Popular discontent was
invested increasingly in the ministers. The absence of arms
diminished the threat of revolt by several fold – and there is
little evidence of agrarian terrorism or intimidation which
were used with some success in contemporary Ireland.
Deaths and serious injuries in the Highlands were almost
entirely on the side of the protesters.

The role of the ministers in the Highlands is a curious one.
'The professed ministers of religion sanctioned the iniquity
. . . prostituted their sacred office and high calling,' wrote
Alexander Mackenzie.[77] It is an extreme view. In reality
their role was not unlike that of catholic priests in the Irish
troubles: they sought to avoid violence. Ministers were, on
occasion, prepared to speak out against landlordism.[78] But
it is true that, bound by an increasingly stereotyped pres-
byterianism, the ministers preached a fatalistic passivity –
they offered spiritual consolation rather than worldly
alternatives.[79] It reinforced the traditional social deference of
the Highlander. Yet religion was an area of life increasingly
separated from the authority of the landlord – thus the fierce
opposition to unacceptable ministers. In matters of religion the
common people believed they possessed inextinguishable
rights totally independent of the landlord. Moreover, the
ministers did not desert their people: they accepted their lot
with their congregations. The mutual commitment increased
and was exemplified in the most striking way by the Disruption in the Highlands. The widespread adherence of
people and ministers to the Free Church in the 1840s – in the
face of considerable persecution – for once showed Highlanders
almost unanimously pitted against secular authority.

The role of women in Highland resistance is another
curiosity – to a remarkable degree Highland riots were
women's riots. In many incidents when the people were in
actual confrontation with the representatives of authority, the
women were found at the head, often taking the worst
injuries. Frequently the menfolk seem to have held back, as a
second line of defence. The transvestite element – of men

dressing as women – was another recurrent feature of Highland disturbances. Parallels with the French Revolution, and the Rebecca Riots, come to mind. Of the former Olwen Hufton has argued forcefully that 'to appreciate the nearness of women to the Revolution one must understand their role in the family economy'.[80] Like the womenfolk of Rebecca's Wales,[81] Highland women shared fully in the most laborious tasks of the peasant economy. Nevertheless it is not altogether evident how family roles are to be related to the propensity to violence and protest. The remarks of the Sutherland agent in 1821 that 'the opinion of the people here is that a woman can do anything with impunity'[82] is clearly not a sufficient explanation.

Any comparison of the patterns of Highland discontent in the nineteenth century with our knowledge of other agrarian societies yields a number of pronounced similarities. Indeed, the forms of social action employed by the Highlanders fit remarkably well into the received models of historical crowd behaviour. The correspondence is closest in those characteristics categorised in 'reactionary violence' as described by Charles Tilly,[83] and in the rural variant of George Rudé's 'pre-industrial crowd'.[84] In terms of leadership, organisation forms of action, spontaneity, composition, and ideology, the Highlanders during the age of the Clearances expressed their discontent in a manner which is now familiar to historians of peasant societies. The fact that food riots occur in the Highlands later than elsewhere in Britain[85] can be associated with the survival of the resolutely pre-industrial character of the region in the middle of the century. Referring to agricultural England of the eighteenth century, E. P. Thompson has commented on 'the comparative rarity of enclosure riots' which, he suggests, was 'not because enclosure was not unpopular, but because the people learned early that to riot was hopeless'.[86] In terms of such a functional approach to social behaviour, the incidence of anti-clearance activity represents a measure of the desperation of the ordinary people of the Highlands – both men and women.

Although Highland discontent failed to check landlord

policies *in toto* it should not be dismissed as futile. The most common response of the Highlanders was a sullen refusal to co-operate, a passive resistance.[87] Symptomatic was the comment of James Loch that, once uprooted, the people would rather emigrate several thousand miles than accept accommodation twenty-six miles away from their old homes. It was a rejection of all the alternatives offered by the landlords. In real terms it was this attitude – itself the product of 'the clearances' – that dealt the fatal blow to several ambitious plans for economic reconstruction. Implicitly the great plans in, for instance Argyll and Sutherland (which required considerable landlord investment) assumed a degree of co-operation which the very act of clearance made impossible. As T. C. Smout has remarked: 'It was madness to assume that any lasting agrarian prosperity could be built except on a basis of carrying the local population with the landowners. The positive response of the tenantry was the whole key to the success in the lowlands.'[88] It may also be the key to failure in the north.

Active resistance helped attract the public attention that eventually, with agonising gradualness, found political expression. More immediately, the prospect of disorder, and the fear of public odium, acted as a brake on the clearance of some estates. At Coigeach, for example, the landlord desisted and the people remained. In 1820 the great Sutherland estate decided that future clearances should be suspended to avoid more obloquy – despite the fact that 'the sheep farmers will continue discontented, and the straths full of sloth and smuggling'. Many of the most notorious of the mid-century clearances were implemented in the name of relatively anonymous legal agents. The agent George Gunn noted in 1841 that 'the state of public opinion is such nowadays, that a Proprietor cannot exercise his just and legal rights without being exposed to all sorts of calumny and mistatements'.[89] It is easy to underestimate the increasing sensitivity of Highland landlords to such attention.[90] This factor, together with the growing sentimentalisation of Highland life in the social conscience of the nation, may help to explain the greater impact of Highland agitation in the 1880s than for any time in the previous century.[91] For between 1790 and 1880 the forms of Highland protest, and its containment, had changed hardly at all.

For the hypothesis and the historical parallels, the question that perplexed Cobbett–the apparent (but perhaps exaggerated) pacifism of the Highlander–remains perplexing. The answer remains embedded in the historical sociology of the Highlands. Some consequences of the social response to the clearances are already visible: efforts to rebuild the Highland economy were dislocated, landlords intent on wholesale eviction were sometimes frustrated, and an atmosphere of permanent indignation was created in which developed the later consciousness of the Highland problem.

Notes

1. I wish to thank Monica Clough, John McCracken, Leon Mann, Roland Quinault, George Rudé and Ron Witton for their thoughts on the first draft of this paper. Some of the findings were presented to a symposium on 'Leaders and Followers in Riots', at Flinders University in July 1972.
2. *The Village Labourer, 1760–1832* (1920), p. 218.
3. Charles Tilly, 'The Changing Place of Collective Violence', in *Essays in Theory and History*, edited by M. Richter (Cambridge, Mass., 1970), p. 141.
4. See Eric Richards, 'Structural Change in a Regional Economy: Sutherland and the Industrial Revolution, 1780–1830', *The Economic History Review*, 2nd series, vol. XXVI (1973).
5. Confusion over this term is widespread. For example, 'The Sutherland clearances were, at least in part, the unintended result of a constructive policy of re-settlement'. H. R. Trevor-Roper, *The Sunday Times*, 26th October, 1969.
6. Ian MacLennan, 'Rape of the Glens', *Spectator*, 18th October, 1963; W. Cobbett, *Hansard*, vol. XVI, 1st March, 1833.
7. Hugh Miller, *Sutherland as it was and is, or How a Country may be ruined* (Edinburgh, 1843), p. 26.
8. Review in *Economica*, August 1958. See also, for example, H. J. Hanham, 'The Problem of Highland Discontent, 1880–1885', *Transactions of the Royal Historical Society*, 5th series, v. 19, 1969, pp. 21–3. In 1830 William Young, the agricultural entrepreneur, calculated that the real rent of the Sutherland estate was worth 20 per cent more than its nominal level because it had 'no *Tythes*, poor *rates* or *Incendiaries* to contend with'. Stafford Record Office, Sutherland Collection (subsequently sc) D593/K/, Young to Loch, 5th December, 1830.

9. Eric Cregeen, 'The Changing Role of the House of Argyll in the Scottish Highlands', in *Essays in Scottish History in the Eighteenth Century*, edited by N. T. Phillipson and Rosalind Mitchison (Edinburgh, 1970), p. 9.

10. It is dealt with at length, though rather impressionistically, by J. Prebble, *The Highland Clearances* (1963) Ch. 1. See also T. C. Smout, *A History of the Scottish People, 1560–1830* (1969), p. 444.

11. Quoted in Eric Richards, 'The prospect of economic growth in Sutherland, 1809, 1813', *Scottish Historical Review*, vol. XLIX (1970), p. 161.

12. sc D593/K/, Young to Loch, 7th February, 1813, 21st February, 1813, Loch to Cranstoun, 15th February, 1813.

13. As Sidmouth's informant pointed out, 'Most of the Local Militiamen are either themselves of the number who are dispossessed or entertain the same sentiments. A Military Force therefore of a different description has become necessary. There are however few Troops in the North of Scotland'. Scottish Record Office (sro) Home Office Papers, Scotland, RH2/4, f. 82, A. Colquhoun to Viscount Sidmouth, 19th February, 1813. *The Military Register*, 14th August, 1815, claimed that Brora colliers (i.e. non-Sutherland men) were sworn in as special constables and armed with 5½ lb. bludgeons to defend Dunrobin Castle.

14. sc D593/K/, Young to Cranstoun, 28th February, 1813, Loch to Cranstoun, 18th February, 1813, Young to Loch, 27th March 1813.

15. See *The Star*, 24th March 1813, letter from 'A Friend of Improvement', and *The Military Register*, 28th June, 1815, 23rd August, 1815.

16. Lord Selkirk was in Sutherland just after the outburst and took a sympathetic view of their problems. He remarked: 'These people had so much of the Old Highland Spirit as to think their land their own, and attempted to resist the change *vi et armis*, but this attempt being soon quelled, they determined on emigrating all in a body.' Selkirk thought them a fine set of people – morally and physically, and 'rigid Presbyterians'. He also considered their disturbance justifiable: 'According to the idea handed down to them from their ancestors, and long prevalent among high and low throughout the Highlands, they were only defending their rights and resisting a ruinous unjust and tyrannical encroachment on their property.' Equally significant was his remark: 'Of the Kildonan people, there is scarcely any who can be pointed out as a leading man.' All had good names, and John Sutherland had actually restrained the young men from violence. Public Archives, Ottawa, Selkirk Papers, Selkirk to MacDonnell, 16th June, 1813, CMG 19 E 1, 1 (2), pp. 650–61.

17. Sidmouth was reassured by his advisers that the outbreak was apolitical in character: 'The riotous proceedings . . . have originated from causes very different from any of those which produced a tendency to disturbance in other parts of Scotland.' It was a purely local and agrarian affair, he was told. Scottish Record Office, Home Office (Scotland) Correspondence, RH 2/4, 100, f. 82, Colquhoun to Sidmouth, 19th February, 1813.

18. The Stafford family was probably glad to settle privately with the offenders. A later critic pointed out that, although Young had committed certain individuals to the County Prison, no case was subsequently brought against them. It was alleged that Young had deluded the people with empty promises. The *Military Register*, 28th June 1815. sc D593/K/, Loch to Young, 3rd April, 1813.

19. *Ibid.*, Loch to Inglis (Home Office), 6th March, 1813.

20. Huw Scott, *Fasti Ecclesiae Scoticanae* (1928), vol. XIII, p. 83.

21. SC D593/K/, Young to Loch, 11th July, 1813, Loch to Cranstoun, 7th August, 1813, Cranstoun to Loch, 8th August, 1813, Gower to Mackid, 7th August, 1813.

22. Donald Sage, *Memorabilia Domestica, or Domestic Life in the North of Scotland* (2nd edn, Wick, 1899), p. 192 (emphasis added). The incident was also described by William Daniel who was in the district quite soon after. Of the common people he said: 'Their piety would be perfectly exemplary were it not impaired, in some instances, by bigotry and fanaticism . . . The promontory of Ru Storr . . . seems to have been one of the last strongholds in which the gloomy and savage supersititions of the country lingered.' *A Voyage Round Great Britain undertaken in the Summer of the year 1813* (London, 1814–20), vol. IV, pp. 74–6.

23. See Eric Richards, 'The Mind of Patrick Sellar (1780–1851)', *Scottish Studies*, vol. XV (1971).

24. SC D593/K/, Young to Loch, 15th June, 1815.

25. *Ibid.*, Sellar to Loch, 28th June, 1815, Loch to Lady Stafford, 9th June, 1815, Sellar to Lady Stafford, 17th July 1815.

26. *Ibid.*, Sellar to Lady Stafford, 17th July, 1815. *The Military Register*, 11th October, 1815. The government-sanctioned *Police Gazette* as well as *The Annual Register* had published accounts assuming Sellar's guilt. Tacksman Robert Gordon told the Highland Society in London that the people 'think they can bring Mr Sellar to a trial that he shall be obliged to give up their old farms again'. SC D593/K/, Gordon to Munro, 12th February, 1816, Grant to Loch, 26th May, 1816, Sellar to Lady Stafford, 17th July, 1815.

27. The minister, Mackenzie, refused to comply with the landlord's request to deny certain allegations in *The Star* – an unusual case of clerical obstinacy in the history of the clearances. SC D593/K, Mackenzie to Loch, 25th August, 1815, Sellar to Loch, 16th October, 1815.

28. *Ibid.*, Young to Loch, 11th October, 1815.

29. P. Gaskell, *Morven Transformed*, (1968), p. 38, suggests that on the evidence of the Trial Report no other verdict was possible. This transcript however, is not necessarily an accurate or even objective record.

30. This was a minor parallel with contemporary Irish rural outrages. Sheep thefts in the northern Highlands reached epidemic proportions in the late 1810s. SC D593/K/, Loch to Young, 30th May, 1816, Loch to Charles Ross, 7th January, 1817, Young to Loch, 26th May, 1816.

31. *The Scotsman*, 10th July, 1819, 25th December, 1820; see also the allegations of atrocity in *The Military Register*, 25th August, 1819.

32. *The Military Register*, 4th August, 1819. The Sutherland regime felt ill-used because, while it made provision for cleared tenants, other Highland landlords (e.g. Lord Moray, and Munro of Novar) simply evicted their tenants.

33. The publicity aroused a considerable degree of respectable sympathy. For example, National Library of Scotland, MS 3890, f. 2368, J. S. B. Morritt to W. Scott; and R. Southey, *A Journal of a Tour in Scotland* (ed. C. H. Herford, 1929), *passim*.

34. SC D593/K/K. Mackay to Suther, 28th October, 1819.

35. *Ibid.*, Loch to Gunn, 17th November, 1819, Loch to Lady Stafford, 9th November, 1819, Loch to Mackay, 14th December, 1819, Mackenzie to

Loch, 10th November, 1819. The Lord Advocate had publicly spoken of 'an unnatural union between the Radical Reformers and the gallant, brave Highlanders'. *The Military Register* considered it an attempt to blacken Dudgeon merely by association (29th December, 1819).

36. This was an echo of the curious allegation made in December 1813 by the Kildonan rebels to the effect that the Northumbrian shepherds had drunk the health of Bonaparte – and that the 'rebellion' was thus opposed to 'sedition'. See *The Military Register*, 17th July, 1816.

37. sc D593/K/, Loch to Brougham, 27th December, 1819, Mackenzie to Loch, 27th December, 1819, Suther to Loch, 15th January, 1820, Loch to Suther, 22nd January, 1820. *The Military Register*, 19th January, 1820. *The Scotsman*, 22nd January, 1820.

38. *Ibid.*, Suther to Loch, 14th February, 1820, Loch to Gunn, 7th February, 1820, Gunn to Loch, 11th March, 1820, 18th March, 1820.

39. *Ibid.*, Mackenzie to Loch, 30th March, 1820, Mackay to Loch, 4th March, 1820, Suther to Loch, 3rd March, 1820, 5th March, 1820. *Military Register*, 22nd March, 1820. *Inverness Courier*, 9th March, 1820. *Scotsman*, 11th March, 1820.

40. Home Office (Scotland) Correspondence, RH2/4 181 ff. 255–6, 284. sc D593/K/, Loch to Suther, 26th March, 1820, 23rd March, 1820.

41. *The Military Register*, 29th March, 1820, concurred in these taunting words: 'It is not very likely that the Sutherland men would do for *strangers* what in eight years, they had too much respect for the laws, to do *for themselves* under trying conditions.'

42. *The Scotsman*, 11th March, 1820. *The Military Register, op. cit.*

43. sc D593/K/, Loch to Suther, 26th March, 1820, Gunn to Loch, 3rd April, 1820, 4th April, 1820, Kennedy to Loch, 15th April, 1820.

44. *Ibid.*, Mackenzie to Loch, 14th August, 1820.

45. *Ibid.*, Loch to Mackenzie, 23rd March, 1821, Loch to Lord Stafford, 20th March, 1821, Suther to Loch, 27th March, 1821.

46. *Ibid.*, Grant to Loch, 17th April, 1821, Suther to Loch, 9th April, 1820, 11th April, 1821, 17th April, 1821, 27th April, 1821, 28th April, 1821.

47. *Ibid.*, Loch to Suther, 30th March, 1821, Sir Charles Ross to Solicitor General, 15th April, 1821, Moneypenny to Mackenzie, 17th April, 1821, Suther to Loch, 27th May, 1821.

48. Described in Hanham, *op. cit.*

49. W. Cobbett, *Rural Rides* (1930 edn), vol. III, p. 819.

50. S. de Sismondi, *Political Economy and the Philosophy of Government* (1857: selections had been printed in British journals in 1843), Karl Marx, *Capital* (Everyman edition, 2 vols, 1930), vol. II, pp. 807–10.

51. J. Barron, *The Northern Highlands in the Nineteenth Century* (Inverness 1903–13), vol. II, p. 251. sc D593/P/22/1/7, Lumsden to Rae, 6th October, 1841.

52. *Ibid.*

53. See Lord Teignmouth, *Sketches of the Coasts and Lands of Scotland and the Isle of Man* (1836), vol. II, pp. 17–24.

54. sc D593/K/, Anderson to Loch, 2nd August, 1841, Loch to Horsburgh, 28th September, 1841, Lockhart to Loch, 3rd November, 1841, Loch to Lord Stafford, 13th September, 1841.

55. *Ibid.*, Horsburgh to Loch, 20th October, 1841, 13th October, 1841, Loch to Anderson, 6th November, 1841, D593/P/22/1/7; Barron, *op. cit.*, vol. II,

314, 316, vol. III, p. xxx. See also W. Findlater, *Disruption Worthies of the Highlands, Another Memorial of 1843* (Edinburgh, 1877), p. 66.

56. Barron, *op. cit.*, vol. III, pp. 10, 15–6, 303; Alexander Mackenzie, *The History of the Highland Clearances* (reprint 1966, Glasgow), pp. 128–134.

57. Barron, *op. cit.*, vol. III, pp. 32–3; sc D593/K/22/1/7, Sinclair to Lumsden, 5th August, 1843, Lumsden to Duke of Sutherland, 7th September, 1843.

58. *Op. cit.*, p. 200.

59. Barron, *op. cit.*, vol. III, pp. 185, 190; *Journal of Henry Cockburn, 1831–1854* (Edinburgh 1874), vol. II, p. 247.

60. Barron, *op. cit.*, vol. III, p. 207.

61. sc D593/K/, Gunn to Loch, 5th March, 1852, 18th March, 1852, 21st March, 1852.

62. Donald Ross, quoted in Mackenzie, *op. cit.*, pp. 211–12.

63. Barron, *op. cit.*, vol. III, pp. 293, 297. See also A. Nicholson, *History of Skye* (Glasgow 1930), p. 382 ff.

64. See Barron, *op. cit.*, vol. III, pp. 289–92, and the account in Mackenzie, *op. cit.*, pp. 170–87.

65. D. Ross quoted in Mackenzie, *op. cit.*, p. 136; Barron, *op. cit.*, vol. III, pp. 302–9.

66. K. Marx, 'Sutherland and slavery, or the duchess at home', *The People's Paper*, 12th March, 1853; H. G. Stowe, *Sunny Memories of Foreign Lands* (1854); D. Ross, *The Scottish Highlanders; their Present Sufferings and Future Prospects* (1852); L. de Lavergne, *The Rural Economy of England, Scotland and Ireland* (1855).

67. sc D593/K/, Loch to Sutherland, 19th February, 1855.

68. See Hanham, *op. cit.*, which suggests that 'once the attention of the outside world had been attracted, the character of the land problem in the Western Highlands changed dramatically' (p. 65). Undoubtedly this was important in explaining the unprecedented effectiveness of the Skye protest. But widespread outside publicity had been attracted by many Highland outbursts in the previous part of the century. The greater responsiveness of public opinion by the 1880s may have been the more decisive variable.

69. *The Northern Ensign*, 7th October, 1884, 16th October, 1884. It was a time when a Scottish writer, Blackie, was prepared to quote the words of the Swiss economist, Sismondi, written some fifty years earlier: 'Let the lords of Scotland beware; if once they believe that they have no need for the people the people may in their turn think that they have no need of them'. The implication of Blackie's own remarks was that the Highlanders should have rebelled long ago. J. S. Blackie, *The Scottish Highlanders and the Land Laws* (1885), pp. xiv, 192 ff.

70. Induction Riots, of course, were not confined to Highland Scotland. See, for instance, John Galt, *Annals of the Parish* (1911 edn) pp. 7–10. I owe this reference to Roland Quinault.

71. See Scott, *op. cit.*, vol. VIII; also H. F. Campbell 'Notes on the County of Sutherland in the 18th Century', *Transactions of the Gaelic Society of Inverness*, 1907, p. 480.

72. sc D593/K, Bairgie to Loch, 10th February, 1834; Barron, *op. cit.*, vol. III, pp. 33–40.

73. The social history of the disruption in the Highlands has yet to be written. It is already evident that there were significant variations in the pattern

of popular response. See G. I. T. Machin, 'The Disruption and British Politics, 1834-43', *Scottish Historical Review*, vol. LI (April 1972), p. 35 n.

74. Barron, *op. cit.*, vol. III, pp. 128-31.

75. There are plausible theories (applied to comparable cases) that emigration acts as a 'haemorrhage from the countryside of the young and the rebellious' (E. P. Thompson in the Foreword to A. J. Peacock, *Bread or Blood* (1965), p. 9). Charles Tilly also believes that rapid emigration acts 'as a damper on violent protest, tending to withdraw the discontented'. The authors of *The Scottish Insurrection of 1820* (1970), P. Berresford Ellis and S. Mac A'Ghobhainn, assert that the people ejected during the clearances moved south 'to the industrial belt . . . were enlisting in the Radical ranks almost to a man', though they give no evidence (p. 113).

76. The old forms of leadership seem to have survived the emigration: for example, see Janet Schaw, *Journal of a Lady of Quality* (ed. E. W. Andrews, 1921), p. 28.

77. Mackenzie, *op. cit.*, p. 21.

78. Outspoken remarks by ministers expressly critical of landlords, can be found in various places: for example, the *New Statistical Account* and in the Poor Law inquiries of the late 1830s.

79. Cf. Smout, *op. cit.*, pp. 324-31, to the effect that Calvinism was deadly to any kind of radical protest.

80. Olwen Hufton, 'Women in Revolution, 1789-1796', *Past and Present*, vol. 53, November 1971, p. 91. See also E. P. Thompson, 'The Moral Economy of the English Crowd in the Eighteenth Century', *Past and Present*, vol. 50, February 1971, pp. 115-17.

81. See David Williams, *The Rebecca Riots* (Cardiff 1955), pp. 100-1. Much of the social history of the Highlands has yet to be written, but see I. F. Grant, *Highland Folkways* (1961) pp. 198-9.

82. SC D593/K/, Suther to Loch, 11th April, 1821.

83. As expounded in Tilly *op. cit.*, and in his essay 'Collective Violence in European Perspective', in H. D. Graham and T. R. Gurr, *Violence in America* (Signet edition, New York 1969), pp. 16-24.

84. See for instance his essay 'The "Pre-Industrial Crowd" ', in George Rudé, *Paris and London in the Eighteenth Century* (1970).

85. Tilly notes that 'the classic food riot virtually disappeared after 1830'. ('Collective Violence', *op. cit.*, p. 17).

86. E. P. Thompson, 'English Trade Unionism and other Labour Movements before 1790', *Society for the Study of Labour History*, Bulletin No. 17 (1968), p. 20.

87. See Hugh Miller, *Leading Articles on Various Subjects* (Edinburgh 1870), p. 420.

88. Smout, *op. cit.*, p. 360.

89. D593/K/, Gunn to Loch, 14th September, 1841.

90. Cf. the remark of Trevelyan in 1852 that 'the existing Highland proprietors are, as a class, more than usually amenable to public opinion'. D. S. MacMillan, 'Sir Charles Trevelyan and the Highland and Island Emigration Society, 1849-1859', *Royal Australian Historical Journal*, vol. XLIX, p. 175.

91. The 'Crofters' War of 1882', in almost every respect, conformed to the classic mould of Highland protest set since 1790.

3

The General Strike of 1842

A Study in Leadership, Organisation and the Threat of Revolution during the Plug Plot Disturbances

F. C. MATHER

In the eyes of contemporaries the semi-revolutionary strike movement, which engulfed the manufacturing districts of Britain in the summer of 1842, assumed an importance which the historian has seldom recognised. Graham, who was then Home Secretary, thought it 'more serious' than the Chartist disturbances of 1839. To Melbourne, according to the Queen, it recalled the tumults of the Reform Bill struggle.[1] Lieutenant Colonel Maberley, the Secretary of the Post Office, whose duties afforded him a unique insight into conditions prevailing in different parts of the country, went so far as to describe it as 'a commotion such as we have not witnessed for half a century'.[2]

It would be unsafe to dismiss these opinions as being wildly exaggerated. There are objective grounds for believing that, limited though they were in duration to a period of two months, the disturbances of 1842 were the most intense of any that occurred in Britain from the time of the French Revolution to that of the Chartist *détente* of 1848. They covered a wider geographical area than Luddism, embraced more trades than the Agricultural Labourers' Rising of 1830, and broke with more concentrated force than the Chartist unrest of 1839 and 1848. No fewer than fifteen

English or Welsh shires and eight Scottish counties were affected by them.[3] The main impact, it is true, was upon the lowlands of Scotland and on a concentrated block of English territory stretching from the Aire and the Ribble in the North to Shropshire and Staffordshire, Warwickshire and Leicestershire in the South. But there were ripples of the main wave in Cumberland and Glamorganshire, on Tyneside, and at Chard in Somerset. Even the capital was stirred. Public meetings were arranged there to take cognizance of the 'awful state of the Country', and a tumultuous procession surged through the City at midnight.

The movement has been described as a 'general strike, the first not only in Britain but in any capitalist country'.[4] The stoppage was never completely general in the sense of nationwide, but in many towns and districts there was, indeed, an almost complete suspension of labour in factories, coalmines and other large establishments, whilst domestic handworkers often turned out to demonstrate and to compel others to join them. But it was also much more than a strike. A local postmaster writing from Accrington at the height of the outbreak observed: 'It is more like a revolution than anything else in this neighbourhood, and we fear that plunder and mischief is not at an end.'[5] Graham and Melbourne, too, harped in their correspondence upon the insurrectionary character of the strike. Nor was this mere moonshine. It would be wrong to conclude that a geuine revolutionary situation existed, for in the last analysis the state's monopoly of power was not in imminent danger of being overthrown.[6] However, authority was undoubtedly challenged. Workmen pledged not to return to work until the constitution was changed, many thousands of strikers took virtual possession of large towns for hours on end, and even thought of marching on London to set the nation right.[7] On one occasion the mob even unseated a detachment of calvalry by pelting it with heavy stones. The speed with which rumour spread provided a further indication of abnormality, found in other societies when in process of dissolution. Sir Robert Peel, writing from his country house in Staffordshire, told of a report brought by a railway guard from London that the Queen had been assassinated at Windsor. This had apparently circulated like wildfire.[8]

The 1842 outbreak furnishes the opportunity, therefore, to study revolutionary processes at work in a normally stable society, and this will be attempted briefly. We shall hope thereby to throw some light upon the extent of the danger to which the country was exposed, and also upon the reserves of stability.

But first the pattern of the disturbances must be briefly sketched. Although there had been sporadic local turnouts, provoked by wage reductions, from the earliest months of 1842, the period of continuous unrest may be dated from a strike which began on the North Staffordshire coalfield on July 8th. From that time forward events unfolded in four main stages. During the first of these, which lasted until August 2nd, the stoppage was confined to the collieries of North and South Staffordshire, and its purpose, like that of previous outbreaks, was the redress of certain economic grievances, notably low wages, truck payments and a fraudulent system of remuneration known as Bildas. Nevertheless, two essential features of the later, more generalised, disturbances became apparent. One was the raking out of boiler fires, and the drawing of boiler plugs, to prevent the pit engines from resuming work. The other was the practice of marching in force from establishment to establishment to compel a suspension of labour. Sometimes the distances covered by the mobs were quite considerable. The North Staffordshire miners got as far as the Poynton colliery near Stockport, a distance of some twenty-five miles, before being repelled by the troops. The second phase opened on August 3rd, and continued until about the 11th of that month. Its principal characteristic was an extension of the geo-graphical and occupational coverage of the strike. On August 3rd 10,000 colliers and ironminers of the Airdrie district of Lanarkshire left their pits, and started to plunder the potato patches of the neighbouring farmers for food. Two days later there was a strike at Bayley's cotton factory in

Stalybridge, and roving cohorts of operatives carried the stoppage first to the whole area of Ashton and Stalybridge, then to Manchester, and subsequently to towns adjacent to Manchester, using as much force as was necessary to bring factories to a standstill. As yet the movement remained, to outward appearances, largely non-political. Although the People's Charter was praised at public meetings, the resolutions that were passed at these were in almost all cases merely for a restoration of the wages of 1840, a ten-hour working day, or reduced rents.[9]

During the third stage, from August 12th to 20th, the strike was at its height. By dint of the exertions of the large armies of turnouts which marched from town to town it quickly became general in the manufacturing districts of Lancashire, Cheshire and the West Riding, and began to spread into Leicestershire and Nottinghamshire. Meanwhile, conferences of delegates assembled in Manchester to direct the movement, and these endeavoured, with some apparent success, to harness it to the People's Charter. It was at this stage that the revolutionary and anti-governmental features of the outbreak were most in evidence. Manchester was placarded, as London had been at the height of the Reform Bill struggle, with notices calling for a run on the banks,[10] and there were sanguinary clashes between the mob and the military at Preston and at Blackburn, in the Potteries and at Salter Hebble in Yorkshire. This was also, however, the period when the central government intervened, with troops and official exhortations, to curb the violence and procure the arrest of the leaders. The fourth phase, therefore, which stretched into late September in some districts was anti-climactic. It was a period of diminished violence and steady trickle back to work, and although certain categories of workers, notably the cotton operatives of south-east Lancashire continued to hold out, it was for wage increases that they contended and not for the People's Charter. The wheel had come full circle. What had begun as a wage dispute was a wage dispute once more.

To return to our main task, discussion of the mechanics of

revolution is bound sooner or later to raise the question of the necessity of leadership. This has long been an open question among writers on the subject, whether they be historians or political scientists, sociologists or active revolutionaries. As Crane Brinton formulates it, the division lies between, on the one hand, 'the school of circumstances', which regards revolution as a 'wild and natural growth', the more or less spontaneous reaction to intolerable oppression, and on the other, 'the school of plot', which sees it as a 'forced and artificial growth', sparked off by 'a series of interlocking plots initiated by small but determined groups of malcontents'.[11] Broadly speaking, the conflict reflects the divergence between the apologists for revolution and the conservative opponents of it, although Communist explanations with their un-ashamed emphasis on the role of leaders consciously planning a revolt provide an exception to this rule. We may perhaps agree with Crane Brinton that both extremes are nonsense. 'Chance', as Pasteur said, 'favours only the mind which is prepared', and while sudden and unexpected events like famines, or slumps, or the dislocations of war, do provide the motive power of revolution, the presence of leaders who can channel the anger or despair of the mob into purposeful activity is essential to the achievement of real success. Depending upon the nature of the objects sought, these leaders need not be instruments of an intellectual elite or concentrated pressure group. They may, as Chalmers Johnson implies,[12] be mere hedge preachers and village prophets, but leadership in some form and to some degree is indispensable.

It will be useful to apply this analysis to the General Strike of 1842. The explanation of this which found most favour at the time was that of 'the school of plot'. The Chartists blamed the Anti-Corn Law League; the Leaguers blamed the Chartists; the Conservative government blamed both, and added the trade unions for good measure. The case against the Anti-Corn Law League need not detain us long. Elaborated by John Wilson Croker in a clever political polemic which appeared in *The Quarterly Review*,[13] it ran to the effect that, pursuant to a long-term plan, the League engineered the strike both by incitement and by the action of its member millowners in effecting a reduction in the wages of the cotton operatives. Croker made many telling points against the League, and there can be little doubt that the continual harping upon the damage inflicted by the Corn Laws, and on the selfishness of landlords, helped to encourage the insurgents and to demoralise the upholders of law and order when the conflict came. Nevertheless, the League can almost certainly be acquitted of direct conspiracy to foment the outbreak. Both in Staffordshire and in southern Lancashire Tory employers shared with free-trading liberals the responsibility for making the offending wage reductions, and Bayleys of Stalybridge, whose stubbornness was immediately responsible for the outbreak in Lancashire, were in the last resort prepared to withdraw their notice of reduction. It was the men who then refused the olive branch.[14]

But what of the Chartists and the trade unions? It was upon these, acting as he supposed in concert, through a conference of trade delegates meeting in Manchester, that the Home Secretary's suspicions first alighted. 'It is quite clear,' he wrote to General Sir William Warre on August 15th, 'that these Delegates are the Directing Body: they form the link between the trades unions and the Chartists.'[15] Later historians, however, reacting sharply against such conspiratorial explanations, have emphasised the strike's total spontaneity. Mr Christopher Thorne writes that 'the Plug Riots, manifestations of utter misery . . . following wage cuts in the summer of 1842, were by no means Chartist-inspired . . .',[16] while Dr Donald Read makes explicit the assumptions of the modern consensus in the words: 'There was no causal connection between Chartism and the outbreak. . . . The Chartists . . . merely attempted to exploit it once it had occurred.'[17] This paper is designed to suggest that the truth lies in between the contemporary and more recent interpretations.

It seems to me that the role of conscious, creative leadership did assert itself at two successive stages in the develop-

ment of the strike. First in the inception. It is true that the
ordinary coalminer or cotton operative, who struck work
and endeavoured to persuade others to do likewise, did so
out of a sense of exasperation induced by a long series of wage
reductions. Without this impetus no amount of oratory would
have produced an outbreak as widespread as the Plug Plot.
Given this factor, however, the importance of leaders, who
suggested when the time was ripe to strike, which factories
should be turned out by force, and what should be demanded
as the price of returning to work, can scarcely be denied.
There is evidence that, in Stalybridge and in the Staffordshire Potteries, the workpeople had local trade committees
to formulate their demands, but enthusiasm was principally
sustained at large open-air meetings, where directions were
also issued as to where the mob should proceed, what should
be their terms, and how they should behave. From the official
reports of the subsequent trials at the Lancaster Assizes, and
from the columns of the *Northern Star*,[18] it is possible to
compile a list of the chairmen and principal speakers at the
meetings in Stalybridge and Ashton, and also in Manchester, in the early days of the outbreak. Research into the
background of these figures shows that they were mostly
Chartists, and that many had no connection with the cotton
industry, where the grievances which provoked the strike
occurred.

The *Star* lists the speakers at a meeting in Stalybridge early
on August 8th, which, after an adjournment, ended in a
resolution to turn out factories in Stalybridge and Dukinfield. Six names were mentioned. The Chairman, Alexander
('Sandy') Challenger, was a hatter, who had once proposed
a memorial to the Queen that she should employ only
Chartist ministers.[19] William Stephenson was nominated as a
representative of Stalybridge to the General Council of the
National Charter Association; so also was John Durham
(mistakenly described as 'Derham'), a Stalybridge news-
agent.[20] Patrick Brophy was an Irishman who had once
been secretary of the Irish Universal Suffrage Association,
and had become a Chartist lecturer.[21] Fenton was pre-

sumably the notorious pike-selling Chartist from Ashton, once described in a piece of local doggerel as one of 'Fergus' dupes'.[22] At a later meeting that afternoon which adopted a resolution 'that the people of Ashton go to Oldham and those at Stalybridge and Dukinfield to Hyde' the principal speakers were Brophy and Richard Pilling, a member of the South Lancashire delegate conference of the National Charter Association.[23] Pilling afterwards headed the Ashton turnouts to Oldham.[24] In Granby Row Fields, Manchester, on August 9th seven speakers were mentioned; four were certainly Chartists and two more probably so.[25] At a further meeting in the same place on the following day Christopher Doyle, who had been a member of the Chartist Convention of 1842,[26] urged the people to form a procession. In the Ashton context mention should be made of William Aitken (Aitkin), a local schoolmaster and Chartist leader, who went with Challenger as a delegate to Preston, to persuade the workpeople there to strike;[27] also perhaps of Thomas Mahon, who formed the link between the Chartists and the Operatives' Committee.[28] Similar evidence of Chartist leadership comes from other regions, from the Potteries, from South Staffordshire, where Arthur O'Neill, the Christian Chartist, attended a meeting at West Bromwich on August 1st and moved resolutions embodying the miners' grievances,[29] and from Scotland.

It would be tempting to deduce from these cases a nucleated Chartist conspiracy to work up a general strike in favour of the People's Charter. Only three years earlier a Chartist Convention had adopted such a plan, to rescind it when it found the project lacking in support. Closer examination of the evidence, however, casts doubt on this interpretation. For one thing Chartism was in 1842 too divided to be capable of devising a single national plan. It was split not only between O'Connorites and Complete Suffragists, but also between O'Connor and his editor of the *Northern Star* on the one hand and the chiefs of the Executive of the National Charter Association on the other.[30] Moreover, the Chartists who put themselves at the head of the strikes in

South Lancashire, seemed uncertain themselves whether it was for the Charter or for the redress of trade grievances that they were contending. John Leach told a meeting at Hyde that 'it would be more proper for them to stand out for the wage than the Charter question', as 'it was impossible for them to get the Charter at present'.[31] At a meeting at the Haigh in Stalybridge on August 11th Fenton and Durham argued for the wages question; Stephenson and Mahon for the Charter.[32] Yet all were Chartists.

Probably, therefore, these local Chartists headed the turnouts over wage grievances not simply to exploit them (although it would be naive to suggest that they were not, in many cases, also feeling their way to turn the situation to the advantage of the People's Charter) but out of a deep-rooted sense of commitment to working-class interests which Chartism engendered. There was an established pattern of Chartist leadership in trade disputes going back for at least several months before the Plug Plot commenced. Aitken and Pilling were to be found taking the lead in resistance to a proposed 10 per cent reduction of wages in Ashton as early as March 1842.[33] The action taken in August was in one perspective merely a legitimate extension of this.

If, however, at first, the Chartists contributed little to the shaping of the objects of the strike, they exerted quite a profound influence on the tactics that were pursued. It is possible to discern in the speeches which they made evidence of a design to unify discontents into a single focus of confrontation with the employers. This was apparent in Chartist contributions to strikes even before the Plug Plot began. O'Neill told a West Bromwich strike meeting in May that 'the whole district should be forthwith canvassed, united and organised to enable them to resist not only the present reduction but also future attempts'.[34] Perhaps there was something in Chartism with its class-conscious appeal to general working-class interests that led its adherents to advise union of forces as an appropriate weapon of defence in trade disputes, for when the strikes broke out in Lancashire in August, it was again the object of the Chartist orators to bring a concerted pressure of the whole area to bear upon the employers. It was resolved at a meeting on Mottram Moor on Sunday, August 7th 'that on the Tuesday, they would march to Manchester, stop all labour, visit the Exchange and teach "the merchants how to give better prices for goods" '. The events of the two following days were fully consistent with such a plan. By a sequence of rallies and turnout marches the operatives of the Ashton, Stalybridge, Hyde and Dukinfield district were slowly shepherded together, until a joint invasion of Manchester became feasible. It occurred on Tuesday, August 9th, when a section of the invading force did in fact make its way at the earliest opportunity to the Exchange.[35] In this way the Chartists helped to expand and to unify the movement when it occurred, though it is by no means clear that they were acting in accordance with any revolutionary plan conceived before the outbreak began. At least they cast their influence against recourse to violence.[36]

Once the strikes had been successfully launched, a second organised intervention occurred – that of the delegate conferences. These were of two kinds – a national conference of the National Charter Association held in Manchester on August 16th and 17th, and a series of regional conferences consisting of delegates from the trades of Manchester and district, which met in the same city from August 11th to 20th. In most historical accounts of the Plug Plot the former plays a central role. The latter, however, was in some respects the more important. It was the trade conferences that gave the first general lead to adopt the People's Charter as the prime object of the strike. On August 12th a meeting of the trades and millhands of Manchester and its vicinity with delegates from various parts of Lancashire and Yorkshire, adopted a resolution: 'that this meeting recommend the people of all trades and callings to forthwith cease work until the above document becomes the law of the land'. This was confirmed at a differently constituted conference in the Carpenters' Hall that same afternoon.[37] The deliberations coincided with and strengthened a growing movement in the country to give the turnout a political colouring.[38] Moreover, in the Manchester district, at least, which was the home of the strike, the trade delegates rather than the Chartists came to be regarded as the leaders. Their continued sessions from August 15th onwards, held after further elections had taken place, were besieged by large crowds, which gathered in the streets outside their meeting halls, eager to know what transpired within, so much so that the delegates themselves, anxious to avoid attracting the attention of the authorities, repeatedly and vainly urged them to disperse.[39]

The assembling of these delegates apparently *ex nihilo*, and their uncompromising stand for the People's Charter, is a phenomenon which calls for explanation. To Home Secretary Graham they formed the nub of the supposed conspiracy, linking the Chartists with the trade unions.[40] Events, however, are capable of a less sinister interpretation. The immediate urge which led to the gathering of these bodies, appears to have been more or less spontaneous. Shortly after the march of the turnouts from Ashton into Manchester two separate initiatives were taken in the town to procure the appointment of trade delegates – one by the power-loom weavers and the other by the mechanics. There may, in fact, have been more than two, but that of the mechanics proved the most fruitful and eventually burgeoned into the conference in the Carpenters' Hall on August 11th and 12th, which adopted the resolution to strike for the Charter. It seems that the mechanics were first goaded into an appeal for support from their fellow tradesmen because one of their own meetings had been interrupted by the soldiery.[41] Behind these occurrences, however, lay a long period of unintended preparation. In Manchester and the surrounding towns the tradition of uniting trades by delegates for mutual support upon a regional basis stretched back at least to the Philanthropic Society of 1818, which included the towns of Manchester, Stockport, Ashton-under-Lyne, Oldham and Bury.[42] During the nine months preceding the outbreak at Stalybridge this tradition was revived by the attempts of both the Anti-Corn Law League and the

Chartists to draw out an expression of support from the trade societies. As early as October 1841 a gathering of the Manchester Operative Anti-Corn Law Association had appointed a committee to invite the trades, mill hands and other bodies of working men to attend a meeting for the purpose of obtaining the extinction of the corn monopoly and compensation for those who had been robbed by it.[43] By New Year's Day 1842 a conference of deputies from the different working men's associations of the Kingdom was being held in the Anti-Corn Law League's rooms in Manchester, and this commissioned a deputation of workmen from Messrs Sharp and Roberts' engineering works in Manchester to organise the trades upon the subject of Corn Law repeal, which was to be accompanied by an 'equitable adjustment' of the National Debt, financed by the landlords out of taxation.[44]

Significantly, the leader of the deputation from Messrs Sharp and Roberts was Alexander Hutchinson, a smith, who was to serve as the standing chairman of the trade delegate conferences held in Manchester in the second week of the disturbances of August. Hutchinson was an Owenite Socialist, who, at the time of his arrest during the Plug Plot, planned to emigrate to the backwoods of America for the purpose of founding or joining a communitarian experiment there. His position was somewhat compromised by the fact that, when he was arrested, the police discovered in his house in Manchester a collection of firearms and gunpowder, which he had intended to take with him on his journey.[45]

But to return to events earlier in the year, Hutchinson and his colleagues fulfilled their commission from the Anti-Corn Law League to organise the trades. Meetings, consisting of delegates from the bricklayers and the mechanics, the silk dyers and the calico printers, the engravers and the glass cutters, the shoemakers and the tailors were duly held. At the last of these, in the Hop Pole Inn, Manchester, on March, 14th, with Hutchinson in the chair, the unexpected happened. Delegate after delegate rose to substitute an agitation for the People's Charter for one in favour of Corn

Law repeal, and eventually a motion for uniting the trades and political bodies of Manchester on the basis of the Charter alone was carried by fifty-nine votes. It was further resolved to invite the trades of Manchester and Salford to attend a demonstration on Good Friday, when Feargus O'Connor would lay the foundation stone of a memorial to Orator Hunt. The lead in favour of the Charter was begun by the representative of the silk dyers and was followed by those of the calico printers and the fustian cutters.[46]

The outcome of this meeting reflects a development, the importance of which historians have only just begun to appreciate. Until recently it has been often assumed that Chartism and trade unionism were two mutually exclusive expressions of working-class endeavour. By some historians, notably Professor Asa Briggs, a pendulum explanation had been invoked to clarify the relationship between them. Working men concentrated upon trade union activity in times of good trade and turned to politics when trade was poor.[47] This thesis is both valid and useful, as a general case, but it must admit of significant exceptions. Certain trades, the skilled handicrafts in particular, retained their organisation through the worst years of depression, and these sometimes turned collectively to Chartism, in response to wage cutting or the threat of downgrading, because reflection had taught their members that a political solution was relevant to their economic difficulties. The columns of the *Northern Star* during the first six months of 1842 furnish many examples of initiatives by various groups of tradesmen to declare for the Charter or join the National Charter Association. The 'cordwainers of Colne', the 'associated shoemakers of Wigan', the fustian cutters of Manchester, the joiners of Manchester,[48] are all cases in point. Particularly interesting is the conversion of the engineering trades of Manchester, which took place in the two months prior to the outbreak of the Plug Plot in Lancashire. On May 31st the mechanics, and on July 12th the hammermen, adopted at their general meetings resolutions to become members of the N.C.A.[49] It is not suggested that these bodies were anything more than local societies or branches or that their conversion to Chartism in any way typified the attitude of national organisations like the Journeymen Steam Engine and Machine Makers Friendly Society, which were often as scrupulous as the Methodists in adopting 'No Politics' rules.[50] Nevertheless, at the regional level, in places like Manchester, London and Glasgow,[51] there was a marked coalescence of Chartism and the trade societies, and this exerted a profound influence upon the character of the General Strike.

Success in converting the unions to the Six Points was partly the result of a deliberate Chartist effort to achieve it. Numerous initiatives were taken in the two or three months before the Plug Plot, some of them local and unco-ordinated, like that of the Preston Chartists in June for the establishment of a standing joint conference of Chartists and trade unionists, which would refuse to separate until it had achieved the protection of trade and the constitutional liberties of the people.[52] As yet Feargus O'Connor and the editor of the *Northern Star* newspaper showed no interest in the movement, but three of the leading members of the Executive of the National Charter Association appear to have been involved in it, whether individually or collectively. P. M. McDouall and James Leach were active in lecturing to the trades on the virtues of Chartism,[53] whilst John Campbell, the Secretary of the Association, published a Letter to the Chartists of Great Britain in the *Star* on June 11th, calling for a union of the Chartists and the trade societies. 'Without union', he urged, 'we are powerless; with it we are everything'.[54] There are strong indications, however, that the missionary activity undertaken by the Chartists was only successful because it coincided with a spontaneous development within the trades themselves. Some groups were clearly influenced in their decisions for the Charter by deputations sent to them by other trades – the hammermen by the mechanics, the mechanics by the carpenters.[55] Moreover, in the dialogue conducted at the lodge meetings, the argument for becoming Chartist which carried the greatest weight was the economic one. Political power was necessary to secure the object for which the unions had themselves been founded – the protection of the labour of working men.[56] This could be made relevant to the needs even of those aristocratic trades, which were merely threatened with wage cutting, dilution of labour and machine competition, and not yet seriously oppressed. In this connection it is useful to note an address issued in June 1842 by the Committee charged with the responsibility of preparing the monument to Henry Hunt in Manchester. It reminded 'the aristocratical portion of the trades', which had hitherto stood aloof from Chartism, that 'the same circumstances are at work still which have brought down the wages of, and impoverished other trades, and will continue, if not checked, and operate upon theirs also'.[57] In an age when, as Mr Edward Thompson has shown, the forces of economic change were operating to produce a widespread insecurity among artisans of all kinds,[58] this was a powerful case to use. Its employment reveals not merely the greater sophistication with which Chartists were coming to present their arguments, but also the extent to which the trade societies were deflected towards Chartism by factors present in their own shop-floor experience.

It would seem, therefore, that the sudden assembling of the trades delegates during the Plug Plot disturbances and their declaration for a strike in favour of the People's Charter can be satisfactorily explained by these features of the recent history of the trades, and without recourse to any notion that the delegates were the instruments of a Chartist plot.

Thus far pursued, our investigation tends in its result to support the generally accepted conclusion that no deep or premeditated nodal conspiracy underlay the disturbances of 1842. We have been led, nevertheless, to attribute to leadership a larger part than has been usually allowed. This leadership was opportunistic and often decentralised, moulding events rather than creating them, arising from disseminated assumptions rather than responding to a single controlling voice. Nevertheless, it existed and its presence rendered the outbreak more serious than it would otherwise

have been. It remains to consider briefly how effectively
direction was exercised when it reached the level of the
conferences of trade delegates.

The men who assembled in the Sheardown Inn, Tib
Street, on 15th August, 1842 to resume the task of directing
the strike took a serious view of their responsibilities. They
clearly regarded themselves as a sort of alternative government, charged with the duty of bringing order out of the
chaos that had arisen. In a published Address to the Trades
of Manchester and the Surrounding Districts they claimed
to be the 'true and *bona fide* representatives of the people of
those districts' and a 'personification of the public will'.[59]
One of their number told the crowds assembled outside their
meeting place that they 'considered themselves a committee
of public safety at the present crisis'.[60] Perhaps this was
largely rhetoric, derived from Tom Paine and the English
Jacobin tradition, which had formed part of the culture of
the artisans since the time of the French Revolution. It had,
nevertheless, practical implications. The delegates were
deeply aware, almost pathetically aware, of the need to
provide the country with leadership. When the magistrates
of Manchester broke up their meeting on August 16th, they
used the last few minutes available to them to pass a resolution re-affirming their recommendation to the people to
cease work until the Charter became the law of the land, and
proposing to send delegates to every part of the United
Kingdom to enlist the co-operation of the middle and
labouring classes in carrying the same.[61] Admittedly, there
was a dissentient minority in their ranks anxious to order a
return to work, but of eighty-five delegates assembled on
August 15th, fifty-eight declared for going on with the strike
until the Charter had been enacted.[62] Even after the disaster
of Tuesday 16th, when the authorities entered their meeting
place at the Hall of Science and gave them ten minutes to
disperse, the delegates met again each day that week, and
carefully explored every avenue of approach for keeping the
strike going. This they did notwithstanding the fact that their
ranks were being continually thinned by arrests.[63]

It is true, of course, that the exertions of the delegates were strangely out of proportion to the extent of their direct authority. Elected upon a local basis, they were in no sense the apex of a nationwide organisation. Although it was claimed that one of their meetings, on August 12th, was attended by delegates from Yorkshire as well as from Lancashire,[64] the subsequent gathering on the 15th, which was more carefully screened, seems to have been mainly constituted by the trades of Manchester and a group of towns and townships lying to the north and east of Manchester. From the lists given in the local press it seems that there were representatives from Oldham, Royton, Clayton and Lees, from Bury, Heywood, Middleton and Radcliffe Bridge, from Ashton, Stalybridge, Hyde and Mossley, and from the cotton spinners of Bolton. But the only delegates from the west of Manchester were from the vicinities of Eccles and Leigh, while none were recorded from the towns to the south.[65] Indirectly, however, the delegates had scope for exercising a much wider influence. If only they could have rallied the trades of the Manchester district behind the strike for the People's Charter, they could have carried far distant regions with them too, for there was a pronounced tendency in many areas to look to Manchester for a lead as to what to do. At Merthyr Tydfil, while the miners hesitated whether to strike or not, the authorities placarded the town with notices of the failure of the turn out in Manchester in order to place a damper on the proceedings. The Chief Constable of Glamorganshire commented as follows on the situation there: 'Unless the news from the North be bad I do not apprehend an outbreak. I believe this to be a shadow of the Manchester affair and their object the Charter, and their cry is now or never.'[66] Likewise at Carlisle, in the week beginning August 14th, public meetings were held on three successive evenings to hear reports from 'the conference of the working classes' and on the state of the Manchester district.[67] At Trowbridge in Wiltshire, also, the working men waited upon information that the operatives elsewhere intended to persist in the struggle before deciding whether to commit themselves to it. They expressed the desire for a public body to sit either in London or in Manchester to direct the movement.[68]

Inasmuch as the trade delegates in Manchester endeavoured to rise to their responsibilities it would be difficult to maintain that the general strike for the People's Charter failed for want of leadership. Why, then, did it fail? There are three main reasons.

Firstly, it failed because it was bound to fail. The time-scale was against it. In a society less artificial than our own, the mere suspension of labour by the industrial working class could not subdue the government in less time than it would take to reduce the strikers by starvation. By their insistence on abstaining from work until the People's Charter had become the law of the land, whilst at the same time refusing to countenance any violence, the trade delegates sitting in Manchester committed themselves to logical inconsistencies which they were ultimately unable to resolve. The dilemma was recognised in their debates. Candelet, a delegate from Hyde, observed in terms which recalled Benbow's fiery pamphlet of 1832, that 'there was plenty of provisions for them on the hills – plenty of good crops with which they might supply their wants', but another member immediately inquired: 'How could supplies be obtained during the turn-out consistently with "Peace, Law and Order"? To be sure they were told to go to the hills and find provisions, but the man who had reared those vegetable productions had a first and inalienable right to them.'[69] The point was a fair one for at their meeting on the previous Saturday the delegates had issued a placard headed 'Justice!!!, Peace!!!, Law!!!, Order!!!'[70] In fact, the only way in which a general strike could have been sustained for a lengthy period without violence was by getting the shopkeepers to extend credit to the workpeople while the turnout lasted; and by drawing on voluntary contributions from the well-to-do. The delegates entertained hopes of being able to effect these purposes, for they negotiated through a friendly shopkeeper named Williscroft both with other shopkeepers and with meetings of dissenting ministers.[71] Almost their last throw before giving up the struggle was to convene a meeting of shop-keepers on Friday, August 19th. Nevertheless, despite the fact that printed invitations were delivered at several thousand shops, the project turned out to be a fiasco. Only a handful of people attended.[72] The truth was that, although the shopkeepers and publicans of Stalybridge and Ashton-under-Lyne formed committees to assist the operatives to obtain 'a fair days wage for a fair days work' in the early stages of the strike, these bodies issued notices threatening to withdraw their support as soon as the movement took a political turn.[73] The delegates could rely on some aid from the lower middle classes in a struggle for higher wages, if only because the repeated wage-cuttings of recent years had diminished the shopkeepers' custom,[74] but they could not have it in a strike for the Charter.

Some delegates – they were in a minority – were ready to cut through the knot by diminishing the insistence on Law and Order. The extremists were mainly Irishmen, like William Duffy, who had once been a lecturer for the Anti-Corn Law League, but had apparently turned against his former employers by the time that the delegates met, because, having threatened the government to stop the supplies if the Corn Laws were not repealed, they had then proceeded, as magistrates of Manchester, to put down public meetings during the strike.[75] Duffy was the principal activist during the meetings of the delegates. He was continually striving to bring the conference into conflict with the author-ities by urging it to issue a placard denouncing a proclama-tion, made by the magistrates against public meetings, as unjust and unconstitutional, and to call for a run on the banks.[76] The wonder is that he was not prosecuted. This could indicate that he was still secretly an agent for the Anti-Corn Law League and that the magistrates of that party managed to protect him. My own conviction is that he appears to have been primarily an Irish nationalist, seeking to make trouble for the Tory government without overmuch concern for the English faction which he happened to be in

league with at the time.[77] The same explanation almost
certainly goes for Patrick McIntyre, who eventually stormed
out of a meeting of the delegates, accusing his fellows of
being 'frightened from their propriety by the very "name"
of an army', affirming his belief that 'the way to an Englishman's understanding was through his belly' and thanking the
Almighty that 'he did not belong to a nation whose intellectual susceptibilities were aroused by such carnal in-
stincts'.[78] The role of Irish discontents in the Plug Plot is a
subject which, so far as I am aware, has never been investigated, but, to judge by the names of men who played
a leading role in fomenting it – Patrick Brophy, Daniel
Donovan, Bernard McCartney, Patrick McIntyre, William
Duffy, Christopher Doyle – one which would repay explora-
tion.

The general strike for the People's Charter failed secondly
because it lacked sufficient support from workers in the basic
industries. This is sometimes obscured by the fact that the
conference of trade delegates had so large a majority in
favour of it. The delegates, however, although they represented a wide range of occupations, were not nicely
proportioned in number to the strength and importance of
their constituents. More than a half of those present on August 15th came from what is loosely designated the aristocracy
of labour: the unrevolutionised skilled handicrafts and the
mechanical or engineering trades.[79] Out in the country, in
the mill towns about Manchester, nothing like a firm
consensus for adopting the Charter developed at any stage
in the outbreak. Some towns like Hyde and Glossop declared
enthusiastically for a Chartist strike;[80] others such as Stockport, Macclesfield, Stalybridge, Mossley, Lees and Bury,
remained basically in favour of keeping to a demand for
higher wages. Chartist orators, or invading mobs from other
towns, sometimes persuaded their inhabitants to declare
temporarily for the Six Points, but the decisions thus
reached were often quickly rescinded.[81] The divisions within
the working classes cannot be easily explained. They were
often more a matter of locality than of occupation.[82] It is,

nevertheless, clear that the proposal to abstain from work until the People's Charter became the law of the land was not endorsed by the workmen in some important sectors of British industry. The dissentients included not only the men of the cotton towns of south-east Lancashire, who had begun the strike for higher wages, but also the colliers of Monmouthshire, who answered an appeal from their colleagues of Merthyr with the words: 'You left us in the lurch at Newport, and now you may go to the devil your own way.'[83]

Finally, the strike failed because of the action taken by the government to restore order. This was swift and determined, more vigorous perhaps than that of any government since Lord Sidmouth was at the Home Office. It quickly removed the leaders, demoralised the participants in the turnout mobs, and created a framework of stability within which a return to work could and did commence. One incidental effect of the Home Secretary's policy was that, by encouraging the magistrates to suppress all large meetings in the disturbed areas on the grounds that in present circumstances they had 'a manifest tendency to create terror and to endanger the public peace',[84] he removed one of the principal means by which advice to strike until the People's Charter became law was disseminated. This was instrumental in robbing the strike of its political character. It did not, however, take away the matter of the discontent on which Chartism fed. Only time and the adoption of a more humane approach to social problems could do that.[85]

Notes

1. C. S. Parker, *Sir Robert Peel from His Private Papers* (London, 1891–9), vol. II, p. 541.
2. Graham Papers, Bundle 53A, W. L. Maberley to Sir James Graham, 1st September, 1842. I am indebted to Sir Fergus Graham, Bt., for permission to use the Graham Papers, and to the Librarian of the University of Cambridge for access to the microfilm copy of those papers in the Cambridge University Library.
3. Staffordshire, Shropshire, Worcestershire, Lancashire, Cheshire, West Riding, Warwickshire, Leicestershire, Nottinghamshire, Derbyshire,

Cumberland, Somerset, Glamorganshire, Middlesex, Northumberland, Fifeshire, Ayrshire, Clackmannanshire, Forfarshire, Lanarkshire, East Lothian, Midlothian and Stirlingshire. In some of these counties, however, the movement was not very serious. Thus at Newcastle upon Tyne, apparently, there were strike meetings but these were not followed by action. D. J. Rowe, 'Some Aspects of Chartism on Tyneside', *International Review of Social History*, vol. XVI; 1971, Pt. I, pp. 17–39. Even so rumours were afloat that most of the colliers in the vicinity had struck. *Manchester Guardian*, 27th August, 1842.

4. R. Challinor and B. Ripley, *The Miners' Association: A Trade Union in the Age of the Chartists* (London, 1968), p. 24.

5. Home Office Papers, 45/249, W. Hutchinson to W. L. Maberley, 17th August, 1842.

6. For a definition of revolution in terms of the abrogation of the state's normal monopoly of power, see P. Amann, 'Revolution: A Redefinition', *Political Science Quarterly*, vol. LXXVII (1962), pp. 36–53.

7. In the Dewsbury district of the West Riding the turnouts had coarse grey blankets strapped to their backs to sleep on when they marched to London. F. Peel, *The Risings of the Luddites, Chartists and Plug Drawers* (London, 1968), p. 341; There were rumours of a similar proposal by the miners of South Staffordshire to march on the capital. HO 45/261A, Lord Aylesford to HO, 15th August, 1842.

8. British Museum Add. Ms. 40, 447 (Peel Papers), Sir Robert Peel to Sir James Graham, 16th August, 1842.

9. It is true that resolutions were passed at Stalybridge and Dukinfield in the week preceding the outbreak envisaging a strike in favour of the Charter, but more importance is to be attached to what was demanded when a strike was determined than to earlier declarations respecting a hypothetical future turnout. The decision of a meeting of workpeople at Oldham on August 9th to stop work for the 1840 wages at ten hours instead of twelve and for reduced rents was indicative of the non-political determinations of the early strike meetings. A. G. Rose, 'The Plug Riots of 1842 in Lancashire and Cheshire', *Transactions of the Lancashire and Cheshire Antiquarian Society*, vol. LXVII (1957), pp. 75–112.

10. *The Times* 17th August, 1842.

11. C. Crane Brinton, *The Anatomy of Revolution* (Englewood Cliffs, N.J., 1952), pp. 86, 93.

12. C. Johnson, *Revolution and the Social System* (Hoover Institution Studies, vol. III, 1964), p. 6. What the author of this pamphlet actually states is that 'it is an error to suppose that the masses will never rise without guidance'. By guidance, however, he appears to mean the intervention of an elitist revolutionary leadership, for his statement is illustrated by a quotation from Professor E. Hobsbawm's *Primitive Rebels* claiming that the adepts of Spanish anarchism were 'hedge preachers and village prophets'.

13. *Quarterly Review*, vol. LXXI (1842–3), pp. 244–314.

14. See Rose, *op. cit.*, for convincing proof of this. Part of Croker's case that the reductions were politically inspired was that trade was improving at the time when they were made, but on his own evidence drawn from the *Manchester Guardian* the improvement dated only from the first week in

July, hardly early enough to have influenced decisions taken by the masters on 2nd or at the latest 9th July.

15. Graham Papers, 52A, Sir James Graham to Sir W. Warre, 15th August, 1842.

16. C. Thorne, *Chartism* (London, 1966), p. 8.

17. A. Briggs (ed.), *Chartist Studies* (London, 1959), p. 54.

18. See especially *The Northern Star*, 13th August, 1842, from which the mention of the activities of these parties during the strike is, unless otherwise stated, extracted.

19. At a public meeting at Thackers Foundry, Ashton, early in July. *Northern Star*, 9th July, 1842.

20. *Ibid.*, 4th June, 1842. Durham was described as 'corresponding secretary'.

21. *Ibid.*, 5th February and 4th June, 1842.

22. W. M. Bowman, *England in Ashton-under-Lyne* (London, 1960), pp. 502–3, gives particulars of this man.

23. See report of delegate meeting on July 24th. *Northern Star*, 30th July, 1842.

24. Rose, *op. cit.*

25. The four definites were Alexander Challenger, P. M. Brophy, Christopher Doyle, and John Leach of Hyde. The two probables were Dixon, probably William Dixon, one of the Chartist delegates of South Lancashire, and Bailey, who may well have been John Bailey, a Chartist lecturer. The seventh speaker bore the name of McLaughlan.

26. *Northern Star*, 7th May, 1842.

27. *Ibid.*, 7th May and 20th August, 1842; Bowman, *op. cit.*, p. 501.

28. He was spokesman for the Charter at a meeting of the Committee at the Moulders' Arms, Stalybridge, on August 7th. J. E. P. Wallis (ed.) *Reports of State Trials*, new series (London, 1892), vol. IV, p. 962.

29. HO 45/260, Dartmouth to HO, August 1842.

30. R. G. Gammage, *History of the Chartist Movement, 1837–54* (London, 1969), p. 208.

31. Wallis, *op. cit.*, vol. IV, p. 963.

32. *Ibid.*, Richard Pilling was another Chartist who supported a strike for higher wages (and for the Ten Hours Bill). *Ibid.*, p. 1107.

33. They advised the operatives to send a remonstrance to the masters rather than to strike, as they had no funds to support a turn-out. What is remarkable, however, is the way in which their lead was followed by a meeting which was previously uncertain and divided. *Northern Star*, 19th March, 1842.

34. Challinor and Ripley, *op. cit.*, p. 25.

35. Rose, *op. cit.*; *Northern Star*, 13th August, 1842. Mention of going to Manchester to meet the masters was also made at meetings in Hyde (Wallis, *op. cit.*, p. 967) and in Ashton (Rose, *op. cit.*), on August 9th.

36. Christopher Doyle, urging the people of Manchester to form a procession on August 10th, told them to 'take especial care not to countenance any man who tells you to break the peace. Consider him your enemy,' he added, 'Recollect the spies of 1816.' *Manchester Guardian*, 13th August, 1842. Similar advice was tendered by Challenger at Stalybridge and by Brophy at Ashton, on Monday, August 8th. *Northern Star*, 13th August, 1842.

37. *Northern Star*, 13th August, 1842.

38. Resolutions in favour of standing out for the Charter were taken at meetings on Mottram Moor on August 11th and 12th, at Preston on August 12th, at Stalybridge on the 13th, at Stockport on the 14th and at Marple on the 15th. Wallis, *op. cit.*, vol. IV, pp. 963, 982, 1000, 1012; *Manchester Guardian*, 17th August, 1842. It is uncertain how far these were influenced by decisions taken by the trades parliaments in Manchester. Most probably the trend began independently but accelerated in response to the Manchester resolutions from the 13th onwards. In some of the outlying districts round Manchester Chartist orators boosted the flagging morale of the strikers by exhorting them to submit to the lead of the trade delegates on the question of whether the strike should be for wages or the Charter. It seems likely, therefore, that the delegates, though they were by no means in control of a unified movement, did by their example help to keep alive hopes that the turnout could be made the instrument of obtaining the Charter, at least in the vicinity of Manchester. Wallis, *op. cit.*, vol. IV, p. 997; *Manchester Guardian*, 18th August, 1842.

39. *Manchester Guardian*, 17th August, 1842; *Northern Star*, 20th August, 1842.

40. See above p. 120.

41. *Northern Star*, 13th August, 1842.

42. G. D. H. Cole, *Attempts at General Union* (London, 1953), p. 161.

43. *Manchester Times*, 16th October, 1841.

44. *Ibid.*, 8th January, 1842.

45. *Manchester Guardian*, 24th August, 1842.

46. *Northern Star*, 19th March, 1842.

47. A. Briggs (ed.), *Chartist Studies*, pp. 13–15; Briggs, 'Chartism Reconsidered', *Historical Studies: Papers Read before the Third Conference of Irish Historians* (London, 1959), pp. 42–59.

48. *Northern Star*, 26th February, 19th March, 9th April and 28th May, 1842.

49. *Ibid.*, 4th June and 16th July, 1842. The hammermen resolved that 'we, the hammermen of Manchester, being convinced of the truth and justice of the People's Charter, do forthwith join the National Charter Association as a body'. It is not absolutely clear in all cases whether the decisions to embrace the Charter were taken at regular meetings of the trades or at selective gatherings of politically minded tradesmen, but the meeting of the mechanics held in the Sherwood Arms, Tib Street, was described as 'a general meeting of the above body', and that of the hammermen, at the Olympic Tavern, Stevenson's Square, as 'a general meeting of the hammermen's body.'

50. J. B. Jeffreys, *The Story of the Engineers, 1800–1945* (Lawrence and Wishart, 1945), p. 22; see also resolution of bookbinders at the Manchester trades conference on 16th August, 1842 'that all trade societies do from henceforth make political enquiry and discussion lawful and necessary in their various lodge's meetings and society rooms'. *Northern Star*, 20th August, 1842.

51. J. T. Ward (ed.), *Popular Movements, c. 1830–1850* (London, 1970), 126–7 – contribution by Alex Wilson; *Northern Star*, 5th March and 18th June, 1842.

52. *Northern Star*, 25th June, 1842.

53. *Ibid.*, 11th June, 16th July and 13th August, 1842.

54. *Ibid.*, 11th June, 1842.

55. *Ibid.*, 4th June and 16th July, 1842.

56. The mechanics informed the hammermen at a meeting of the latter on July 12th that their trades 'after maturely examining the subject, had found that the trades' unions had not accomplished that for which they had been formed, namely the protection of the labour of the working man; and, therefore, they had come to the conclusion that nothing short of a participation in the making of the laws by which they were governed would effectively protect their labour'. *Northern Star*, 16th July, 1842; Whittaker of the carpenters made the same point at the mechanics' meeting on May 31st. *Ibid.*, 4th June, 1842.

57. *Ibid.*, 18th June, 1842.

58. E. P. Thompson, *The Making of the English Working Class* (London, 1963), pp. 234–68.

59. *Manchester Guardian*, 17th August, 1842.

60. *Ibid.*

61. *Northern Star*, 20th August, 1842.

62. *Ibid.*

63. *Manchester Guardian*, 20th and 27th August, 1842.

64. *Northern Star*, 13th August, 1842.

65. The lists are those in the *Manchester Guardian*, 17th August, 1842 and the *Manchester Times*, 20th August, 1842. They purport to include only those who were present when the chair was taken on August 15th, but the numbers present at the opening of the following day's session were approximately the same. *Northern Star*, 20th August, 1842.

66. HO 45/265, Captain Charles Napier to HO, 22nd August, 1842; A. Hill to HO, 21st August, 1842.

67. *Northern Star*, 27th August, 1842.

68. *Ibid.*

69. *Manchester Guardian*, 17th August, 1842.

70. *Northern Star*, 20th August, 1842.

71. *Manchester Guardian*, 17th August, 1842.

72. *Ibid.*, 20th August, 1842.

73. See placards issued by the shopkeepers on August 13th and 15th. *Manchester Guardian*, 18th August, 1842; John Leach told a meeting at Hyde on August 10th that the shopkeepers had met at the Mechanics Institution and had resolved 'that they would keep the turnouts for two weeks', but that was before the strike had taken on a political complexion. Wallis, *op. cit.*, vol. IV, p. 968.

74. Public meetings of shopkeepers and publicans had been held in Manchester, Stockport and elsewhere in Lancashire in June and July 1842 to protest against the distress of the tradespeople, which was attributed to the misery of the working classes. Except at Burnley, however, where a Chartist resolution was adopted, these meetings favoured free trade as a remedy. *Manchester Times*, 18th June, 1842; *Stockport Chronicle*, 8th July, 1842; *Northern Star*, 23rd July, 1842.

75. His speech at the delegate meeting on August 15th was hostile to the Leaguers, who 'were one day exciting the people' and 'the next day . . . sending the special constables upon them'. *Manchester Guardian*, 17th August, 1842.

76. *Northern Star*, 20th August, 1842; *Manchester Guardian*, 17th August, 1842.

77. In a speech at an Anti-Corn Law meeting in Manchester on 15th February,

1842 he had proclaimed himself to be not only a Chartist and an advocate of repeal of the Corn Laws but also 'a son of Ireland' who 'hated the tories with a holy hatred'. He denounced 'the dirty Orange Peel'. *Manchester Guardian*, 16th February, 1842. Less than a month earlier he had taken a prominent part in a joint demonstration of Irishmen and Corn Law repealers against some outrages committed by Orangemen in Ulster. *Manchester Times*, 29th January, 1842. In March 1842 he led a group of Irish Repealers in a 'punch-up' directed against Feargus O'Connor at the Manchester Hall of Science, *Manchester Guardian*, 12th March, 1842. He seems to have been one of the Irish allies enlisted by the Manchester Operative Anti-Corn Law Association to protect its meetings against Chartist interruptions but to have retained his own Irish purposes.

78. *Manchester Guardian*, 20th August, 1842; *The Times*, 20th August, 1842.

79. After eliminating overlaps and repetitions a list of 133 delegates from specified occupational groups may be culled from the *Manchester Guardian*, 17th August, 1842 and the *Manchester Times*, 20th August, 1842. Of these, the largest single grouping consisted of representatives of the traditional skills (44 delegates). Some of the most aristocratic trades such as the book-binders and the hatters sent delegates, but the most numerously represented trades within this category were the lesser or declining aristocrats, e.g. the boot and shoemakers (with 8 delegates), the silk weavers (8) and the sawyers (5). The other main groupings were the iron manufacturing and engineering trades (26 delegates); the textile factory operatives (40), who included a number of quite skilled workers such as engravers to calico printers and grinders and strippers; and coalminers (6). Depressed out-workers like the handloom weavers and fustian cutters sent 11 delegates, the labourers only 3. The evidence, such as it is, suggests that the leadership in this phase of Chartism came not from Proletarians but from moderately well-paid workers who were, nevertheless, not so comfortable as to be outside the reach of cyclical distress and downgrading.

80. Wallis, *op. cit.*, vol. IV, pp. 963, 992–3.

81. For such behaviour at Stockport, Macclesfield and Bury see *Manchester Guardian*, 17th and 20th August, 1842; HO 45/249, R. Walker to HO, 17th August, 1842.

82. Thus the people of Hyde showed enthusiasm for the Charter while those of the substantially similar neighbouring cotton town of Stalybridge displayed extreme reluctance to adopt it. The cotton spinners of Oldham decided against the Charter whilst those of nearby Royton agreed to move in its favour. Some colliers from Eccles sent a delegate to the Manchester trades conference, but the men of Lord Francis Egerton's nearby Bridgewater collieries drew up a loyal address to their master. The key to the under-standing of these differences lies, no doubt, in the character of the local communities: the nature of class relations within them and relationships between the different occupational groups within the working classes, in the areas in question.

83. HO 45/265, Captain Charles Napier to HO, 6th September, 1842.

84. HO 41/17, HO to Lyttleton, 19th August, 1842.

85. This chapter was first published in Exeter Papers in Economic History, No. 4. I am grateful to the editors, Professor W. E. Minchinton and Dr J. H. Porter or their permission to reproduce it.

4

Riots and Public Order in the Black Country, 1835–1860

D. PHILIPS

I

This article deals with the question of public order and disorder, as it arose in the Black Country in the period 1835–60. These dates are chosen because they cover the period of the Black Country's greatest industrial and population growth, span the years of the largest riots and disorders and of the introduction of a professional police force, and include the period when a shift becomes noticeable away from relatively unorganised riots to peaceful organised mass activities. The Black Country can be taken as one example of what was happening in the industrialising areas of England – although it was clearly not typical of all industrial regions, being obviously influenced in a number of ways, by purely local factors.

In the 1830s and 1840s, the problem of public disorder and riots was still one of the chief sources of concern to the authorities of law and order in England, particularly in the large cities and industrial areas. The Chartist period provided much evidence to reinforce this fear,[1] and even well after 1848 it was not abnormal for troops to be held ready to assist the civil authorities against the threat of disturbances. A fear of some sort of uprising of the lowest classes and a breaking down of the order of civil society was added to a long-existing concern about, and fear of, the 'dangerous

classes' of the cities.[2] The report of the Royal Commission on
the Establishment of a Constabulary Force, which was
concerned with presenting the most frightening picture of
crime in England and Wales so as to ensure that its recommendation of the need for a national police force would be
adopted, devoted twenty of its pages to setting out the
dangers presented by trade union strikes and urban mobs; it
stressed the advantages which a police force could offer, by
enabling employers to prevent 'intimidation' of their workmen by trade unions during strikes, and preventing violent
brawls by urban mobs.[3] In the Black Country itself, it was
not concerned about ordinary crime, but the experience of
the strikes and riots of 1842, and fear of further large-scale
disorders, which led to the establishment of a county police
force for Staffordshire.[4] The force was subsequently used to
combat ordinary crime as well, but it had been brought in
specifically in response to the fear of disorder.

The Black Country (known by that name since about
1830) is the area immediately to the north-west of Birmingham; it is roughly co-extensive with the southern part of the
South Staffordshire coalfield, a rich source of coal until the
1870s; its name derives from its extensive coal and iron
mines, ironworks, and iron-using domestic outwork trades,
such as nail-making, which characterised the area until the
1870s and provided by far the largest local industries and
sources of employment. Geographically, it is a rough oblong
shape, bounded by a line from Wolverhampton in the north-
west corner, running south to Stourbridge in the south-west
corner; from there, east to Halesowen and then north-east to
West Bromwich; roughly north from West Bromwich up to
Walsall and Bloxwich, the north-east corner, and from there,
west to Wolverhampton. Its population lived in a number of
different-sized units, ranging from large towns like Wolverhampton, Dudley, West Bromwich, Walsall and Bilston,
through smaller towns to small industrial and mining
villages.[5] Administratively, about three-quarters of the area
fell into South Staffordshire, but the towns of its south-
western corner were in Worcestershire, as was the town and

parish of Dudley, which formed a detached part of Worcestershire, although it was in the centre of the Black Country and surrounded by Staffordshire on all sides. The whole area formed an economic and industrial unit because of its coal and iron resources; and it enjoyed its period of greatest importance as a coal and iron producer, and period of greatest industrial and population growth, between 1830 and 1870.[6] Today, this area is part of the large conurbation stretching out of Birmingham, and even in the 1840s, it had something of this character, as the following extract from the report of a commissioner sent to the area in 1843 shows:

'In traversing much of the country included within the above-mentioned boundary [of the South Staffordshire coalfield] . . . the traveller appears never to get out of an interminable village, composed of cottages and very ordinary houses. In some directions he may travel for miles and never be out of sight of numerous two-storied houses; so that the area covered by bricks and mortar must be immense. These houses, for the most part, are not arranged in continuous streets, but are interspersed with blazing furnaces, heaps of burning coal in process of coking, piles of ironstone calcining, forges, pit-banks and engine chimneys; the country being besides intersected with canals, crossing each other at various levels; and the small remaining patches of the surface soil occupied with irregular fields of grass and corn, intermingled with heaps of the refuse of mines or of slag from the blast furnaces . . .'

This same commissioner also said of the area: '. . . its enormous stores of mineral wealth and the consequent density of its population, give it an importance, in an economical and moral point of view, to which I believe no other tract of equal extent can lay claim'.[7] We shall see, a little further on, why he was concerned with the area's 'economical and moral' structure.

To discuss now the sources used for this article, and the

general methodological problems raised by studying riots. The sources used are the court records (Assizes and Quarter Sessions) for this twenty-six-year period; the Home Office Disturbance Papers in the Public Record Office; correspondence between the Lord Lieutenant and magistrates of Staffordshire; local newspapers.[8]

The methodological problem centres on two basic questions: firstly, the definition of a 'riot' or disturbance; secondly, the problem of quantifying riots – on what basis one assesses their size, seriousness and importance.

To take the question of definition first, I propose to use the legal definition of the offence 'riot' as the basis from which to work. This article will concentrate on those incidents in which actual clashes with the authorities took place, and prosecutions were instituted, rather than on all occasions of demonstrations and activities by massed crowds. Since the official reaction played a large part in defining and helping to create riot situations themselves, and since the question of whether a gathering became a disturbance or 'riot' was often decided by how the authorities labelled that gathering, or what action they took or did not take, to disperse it, this official legal definition of riot is the most satisfactory one to use for purposes of definition and quantification. To summarise the legal position briefly, the offence of riot could be a very serious or relatively trivial offence, depending on the circumstances. At common law, riot, which could apply to any disturbance involving three or more people, was only a misdemeanour, and thus could only be punished by imprisonment or a fine; but by statute, the Riot Act of 1715[9] could make riot a felony punishable by death; this latter case came about if twelve or more persons were assembled riotously, and failed to disperse within one hour of the reading, by a peace officer, of the proclamation ordering the crowd to disperse, which was laid down in the Riot Act. Because riot became a felony once this Act was invoked, this entitled the authorities to use force to put it down, involving the possible death or wounding of rioters, such as would result from troops firing on a crowd; whereas for a mis-

demeanour, only 'reasonable means' might be used to put a
stop to the offence, and actual infliction of death or injury
for this purpose might subsequently be ruled in court to have
been illegal. (The death penalty for riot as a felony was
abolished in 1841.)[10]

Which of these classifications of the offence, and which
potential penalties, would be invoked, would depend on the
circumstances of the particular disturbance, and the decision
of the authorities on the spot. For instance, in May 1835, a
magistrate, Rev John Clare, read the Riot Act proclamation
(or 'read the Riot Act', as this procedure is normally, but
slightly inaccurately, described), and ordered the troops to
fire on a Wolverhampton crowd; this caused a great outcry
and a Parliamentary demand for a Commission of Inquiry,
which was granted. The Commissioner found that the conduct of both the magistrate and the troops was justified, on
the grounds that the actions, numbers and mood of the
crowd constituted a serious threat to order. Similarly, in
June 1858, in sentencing a man for taking part in a Wolverhampton riot in which the Mayor had read the Riot Act,
the Judge merely bound him over to keep the peace on his
own recognisances for £50, on the grounds that the chief
police witness had testified that he had not been frightened,
and it was an essential element of the Riot Act that the
conduct of the crowd should be such as to inspire fear.[11] In
other words, an essential element in defining a riot was the
attitude and reaction of the authorities to the assembled
crowd; and the test the law applied was the essentially
subjective one of what the peace officer on the spot at the
time, felt the situation to be.

The flexibility of the legal definition of riot meant that an
indictment for the offence 'riot' could cover a wide variety of
types of behaviour and degrees of seriousness; it could be a
serious riot, such as the two mentioned above, in which the
Riot Act was read; or it could be, and frequently was, a
crowd brawl or a crowd assault on a policeman. For instance, a typical example of the latter sort of incident, taken
from 1835:

A man, Joseph Phillips, and his brother, were taking to the pound three horses which had broken into Phillips' garden and damaged his vegetables. On the way, they were stopped by a crowd of fifty to sixty people armed with sticks and bludgeons, led by the owner of the horses, who demanded that the horses be given back to him. Phillips and his brother refused, and were then attacked by the crowd and injured. Two men were charged with riot and assault for this; one man was found guilty and was fined £5.[12]

Similar prosecutions for riot involve crowd disorders at prize-fights (which were themselves illegal), mass attempts to resist eviction from houses, and street brawls. These were generally punished, if those taking part were found guilty, by fines, being bound over on recognisances or sureties, or light prison sentences.

Now to deal with the second problem, quantification of riots – on what basis does one assess their size, seriousness and importance? I would stress that I am not here concerned with investigating in detail one or two particular riots (such as Professor Rudé, for instance, did with the Gordon Riots or Wilkes disturbances);[13] I am taking a period of time, and looking within that period, at all the riots and disturbances which came to the attention of the authorities, their degrees of importance and violence, and changes within the pattern which can be discerned during the course of this period. In assessing the size and intensity of any given disturbance within this period, the number of people indicted in court for that disturbance does not offer any firm evidence on this point, since that simply represents the number of people arrested and charged, which is in no way representative of the total number of people involved. To count the number of indictments alone, in order to determine the relative importance of riots or their relative frequency, would be misleading; two riots, for each of which four people were prosecuted, may together have involved no more than those same eight people; yet another single riot, for which eight people were prosecuted, may have involved hundreds of people. To call each of these incidents a riot, and rank them as being of equal importance, would be absurd; there must be a qualitative as well as a quantitative test. I have already argued that the question of how the authorities labelled a riot, and what action they took, is the only satisfactory way one can define a riot; and, in trying to estimate the seriousness and importance, the vital point seems to be the degree of threat which the disturbance posed in the eyes of the authorities, and the extent of the action which they took to prevent or repress disorder. So I propose to use a somewhat crude, but simple, distinction of riots and disturbances into two basic types: type A: the more serious type, and type B: the less serious. The criterion for this division is the assessment of the authorities on the spot at the time. Thus, type A will comprise those disturbances which the magistrates considered serious enough in their implications for the maintenance of general order, to warrant their being reported to the Home Secretary and/or the Lord Lieutenant, and, usually, to warrant the taking of such precautionary measures as the swearing in of special constables, calling out the Yeomanry, and the Enrolled Pensioners, or calling in regular troops;[14] type B will comprise all other incidents prosecuted as riot or an analogous offence (such as assault on a constable by more than one person) during this period, which fell short of this degree of seriousness.[15] A clear qualitative difference can be seen between type A and type B riots in the period under consideration: type A covers political, semi-political, or industrial violence; type B covers the less serious riots mentioned above – crowd assaults on policemen, attempts by crowds to rescue arrested people, crowd disturbances at semi-legal public occasions such as prize-fights or bull-baiting, or simple street brawls. The type B are much less dramatic and less attached to discernible motivation and causes than the type A: but they occur more regularly than the type A, and, in their frequency and degree of violence, can perhaps give some insight into the society in which they take place.

Before proceeding to discuss the disturbances themselves, I must say something about the forces of law and order in the

Black Country for this period. Before 1835, it had no professional, uniformed police; the towns, like other provincial towns, relied on parish constables, with local watch forces, set up under local Improvement Acts, in Wolverhampton, Dudley and Walsall. In 1835, Walsall, the only corporate borough among the Black Country towns, set up its own small force in terms of the requirements of the Municipal Corporations Act of 1835. In 1839, the County Police Act permitted (but did not compel) the Justices in Quarter Sessions to set up forces for all or part of their counties. Worcestershire immediately set up a county force, which policed all the Worcestershire parts of the Black Country, with the important exception of Dudley, which, being a detached part of the county, could not by law be included within the ambit of the county force. (It was only brought under the county force in 1845.) Staffordshire Quarter Sessions decided against setting up a force for the whole county, but, at the request of the magistrates of that Division, established a small force (which came into operation in January 1840) for the Southern Division of the Hundred of Offlow South – that area of Staffordshire immediately adjacent to Birmingham, comprising just under half of the area and about one-third of the population, of the Black Country.[16] However, this Offlow South force was only twenty-one men for a population of over 70,000 and an area of 22,090 acres; it operated at night only; and did not function very efficiently for the three years of its existence.[17]

So, in the crucial year 1842, just over 40 per cent of the Black Country towns and population were under a professional 'New Police' force;[18] but those towns without a 'New Police' force included Wolverhampton, Dudley and Bilston, three of the most important towns. In 1842, for reasons discussed earlier,[19] Staffordshire introduced a county force for the entire county; thereafter, the only part of the Black Country without a professional 'New Police' force was Dudley, which came under the Worcestershire county force in 1845. For police purposes, Staffordshire was divided into three police districts, of which one, known as the

Mining District, was roughly co-terminous with the Stafford-shire Black Country area; the force for the Mining District was initially ninety-nine men, increasing to 135 by 1860, so that, even allowing for the greater area and population now covered, this was an improvement on the Offlow South force in terms of numbers and co-ordination of police action over the whole area. The only further change in our period came in 1848, when Wolverhampton became a borough and set up its own force.[20] There is considerable evidence that, by the mid-1850s, these forces were operating efficiently as enforcers of public order, as will be seen later.

II

To start now with a discussion of the type A, more serious, riots: the Black Country experienced six such riots or pro-longed periods of unrest, during the period 1835–60. They come, chronologically, in three rough clusters.

The first cluster comes in 1835, which had two separate riots requiring the calling in of troops, one at Dudley and Stourbridge in January, and the other involving, over the course of two days, riots in May, in the towns in the two opposite corners of the Black Country, Wolverhampton and West Bromwich. Both sets of riots were connected with elections (the general election of 1835 in January, and a South Staffordshire county by-election in May); hence, they can be regarded as somewhat more 'artificial' and less directly connected with social and industrial conditions than most of the later type A riots – although the fact that there were serious riots during both the elections held in 1835 suggests that there was considerable tension and hostility waiting to be released on the part of at least a section of the Black Country populace. In all three cases, Dudley, Stour-bridge and the South Staffordshire by-election, the riots began as attacks on the Tory candidates and their supporters. The Dudley and Stourbridge riots, though requiring troops to be called in, were very small affairs, quickly over, with only one injury recorded.[21] But the May riots were much more severe than the normal (and quasi-tolerated) election riot[22] – at both Wolverhampton (on two successive days) and West Bromwich, the Riot Act was read, and at Wolverhampton, the troops were ordered by a magistrate, Rev John Clare, to fire on the crowd; they did this, and wounded four people. The crowd was annoyed at the victory of the Tory candidate, and had been pelting his supporters with mud; in the evening some began throwing stones at the hotel where the Tory campaign organisers were. Troops were called in, but the crowd kept them at bay with stones, until Clare ordered the troops to fire, after which they cleared the streets. It is hard to discover very much about fhe rioting crowd, but they seem to have been mostly workers in the local metal crafts, presumably demonstrating their discontent at their lack of the vote, and at the Tory victory.

This shooting attracted great attention in the national press,[23] and a demand in Parliament for a commission of inquiry. The calling in of troops, reading of the Riot Act, and firing on the crowd were strongly condemned by Liberals and Radicals, and charges made that this was a deliberate attempt to use the military to repress the people.[24] The Home Secretary, Russell, granted the request for a commission of inquiry, which approved the conduct of the magistrates and the troops in those circumstances.[25] An old, staunch Tory, Staffordshire landowner and J.P., Dyott, saw the whole incident as a simple one in which

'. . . the military were required, and obliged to fire, by which some mob were wounded. . . . It did not appear that the magistrate could be blamed, or that the troops had at all overstepped the line of their duty. The manner of taking up the business by the interference of the House of Commons, appeared to me to be an abominable attempt to reflect on the magistrate (Mr Clare), and an act of great injustice both to the civil and to the military authorities.'[26]

But, Dyott's view of the episode notwithstanding, it was important in showing how strong the opposition was that could be relied on to protest vigorously against any use of troops to fire on a crowd; a magistrate or a military commander could be sure that if he authorised troops to fire on a crowd, he would have to face some sort of inquiry and produce some explanation. This helps to explain why, although troops were freely employed to help put down civil disorders well into the 1850s, they very rarely used their firearms, even at the height of the Chartist agitations, and very few people were injured by action of the troops. It was not philanthropy, but fear of another Peterloo, which led the authorities to keep the armed forces under fairly tight control in cases of internal disorder. The Home Office was always careful, in cases of repression of disorder, to exercise control and restraint on the use of troops, and to keep tight control on the issuing of firearms to police or special constables; and Russell and Graham, as Home Secretaries during the Chartist period, increasingly urged local authorities to make use of policemen instead of troops as enforcers of civil order.[27] Police were a more flexible form of riot control, who could work in small groups, and break up a crowd and make arrests without having to make use of the full force of a volley of bullets or a cavalry charge. As Edwin Chadwick noted in the 1839 Royal Commission on the Police:

'Of the military force it may be observed, that the private soldier has both hands occupied with the musket, with which his efficient action is by the infliction of death by firing or stabbing. The constable or policeman, whose weapon is the truncheon, or, on desperate occasions, the cutlass, has one hand at liberty to seize and hold his prisoner, whilst the other represses force by force.'[28]

And for the Black Country itself, it is interesting to note that, although the Riot Act was again read between 1835 and 1860, there was no other occasion, following the Wolverhampton riot, when troops fired on a crowd.

The next cluster comes in 1840–2, during the depression years which really deserve the name which has been given to the whole decade, of the 'Hungry Forties'. The first major riot here was one in Bilston, against a dinner held by the Bilston Operative Conservative Association. This dinner was held in a marquee erected in Bilston market place, and present at it were a number of the most prominent Tory J.P.s and dignitaries of the Black Country, including Viscount Ingestre, son of the Lord Lieutenant of Staffordshire and M.P. for South Staffordshire, and about 500 others, chiefly 'operative (i.e. working-men) Conservatives'. A crowd of several hundred colliers and puddlers (skilled iron-workers) attacked the small police detachment guarding the meeting,[29] forced them back, and attacked the tent with stones and brickbats. The meeting was broken up, one policeman was stabbed, and some of the Tory dignitaries were badly injured. The motive here seems to have been a mixture of political and economic grievances fused into an attack on the local Tory establishment. The year 1840 was one of depression in the local coal and iron industry,[30] and the labour force of Bilston was heavily dependent for employment on the coal and iron trades – even more than the normal Black Country town; the crowd was made up of colliers and ironworkers, and most of the important Tory figures at the dinner were the local large coal and iron masters. So the riot may represent the frustration engendered by unemployment or under-employment. But more narrowly political motives are suggested by some of the evidence, attacks on the Tory party and its identification with the Church of England and church rates. One police witness at the trial of the rioters testified: 'The mob said they should have a b - - - - y church rate to pay for the dinner, and they would have the tent down before the night was out', and another witness, identifying one of the rioters, said that he had seen him with a large stone in his hand and had asked him to put it down: 'He said he would not till he found some Tory devil to throw it at. He threw it at some gentleman in the Market-place.'[31] The idea of a narrowly political conspiracy being behind the riot was taken up and at least partially believed; the Staffordshire Grand Jury brought in a true bill of indictment for inciting the populace to commit riot at Bilston, against the publishers of the *Staffordshire Examiner*, a short-lived Radical Anti-Corn Law newspaper published in Wolverhampton.[32] The leading article complained of, was published a week before the dinner; it noted that the dinner was to be held and to be attended by Viscount Ingestre. The leader suggested that if 'our friends' should see 'the man-starving Ingestre' as he came into Bilston,

'let them peacefully, and with due regard to the fact that the Tories are very apt at swearing in special constables – let them, we say, peacefully, if not quietly, mark their disapprobation of a man who assisted in parliament to cry down Mr VILLIERS and all those who tried to plead for more food for the starving artisans of Bilston. Let them at such a time bear in mind that INGESTRE is going to gorge the bread he denies to them, and that, as he has more of it than he wants, his appetite may require a sharpener.'[33]

The language is certainly inflammatory, and the Anti-Corn Law League was strong in Wolverhampton and its surrounding area; but the Bilston operatives tended to be Chartist-inclined,[34] rather than supporters of the League. Given the depression and unemployment in the local industries, the absence of any effective relief, and the growth of both Chartism and the League in the area, the hostility of the crowd to such a meeting probably did not require much incitement, though the *Examiner* article probably drew attention to the meeting. The prosecution against the *Examiner* seems to have been dropped, at any rate.

The next series of riots in this cluster have a more direct link with political agitation and Chartism. From late 1841, the magistrates showed great anxiety about the possible effects of the Chartist activity, which had been growing in the Black Country since the late 1830s,[35] and which, by 1841, was attaining considerable strength; but all the Chartist meetings in the early part of 1842, even a huge rally to welcome Feargus O'Connor, went off peacefully.[36] But in April, the hand-made-nail makers around Dudley went on strike, from which arose a riot for which regular troops were called in; the riot was fairly easily put down, though the strike continued for a few weeks.[37] Then, in August, came the great miners' strike with its attendant riots, which, together with the much more severe rioting in the Potteries of North Staffordshire at the same time, severely shook the structure of authority in Staffordshire; they form part of what is usually known as the 'Plug Plot' – the general series of strikes and riots in August/September 1842, which affected Staffordshire, Lancashire, the West Riding, and the East Midlands–which provided the greatest test during the Chartist period, of the authorities' machinery for repressing disorder.[38] Peel felt that the strike revealed serious grievances in the Black Country, and sent a commissioner, Thomas Tancred, to investigate conditions there; his report is the *Midland Mining Commission* already cited. This report, and all other evidence of the strike, make it clear that the strike was primarily concerned with the miners' grievances, and not directly with securing implementation of the Charter; Chartist organisers took the lead in organising the strike and concerting the miners' grievances, but it is clear the grievances, and not the Charter, took priority in the miners' minds. One can certainly criticise the objectivity of Tancred's report, which is based primarily on information given to him by magistrates, coal and iron masters, and clergymen –the only miners it quotes are a few nameless men who testify to the unpopularity of the Chartists, and there is no indication that Tancred even consulted the leaders of the strike or the main Chartist organisers of the area. One can conclude from this that the report is, consciously or unconsciously, weighted towards giving the answer that the government wanted, namely, that the strike was for purely industrial objectives and that political motives nowhere entered into it. But this conclusion of Tancred's is supported by a mass of other evidence, notably, by the resolutions passed by the miners' meeting which took the initial decision to strike. These called for: restoration of the cut in the miners' wages made by the coal and iron masters; regularity of the hours worked per day; an end to 'buildas' (a highly un-popular Black Country usage enforced by some mine con-tractors, which effectively meant that men worked for half a day for only a quarter of a day's pay, or for a number of hours without any pay); and an end to the Truck system, which was notoriously prevalent in the northern part of the Black Country coalfield.[39] No mention was made in these resolu-tions of aspirations to the Charter,[40] and this despite the fact that the resolutions were proposed and seconded by Arthur O'Neill and Joseph Linney, the two most prominent Chartists in the area; it would indicate that the Chartists realised that the Charter in the abstract, did not yet have a strong enough appeal to the Black Country miners, and were capitalising on the specific local grievances.

The statement of a Dudley whitestone miner, quoted by Tancred: 'The men did not follow the chartists for the chartist principle, but they fled to them for refuge, and were glad for anyone to come and instruct them about the prices of iron and so on'[41] has a very plausible ring to it; and the causes of the strike are best summed up in the answer given by a magistrate to Tancred; asked: 'You did not attribute the outbreak, then, merely to the insti-gation of designing persons?' He replied: 'The chartists sowed the seeds of faction in ground well prepared to receive it.' On which Tancred comments, uncharacteristi-cally sharply: 'The most plausible course to pursue in ex-plaining a phenomenon which *prima facie* seems to imply some measure of ill treatment on the part of the employers, was to throw the whole blame upon chartist agitators.'[42] On the other hand, it is clear that the Chartists had an important influence on the strike, helping to organise it and give it purpose and cohesion, and providing much of the inspiration which enabled solidarity to be maintained for six weeks of strike. One of the Staffordshire magistrates unwittingly paid tribute to this, in his speech at the meeting of magistrates called by the Lord Lieutenant to consider action by the authorities to counter the colliers' turn-out bands:

'Politics had had little to do with former strikes, and those strikes had also been insulated; there had been no connection between the different parties, and after a few weeks' cessation from labour, a few breaches of the peace, followed by a few examples of summary punishment, the men had generally returned to work on the master's terms, till a better trade had raised the prices to the former standards. In the present instance the difference was evidently owing to the insane spirit of Chartism. (Hear, hear) . . . It was to Chartism that they must attribute the sullen spirit of discontent, and also the organisation and combined movements which had been so striking on the part of these mobs.'[43]

In fact, Tancred's report substantiates the miners' grievances, especially, the operation of the Truck system and the 'butty' system.[44] A number of the magistrates and ironmasters interviewed by Tancred, condemned the practice of both these systems, yet they seem to have been unable or unwilling to ensure the enforcement of the provisions of the Truck Act of 1831, or those provisions of the Mines Regulation Act of 1842 which outlawed the payment of wages in public houses,[45] or to take the necessary steps to see that the butty system was phased out of mining.[46]

These were the underlying grievances of the strike; the masters' wage cut precipitated the strike itself. Once it had begun, the magistrates called in troops, called out the Staffordshire and Worcestershire Yeomanry and the Enrolled Pensioners, and swore in special constables in large numbers. Bands of colliers moved around the area, trying to enforce a total shutdown of pits; the magistrates' reports complain of 'intimidation' by these groups, of miners who wanted to go to work – and there are undoubtedly a number of cases in which men resisting the strike call were thrown in canals or beaten up. The magistrates also expressed concern about these large groups 'begging' from shopkeepers and 'respectable property owners', which, in view of the size and strength of the groups, and the relatively weak and dispersed state of the authorities, could amount in effect to a form of demanding; this was one of the chief ways in which the miners were able to support themselves during the strike.[47] The actual clashes came when some mine-owners defended their pits with special constables, regular troops and Yeomanry against the turn-out groups, and when the authorities, growing more confident towards the end of August, began to break up meetings and arrest the leaders. Most of the serious clashes with troops and Yeomanry came in this latter period, in the last week of August and first week of September, as it became clear that the employers were not going to give way, and as some of the miners began to trickle back to work; the Riot Act was read three times in three days between August the 26th and 28th, once in Kingswinford and twice in Dudley.[48] During this same period, the Potteries of North Staffordshire experienced a miners' strike attended with far more serious violence, in the course of which large crowds pulled down houses and public buildings, and attacked the houses of magistrates and other local notables, in the towns of the Potteries.[49] This double threat to order in the county seriously shook the forces of authority in Staffordshire; and in October, the Government appointed a Special Commission of Assize to try those arrested during the strike (including most of the local Chartist leaders). In all, 276 people were tried by the Commission, 80 per cent of them being from the Potteries, but with 44 from the Black Country; these 44 were charged with riot plus: sedition, unlawful assembly, preventing miners going down the pits, wounding special constables, etc.; most were given fairly long prison sentences, and 5 were transported for life. In addition, a number of Black Countrymen were tried at the Staffordshire, Worcestershire, and Shropshire Quarter Sessions in October 1842, for riots arising out of the strike; and there were a number of men summarily convicted by J.P.s, of public order offences connected with the conduct of the strike.[50]

I have dealt with the 1842 strike in some detail, for a

number of reasons; firstly, these riots were by far the most serious which the Black Country experienced in the period 1835–60; secondly, they provided the decisive impetus, as mentioned earlier, in pushing the Staffordshire Quarter Sessions into setting up a county police force, which had decisive effects on the handling of questions of public order in the years following; and finally, they show an important pattern, which was repeated in the major disturbances of the 1850s.

There was no further type A disturbance from 1842 through to 1854; even in 1848, the year of industrial depression and Chartist revival in many parts of England, Black Country Chartism showed little activity. There were some fears of disorder and calling in of troops by the Dudley magistrates, but there were few Chartist mass activities and no serious disturbances.

This peace was broken by a riot by striking miners in Bilston in March 1855, the beginning of the third cluster of disturbances. The winter of 1854–5 had been one of depression in the Black Country coal and iron industries;[51] unemployment in these industries was high, and the magistrates' letters to the Lord Lieutenant just before the outbreak, stress the amount of distress and 'excitement' (i.e. unrest) prevailing.[52] Once again, as in 1842, the riot arose from large groups of colliers being on strike; once again, the strike was brought about by a reduction in the colliers' wages; once again, the bands of colliers were found to be begging, attacking provision shops to get food, and intimidating blacklegs. Once again, the miners of the Potteries were on strike at the same time, thus stretching the forces of the law; once again, the strike spread within the Black Country from the northern part of the coalfield around Bilston, to the southern part around Dudley. Even many of the magistrates were men who had been in office in 1842, and they expressed the same fears about public disorder and took the same precautions – they called for military assistance, called out the Yeomanry, assembled the Pensioners, and swore in a large number of special constables.[53]

Yet this strike did not lead to a large rash of riots as the 1842 strike had done, nor do the Lord Lieutenant and Home Secretary seem to have been as worried about the possible consequences as they had been in 1842. The chief points distinguishing the situation from that of 1842 seem to have been: firstly, by 1855, Chartism was effectively dead as a serious national movement, and with it had gone the threat of any national insurrection or strike, which had been a real possibility in 1842.[54] Secondly, by the mid-1850s, the Black Country had a Staffordshire county police force, efficient in dealing with public order disturbances, co-operating with the Wolverhampton borough police force, to anticipate and prevent trouble. The Staffordshire Chief Constable was in communication with the Lord Lieutenant and with the Wolverhampton police before the riot, making arrangements in anticipation of trouble; when the riot occurred, a force of thirty police dispersed, within an hour, a crowd of 3,000 miners armed with sticks and stones, and thereafter prevented any serious rioting taking place.[55] It is not intended here to exaggerate the feats of the police force, or to take the official view uncritically at face value. It is clear, for instance, that the decision to reduce wages was taken by a meeting of coal and ironmasters, many of whom were also magistrates, in the full knowledge that it might lead to disorder, which they could then use the police to repress; and much of the helping role in these weeks was to escort and protect groups of blacklegs, thus helping to break the strike.[56] There can be no doubt that the machinery of law and order operated in the Black Country to the disadvantage of the working class. Power lay with the Lord Lieutenant and the J.P.s who, collectively in Quarter Sessions, were the local legislative, administrative and judicial authorities for the whole county; in Petty Sessions they dispensed local administration and summary justice for their districts; they had influence over the county police force through the Quarter Sessions and through the Chief Constable, whom they appointed. They could command bodies of police, troops and special constables in times of emergency; and in the Black Country, a

large number of the J.P.s were themselves large coal and iron
masters, the largest employers and the most powerful
economic forces in the region; they could exercise this power
to protect their own interests and property through the
normal forces of authority and law and order.[57]

But (to return to the police force role in the 1855 strike) a
significant point of difference distinguishing 1855 from 1842
is the restraint shown by the forces of law; although the
troops, Yeomanry and Pensioners were called out, they were
kept in reserve the whole time, and all the actual work of
enforcement of order was done by the Police – and successfully too, judging both by the absence of serious clashes and
any casualties, and by the commendation of their conduct by
Lord Lieutenant, magistrate, and Chief Constable.[58] Such
commendation, where it had come at all in 1842, had been
reserved for the military, and that, of necessity, had been
only in situations of clash and crisis. The authorities in the
Black Country had found their more flexible response to
crowd activity and violence.[59]

But not all the credit for the diminution of violence belongs
to the police. Historians of the police, such as Critchley,[60]
note the general trend in the 1850s and 1860s away from the
large crowd violence of the earlier decades, and tend to
attribute this to increased efficiency and sophistication in
police methods of handling crowds. But we should look at the
other side of the riot equation as well – it takes two sides to
make a riot. In the Black Country, the 1855 strike was
followed by another colliers' strike in November 1857 –
again in times of depression, again provoked by a wage cut;
again the police took precautions, and the Yeomanry and
Pensioners were held in readiness for trouble. But no trouble
came, even though the strike failed, as did a strike of puddlers
immediately following.[61] Then, in August 1858, with the
Black Country coal and iron trades still in depression, the
colliers struck again. Most of the familiar features are here
again – it began over a wage cut, parties of colliers were out
begging, the police protected blacklegs against 'intimidation', and the magistrates feared violence and kept in regular

touch with the Lord Lieutenant and the Home Office.[62] The strike lasted nine weeks and was bitterly contested; yet this time there was no summoning of troops, Yeomanry, Pensioners or special constables, nor did individual magistrates even ask for them; even the magistrates, who usually emerge as the most alarmist group, wanting military protection for their towns and districts,[63] seem to have had faith in the ability of the police force to handle the situation.

But, at least as important as this growth of confidence of, and in, the police,[64] is the restraint and control shown by the striking miners. The strike lasted nine weeks, and the colliers could only maintain themselves during this time by begging in parties and selling 'papers' and sheets of songs composed for the strike; the colliers' attempts to enforce a general colliers' strike was resisted by the police, who gave protection to blacklegs; the wage claim was strongly urged by the colliers, backed up by a number of bitter grievances (including those of 1842 concerning butties, and payment in truck or beer which were still unredressed), but was fiercely and ultimately successfully resisted by the masters.[65] Yet, despite these difficulties and the atmosphere of bitterness, the conduct of the strike remained organised and restrained, with special emphasis on the need to avoid violence or disorder. As John Caffery, one of the speakers at an open air meeting of 800 colliers held during the strike, said: 'The Colliers had been looked upon as ignorant men, a little bit stupid, and sometimes a bloodthirsty lot. During the present time however there had been no breach of the peace. This was a matter they should rejoice in.' It is notable that the first speaker at this meeting was the old Chartist Joseph Linney, who emphasised the fact he was a Christian and a teetotaller, and stressed the need for non-violence.[66] Throughout the nine weeks of the strike, there was no outbreak of violence or disorder on the part of the strikers.[67] This was acknowledged even by Lord Hatherton, Lord Lieutenant of Staffordshire, and certainly no friend to the striking miners; he said in a letter to the Home Secretary:

'During nearly fifty years that I have observed the state and conduct of the population at similar periods of depression, this, the longest "strike" that I remember has been un-attended with a single instance of violence, as far as I have heard. It is generally attributed by the masters to improved Education and means of Information by the more general circulation of the Press.'[68]

I cannot here go into the question of whether this represents a 'taming' of the working class, in which increased working class education played a part.[69] But clearly, working-class organisation in industries such as mining and the iron industry was becoming more controlled and sophisticated, and, although no miners' trade union had managed to establish itself firmly in the Black Country by 1860,[70] none-theless the strikes seem to have moved out of the era of open confrontation and violence. This impression is strengthened by the fact that in November/December 1855, there was a Black Country agitation, led by another of the Black Country and Birmingham Chartist leaders of the 1840s, George White, in favour of cheaper bread. They held a series of well-attended open air mass meetings at which it was agreed that they would petition the Queen to take executive action to reduce the price of bread; but it died away after about six weeks, in a dispute among the leaders. The police were present at every meeting, and full shorthand reports were sent to the Lord Lieutenant and Home Secretary;[71] not only was there no actual violence or disorder in this campaign, but the language of the speakers was far more peaceful and less inflammatory than had been the case in the Chartist period. This may have been simply a realisation that a working class movement was in no position, in 1855, to achieve anything by threatening or attempting violence or large-scale dis-order, but it could also be seen as reflecting this trend to-wards more organised agitation and less spontaneous disorder.

However, this general trend of industrial disputes away from violence and attacks on property, seems to apply only to those industries, such as mining, which had a secure future in the industrial age, where the workers could negotiate from the strength of that long-term security, even if they were hit by cyclical depression from time to time; this does not seem to apply to industries whose whole position was threatened, and ultimately destroyed, by industrialisation. The militancy of groups of outworkers such as the handloom-weavers of Lancashire is well known; much the same was true of the Black Country nailers. Black Country nailmaking had been an industry based on outworkers which had been a prosperous and major industry until 1830, when it had been hit by competition from machine-made nails; thereafter, prices and wages in the industry steadily fell, and with them fell the living and working conditions of the nailers; yet in 1860, there were still about 18,000 nailers in the Black Country, mostly in the small villages of its eastern borders.[72] In the 1850s, as their position worsened, they staged a series of strikes, which grew more, rather than less, violent as the decade progressed, culminating in a twenty week strike from February to July 1859, followed by a lockout by the nailmasters from August 1859, which eventually destroyed the union of the Dudley horsenail-makers in 1860.[73] During the strike, the nailers used the tactic of cutting and rendering useless the nail-making bellows of blacklegs; as the lockout progressed, cutting the bellows of blacklegs and non-union members, and attacks on the shops of some nailmasters, increased.[74] The authorities took a strong view of this, and there were a number of prosecutions for such offences at the 1859 and 1860 Assizes; most received prison sentences, and five received long terms of penal servitude.[75] Baron Bramwell, in sentencing one of the Worcestershire men,

'made some very severe strictures upon trade unions and strikes. He said no society or union had a right to make rules as to the manner in which others should conduct themselves. These unions were mischievous in the extreme, they were against the interests of the workmen themselves, against public opinion, and would not be tolerated in this country.

These crimes were committed in a dirty sneaking manner, and were deserving of the strongest reprobation.'[76]

But these activities of the nailers did not cause the concern among the Black Country authorities which the miners' strikes did; they were essentially part of the power struggle within the local nailmaking industry, and, as such, much closer to the early nineteenth-century primitive trade union tactics such as frame-breaking – what Hobsbawm has called 'collective bargaining by riot.'[77]

The remaining type A riot of this period came in June 1858, and this had no connection with industry. In June 1858, a man calling himself 'Baron de Camin', an anti-Catholic lecturer, came to Wolverhampton to give a series of lectures attacking the Pope and the Catholic Church; what resulted can be seen as a forerunner of the better-known Wolverhampton riot provoked by the Orange lecturer William Murphy, in February 1867.[78] His first lecture was broken up by a large crowd of Irish labourers; the police gathered in force at the second lecture to prevent another disruption. A large Irish crowd gathered, and started throwing stones at the hall where the lecture was to be held; the Mayor read the Riot Act and sent in the police to disperse the crowd. The crowd resisted with sticks and stones, but were dispersed, and two men were arrested. The Mayor and Council of Wolverhampton then seem to have anticipated a series of disturbances following this, as they took great precautions – they called in a body of regular troops, called out the Wolverhampton Yeomanry Troop and the Enrolled Pensioners, called in a body of Staffordshire county police (Wolverhampton having its own borough force as well) and swore in special constables. However, no further disturbance occurred.[79] This riot and the subsequent Murphy riot are an indication of how easily violence and hostility between sections of the working class could be stirred up by anti-Catholic propaganda delivered in a city with a substantial immigrant Irish population.

III

I turn now to the other form of riot or disturbance mentioned in my initial classification, the type B – the less serious, non-politico-industrial riot or disturbance.

The early years of the period, 1835–42, are reasonably disturbed years, with an average of seven type B prosecutions being brought each year. Their incidence seems to have no special connection with that of the type A disturbances; their number is high in the years in which type A disturbances took place, but also in years in which there were no type A disturbances (see Table 5).

After 1842, as mentioned earlier, there is no serious riot again until 1855; and even the riot and strikes of 1855–8 show a distinct trend away from the earlier violence. The same trend away from disturbance and violence seems broadly true for the less serious riots, with one significant exception. The average number of type B disturbance prosecutions for the eighteen years 1843–60, is slightly less than four per year; but the distribution is very uneven – for the three years 1843–5, the average is eleven per year, and for the remaining fifteen years, about two and a half per year (see Table 5). I shall return to what I see as the significance of the figures for 1843–5 below. The figures for 1846–60 seem to show a definite decline in the number of type B prosecutions (see Table 5). In 1856–60 the Irish seem for the first time to come into prominence as potential riot material in the Black Country; incidents involving Irish brawls, or fights with the police figure in the newspapers, and virtually all those indicted for non-industrial rioting between 1856 and 1860 have Irish names. This seems to be connected with the time of the greatest Irish immigration into the area; its significance will be discussed below in the conclusions.

To return now to the significance of the years 1843–5. In these years, there were no serious riots, and no apprehensions expressed by the authorities about serious social tensions, and they were followed by a fifteen-year period of incontestable decline in the number of type B prosecutions; why,

TABLE 5

Number of sets of prosecutions, and individual indictments for riot and allied offences, in the Black Country, 1835–60

Year	Type B		Type A	
	Prosecutions	Indictments	Prosecutions	Indictments
1835	7	35	7	23
1836	6	18		
1837	7	15		
1838	4	14		
1839	7	24		
1840	10	34	1	8
1841	7	25		
1842	8	52	26	83
1843	12	48		
1844	10	41		
1845	11	26		
1846	3	5		
1847	3	7		
1848	5	20		
1849	2	5		
1850	1	4		
1851	2	3		
1852	2	11		
1853	2	14		
1854	3	9		
1855	2	13	1	8
1856	2	13		
1857	1	1		
1858	2	3	1	1
1859	1	1	2 }	4 } nailers'
1860	6	6	4 }	9 } bellows cutting.

Source: Staffordshire and Worcestershire Quarter Sessions and Assizes records 1835–60, and Shropshire Quarter Sessions and Assizes records 1835–44 (until 1844, the parish of Halesowen, in the Black Country, was in Shropshire; in 1844 it was transferred to Worcestershire). The figures for prosecutions are the number of *actual riot or disorder incidents* which were prosecuted; the figures for indictments are the *number of individuals charged* with these offences. The Type A prosecutions are for serious riots; the type B prosecutions are for offences of riot, offences involving collective disturbance or collective assault, and assaults on peace officers.

then, the sudden increase for these three years? I would stress here that the quantification for assessing these riots is necessarily crude, so this cannot be presented as more than a hypothesis; nonetheless, the increase in such prosecutions, plus the fact that most of the incidents seem to be crowd assaults on policemen and/or attempted rescue of prisoners, riots by crowds at illegal gatherings such as prize-fights, or street brawls, suggest that the increase is attributable to the coming into operation in March 1843 of the Staffordshire County Police Force. As has been stated, the police force was not entirely new for the whole area, but it did bring a considerable increase in numbers, central co-ordination, and efficiency in dealing with public order issues.[80] It is likely that the introduction of the force led to a more vigorous official policy of breaking up brawls and cracking down on previously tolerated popular activities. Studies of the introduction of a police force into other communities, have shown that they result in a great increase in prosecutions for minor public order offences, such as drunkenness and minor breaches of the peace, as the introduction of the police force leads to a heightened sensitivity to, and a lower tolerance for, disorder.[81] From its establishment, the Staffordshire County Force cracked down on the popular and rowdy recreations of the Black Country – the wakes and fairs, the prize-fights, and the animal sports – bull-baiting, cockfighting, dog-fighting.[82] This policy of general surveillance and the imposition of a higher standard of public order by the force led to a marked increase in the number of *summary* prosecutions for offences such as drunkenness, disorderly behaviour and breaches of the peace, and this number continued to grow.[83] But the *indictable* prosecutions for public order offences, as we have seen, increased for 1843–5, but then declined markedly; this upsurge, I would suggest, is due to the initial reaction of hostility provoked by the new police and their policy. There is a notable increase in the number of prosecutions for assaults on the police in these years; there had been such prosecutions before 1843 (under the general name of 'assault on a peace officer', which could refer either to a parish constable or to a paid policeman) but there is a distinct increase in 1843-5 – not surprising when you consider that there are then considerably more policemen around to be assaulted, and doing more to provoke such assaults.

The decline in the number of indictable public order prosecutions after 1845, at a time when the population was still growing and a higher standard of public order being imposed, would suggest that, on the whole, the police were successful in imposing this higher standard; the police presence and interference became less new and unusual, and more accepted and commonplace. Hence resistance to the police interference gradually diminished, the new standard of public order became accepted by the mass of the population as the norm, the proscribed sports died out, and thus the number of indictable public order prosecutions decreased.[84] If we accept that the introduction of the force led to a heightened official sensitivity to disorder, then the fact that the number of type B disturbance prosecutions *falls* after 1845, would imply a genuine reduction in the actual incidence of such disorders, paralleling the trend away from crowd violence in industrial disputes. Alternatively, it may mean that such disorders which were previously being tried on indictment at Quarter Sessions were now being tried summarily, or not being prosecuted at all. The heightened sensitivity to disorder seems to be a fact, as indicated by the great increase in summary prosecutions for drunkenness and minor disorders after 1843; so the latter possibility (that they were not being prosecuted) is unlikely to be correct; if the former is correct (summary rather than indictable trial), this would imply that type B riots were being treated less seriously than before. In fact, since there was no statute in this period transferring the trial of certain public order offences from indictable to summary trial, and no indication given by the Quarter Sessions and magistrates of the time, that such a transfer was taking place informally, it is likely that this decline in the numbers of public order offences tried indictably, represents a real decrease in the number of incidents taking place. In the 1850s, public disorder was becoming viewed officially with less concern; in the 1830s and 1840s, it was seen as a serious social threat; in the 1850s it was viewed more as a public nuisance – to be attended to, but not likely to create alarm and fears of social upheaval.

IV

To summarise briefly the trends that emerge from this article. Firstly, during this twenty-six year period, there were only six disturbances or groups of disturbance, which can be characterised as major or type A. Some significance must attach to the timing of the clusters of years in which they fall: 1840 was part, and 1842 the trough, of the worst depression of the nineteenth century; 1855 and 1857–8 were periods of depression for the industries of the Black Country; 1835 was a year of prosperity, but the riots here seem to be mainly due to the fortuitous fact of two elections being held in that year, and the opportunity and virtual licence which elections offered for disorderly demonstrations and riots. The fact that the type A riots do fall into clusters so neatly over this period suggests that there must be some connection with the economic state of the area for all except the election riots. From another point of view, all these riots could be seen as expressing a type of political frustration (taking 'political' in its broadest sense to cover the miners' struggles against the entrenched economic, social and legal power of the coal and iron masters, and the Irish desire to put a stop to anti-Catholic propaganda). The 1835 and 1840 riots were expressions by the voteless crowds of their political feelings; the 1842 strike and riots were overlaid with Chartist overtones, but were primarily aimed at certain economic and legal objectives which the local Chartists had pointed out; the 1855–8 strikes were aimed at the same objectives, and show how organisation and peaceful demonstration were replacing spontaneous violence as the chosen means; the 'Baron de Camin' riot was an attempt by the Irish to silence a lecturer who stirred up popular anti-Catholicism. Rela-

tively little sophisticated ideological motivation can be seen
in any of these riots however; Chartism and the Anti-Corn
Law League had some influence on the riots of 1840 and
1842, but the others were straightforward expressions of
opposition to Tory candidates or anti-Catholic lecturers, or
demands for higher wages and better working conditions.
What does stand out, in fact, is the relative absence from the
Black Country in this period, of serious riots; in all, the Riot
Act was read on no more than ten occasions during these
twenty-six years. Even giving the fullest attention to the
potential for violence and conflict in the type A riots of this
period, they cannot be seen as in any way seriously threatening an overthrow or even a weakening of the existing
structure of authority – even 1842 was primarily an industrial
conflict which frightened the authorities by its rapid and widespread growth, its solid support, and its Chartist links,
rather than a genuine threat of insurrection. There has
perhaps been a tendency to play down the elements of
violence and conflict, and the use made of armed force, in
mid-nineteenth century England; but, in correcting this, one
should not fall into the opposite trap of investing the violence
and disturbances which did take place with more significance than they deserve. It is clear that in the Black
Country, between 1835 and 1860, the disturbances were
sporadic and mainly unconnected; they reveal no central
revolutionary impulse.

Secondly, to look at the developments in the forces at the
disposal of the authorities, there was an improvement in
those forces and in their ability to control and disperse a
crowd. In 1835 the troops fire on the crowd, in 1840 the
band of police is overwhelmed and beaten back by the
Bilston crowd, in 1842 the troops, Yeomanry, Pensioners and
special constables have difficulty coping with the widespread turn-out bands; yet in 1855–8 the police successfully
cope with the groups of striking miners, and on the whole
violence is avoided. This implies not simply a technical
improvement in the police as riot-controllers (and we have
already noted the credit which the miners themselves must

receive for the peacefulness of the strikes); but also that one cannot overlook the role of the authorities in defining and creating a riot. The forces of authority, clumsily used, may provoke a crowd and offer it something to unite against, thus turning a disorganised protest into a riot. In the Wolverhampton riot of 1835, one could say that the riot was partially created by the act of the magistrate reading the Riot Act and ordering the troops to fire on the crowd – that act changed them from a hostile crowd jeering and throwing mud and stones, into a riotous crowd, and also made it likely that there would be serious injuries caused, by giving the troops the authority to shoot. Similarly, in 1840, the policemen guarding the Tory tent gave the demonstrators something against which to unite and fight; even in 1842, most of the violence came only when the strike was losing impetus and some miners were going back to work, and the turn-out bands found the pits and the blacklegs guarded by special constables and troops. In the 'Baron de Camin' incident, the first lecture had been broken up forcibly, but without occasioning a proper riot; it was the presence of the police at the second lecture, and their determination to prevent another disruption by the crowd, which sparked off the riot. Riots thus require more than simply a crowd temporarily united for some action which infringes the law; their progress will be crucially affected by the reaction or lack of reaction of the authorities; a crowd action which is unlawful, but not in itself violent or seriously illegal, may be provoked into a full-scale riot by clumsy action by the authorities. The merit of the police role in the 1855–8 strikes was that, unlike the troops, they could operate in small groups, and they were able to break up the bands of colliers when they were felt to be too large, without provoking a full-scale confrontation; they also, on the whole, avoided provocation, and were concerned to prevent situations arising in which a large crowd of colliers faced a large force of police. The result was that they successfully avoided riots, though they were involved in a number of situations which, had they been reacting less flexibly and subtly (like the troops twenty years before), they would have labelled 'riot' situations and acted on accordingly, thus, in effect, contributing to the creation of a riot.

Thirdly, there appears to be no easily established direct relationship between the incidence of type A and type B disorders: although the number of prosecutions for type B disorders is high in the years of type A outbreaks, in 1835, 1840 and 1842, there is no corresponding increase in type Bs in the years 1855–8 with the recurrence of riot and strike disorders; and the most notable increase in type Bs comes in 1843–5, where it can be attributed to official action, as I have argued. But there does seem to be a less direct link between the type A and type B disturbances, in the sense that in the period that the element of violence is diminishing in the type A disturbance (as I have argued it was doing in the 1850s), the number of type B incidents also declines, suggesting an overall decline in violence in normal social life, not merely in the use of violence in industrial disputes. Taking disturbances as a whole, type A and type B, there are 168 prosecutions or sets of prosecutions over the twenty-six year period (see Table 5); if one divides the period at 1842, then in the first *eight* years there are *ninety* sets of prosecutions for disturbances; in the next *eighteen* years there are only *seventy-eight* – and this at a time when, as I have argued, one could expect greater police and public sensitivity to questions of public order, and hence an artificial *increase* in the figures; even static figures at a time of increased police activity might imply a reduction in the number of actual incidents, and a *decrease* in such conditions must reflect a real decrease in incidents of public disturbance.

The contrast becomes even more striking if one divides the period at 1845; the eleven years 1843–5 yield 123 sets of prosecutions; the fifteen years 1846–60 yield only forty-five sets, that is, 75 per cent of the prosecutions take place in the first 40 per cent of the period. Or, if one divides the period at half-way, then in the first half there are 129 and in the second half thirty-nine. The conclusion would seem to be that the late 1840s and 1850s in the Black Country saw a decline, not only in working class political unrest and violence, as has often been remarked upon, but also a general decline in social violence and disturbances. The fact that the Irish become prominent among those prosecuted for type B disorders in the late 1850s might serve to emphasise this point. The Irish were more recent immigrants to the Black Country towns than were most of the Englishmen there, and they had a reputation for violence and disorderliness. It is not surprising that the police should have concentrated much of their public order attention on the Irish, nor that the Irish should have responded with brawls and mass attacks on the police or attempted rescues of arrested people. They had not been in the towns long enough to have absorbed and accepted the new police-enforced 'respectable' standards of order, nor do they seem to have accorded the police the same degree of legitimacy which the native English working class seem to have come round to doing. This would explain why most of those prosecuted for type B disorders in the late 1850s have Irish names: it also casts some incidental light on the movement towards relative orderliness of the native English by the late 1850s.

Notes

1. See F. C. Mather, *Public Order in the Age of the Chartists* (Manchester, 1959).
2. See A. Silver 'The Demand for Order in Civil Society' in D. Bordua (ed.), *The Police: Six Sociological Essays* (New York, 1967), pp. 1–24. A specific application of this fear of insurrection and terminology of the 'dangerous classes' was made by a writer in Blackwood's in 1844:

   'Meanwhile, destitution, profligacy, sensuality and crime advance with unheard-of rapidity in the manufacturing districts, and the dangerous classes there massed together combine every three or four years in some general strike or alarming insurrection, which, while it lasts, excites universal terror'.

   [Anon], 'Causes of the Increase of Crime', *Blackwood's Edinburgh Magazine*, vol. LVI, no. CCCXLV (July 1844), pp. 1–14, at p. 2.
3. *First Report of the Commissioners appointed to inquire as to the Best Means of establishing an efficient Constabulary Force in the Counties of England and Wales*, Parl. Papers 1839, XIX, pp. 68–88, 136, 185–6.

4. In 1839 the Staffordshire Quarter Sessions had declined, on the grounds of expense, to set up a force for the whole county, and had set up only a small force for a portion of the Black Country. At the Quarter Sessions held in June 1842 (*before* the large strikes and riots of August/September 1842), notice was given of a motion to remove even this small force from the town of Darlaston on the grounds that it was 'a vexatious and useless burthen on the rates', and the towns of Wednesbury and West Bromwich petitioned in similar terms. At the next Quarter Sessions, however, (*after* the riots) this motion was withdrawn on the grounds that 'circumstances had since taken place which rendered it inexpedient to reduce the police force'; and a number of magistrates plainly stated that experience of their unprotected exposure to the disturbances had overcome their objections to a police force. At the following Adjourned Sessions (November 1842) a police force was established for the whole county. *Staffordshire Advertiser* (cited hereafter as *S.A.*) 2nd July, 1842 – report of Midsummer Quarter Sessions; 22nd October, 1842 – report of Michaelmas Quarter Sessions; 12th November, 1842 – report of Adjourned Sessions.

5. *Population of the Black Country*

	1831	1861
TOTAL	211,323	473,946
Large towns		
Wolverhampton	24,732	60,860
Dudley	23,430	44,951
West Bromwich	15,327	41,795
Walsall	14,420	37,760
Bilston	14,492	24,364

6. See G. C. Allen, *The Industrial Development of Birmingham and the Black Country* (London, 1929), p. 32.

7. *First Report of the Midland Mining Commission (South Staffordshire)* (cited hereafter as *Midland Mining Commission*), *Parl. Papers 1843*, XIII, p. iv.

8. Quarter Sessions and Assizes Calendars and Indictment Rolls 1835–60 found in Staffordshire Record Office (SRO), William Salt Library, Stafford (WSL), the Public Record Office (PRO), and the office of the Clerk of the Peace, Walsall. Home Office Disturbance Papers – PRO: HO 41 Out-letters: HO 40 and 45 In-letters. Lord Lieutenants' correspondence – SRO D649/10, Out-letter Book of Lord Talbot (Lord Lieutenant 1812–49) 1822–42; SRO D260/M/F/5/6/1–2, Correspondence of Lord Hatherton (Lord Lieutenant 1854–63) relating to disturbances 1855–8.

9. 1 Geo. I, stat. 2, c. 5.

10. Substitution of Punishment for Death Act 1841 (4 & 5 Vict. c. 56). See L. Radzinowicz, *A History of the English Criminal Law and its Administration from 1750* (London, 1948–68), vol. IV, p. 320.

11. *S.A.*, 20th June, 1835, 4th July, 1835; *S.A.*, 31st July, 1858, report of the Summer Assizes.

12. *S.A.*, 31st October, 1835, report of Michaelmas Quarter Sessions.

13. G. Rudé, *The Crowd in History* (New York, 1964); *Wilkes and Liberty* (Oxford, 1962); *Paris and London in the Eighteenth Century* (London, 1970).

14. On the organisation and use of such forces against serious disorders, see Mather, *Public Order*, Chs. III, V.

15. This distinction does not coincide fully with the legal distinction of riot as felony from riot as misdemeanour, since participants in the same serious

riot could be differently prosecuted, some for a felony and some for a misdemeanour.

16. For the history of the establishment of the police forces of England and
Wales, starting with the Metropolitan Force in 1829, see: Radzinowicz,
op. cit., vols. II–IV; Mather, *op. cit.*, Chs. III, IV; T. A. Critchley, *A
History of Police in England and Wales, 1900–1966* (London, 1967); C.
Reith, *The Police Idea* (London, 1938) and *A New Study of Police History*
(Edinburgh, 1956). For the establishment of the early Black Country
forces, see *Return of the Several Cities and Boroughs of Great Britain, their
Population respectively, the Number of Police, and the Cost of the same in each year
from their Establishment, Parl. Papers 1854,* LII (345), p. 509; *Returns of
Police established in each County or Division of a County in England and Wales
under Acts 2 & 3 Vict. c. 93 and 3 & 4 Vict. c. 88, Parl. Papers 1842,* XXXII,
pp. 649–75; J. H. A. Collins, *History of the Former Walsall Borough Police
Force* (Brierley Hill, 1967); [Anon], *Worcestershire Constabulary: History of the
Force* (Hindlip, Worcs., 1951); *S.A.,* 23rd November, 1839.

17. 1842 *Returns of Police.* See *S.A.,* 23rd November, 1839, speech of Earl of
Dartmouth – he there gives a ratio of one policeman per 2,000 inhabitants
for this new Offlow South force. But the force was only twenty-one in
strength, and the population of the area was 78,275 (1841 Census) – a
much lower ratio of one policeman to cover 3,700 inhabitants. On the
force operating at night only, see First Report to Quarter Sessions of the
Superintendent of the Offlow South Force (SRO Q/April 2nd, April
1840).

18. Using 1841 Census figures – total population 293,301; policed by the
Walsall Worcestershire or Offlow South forces 130,726; not covered by
these forces 162, 575.

19. See p. 142 footnote 4.

20. The mining District ratio of police to population in 1842 was ninety-nine
men to a population of 210,534, or one to about 2,100; it was maintained
at about that in the 1850s. The Walsall and Wolverhampton forces slowly
improved their ratios of police to population, especially after 1856.

21. *Worcester Herald,* 3rd January, 1835; 10th January, 1835; 17th January,
1835.

22. See the comment of counsel prosecuting those involved in the West
Bromwich riot – the rioters went beyond 'the normally-tolerated excesses
of a contested election, and so far forgot themselves as to injure people and
destroy property'. (*S.A.,* 4th July, 1835, report of Midsummer Quarter
Sessions.) See also N. Gash, *Politics in the Age of Peel* (London, 1953), Ch. 6.
In this chapter, which deals with election riots, Gash singles out the May
1835 Wolverhampton riot as an exceptionally serious one, but states that
it was not all that different from other election riots. He uses this as an
opportunity to add the comment: 'It is clear that in Wolverhampton, and
probably in many other towns, violence was endemic among the lower
classes, and election time provided merely the provocation and the
opportunity.' (*ibid.,* p. 152.)

23. See the leaders from *The Times* and *Morning Chronicle,* reprinted in *S.A.,*
6th June, 1835.

24. See, for instance, the *Morning Chronicle* leader cited above: 'Strong ground
for suspicion exists that the conduct of the military at Wolverhampton is the

result of systematic attempts on the part of the officers, who are nearly all Tories. . . . if the Tories are insane enough to suppose that they can reconquer their lost power through the instrumentality of the army, they will find themselves wofully mistaken . . . We apprehend that there can be no justification of the cruelty of the military towards an unarmed population.' And Scholefield in Parliament specifically invoked Peterloo in condemnation of the troops' actions.

25. See p. 5 above, on the Commission's approval of Clare's action. For full details of the Commission's hearings and its report, see *S.A.*, 13th June, 20th June, and 4th July, 1835.

26. *Dyott's Diary 1781–1845*, ed. R. W. Jeffery (London, 1907), vol. II, pp. 202–3.

27. See, for instance, PRO: HO 41/16, Graham to Dartmouth, 15th December, 1841; Graham to Dartmouth 20th July, 1842, 25th July, 1842 and 8th August, 1842; also Mather, *op. cit.*, p. 132.

28. 1839 *Royal Commission on Constabulary*, p. 83.

29. The Superintendent and twelve men from the Offlow South force had been sent in to Bilston especially for this purpose, although Bilston was outside the Offlow South area.

30. G. J. Barnsby, 'The Standard of Living in the Black Country during the Nineteenth Century', *Economic History Review*, 2nd series vol. XXIV (1971), pp. 220–39, at p. 234.

31. *S.A.*, 31st October, 1840, report of Michaelmas Quarter Sessions; see also the reports of the riot in *S.A.*, 8th and 15th August, 1840, depositions of witnesses at the committal to trial of the rioters (SRO Q/SB M.1840), and the account given in Rev J. B. Owen, *A Memoir of the late G. B. Thorneycroft Esq.* (London, 1856), pp. 90–6. Owen, like most magistrates in such situations, tried to maintain that the rioters were not local people 'but a wholesale importation of strangers from a distant part of the county', but the newspaper reports and the trials make it clear that the rioters were Bilston colliers and puddlers.

32. *S.A.*, 24th October, 1840; *Wolverhampton Chronicle*, 28th October, 1840.

33. *Staffordshire Examiner*, 1st August, 1840.

34. See G. J. Barnsby, 'The Working Class Movement in the Black Country' (University of Birmingham M.A. thesis, 1965), pp. 115–73.

35. *Ibid.*, pp. 115–48.

36. The Black Country Chartist meetings in this period are described in a series of reports by an informer to the Home Office – PRO: HO 45/260, Talbot to Graham, 4th February, 1842 (5 reports enclosed); Talbot to Graham, 21st February, 1842 (2 reports enclosed); Talbot to Graham, 8th March, 1842 (1 report enclosed).

37. PRO: HO 45/260, Talbot to Graham, 4th May, 1842; HO 41/16, HO to Dudley magistrates, 26th April, 1842.

38. On the Plug Plot, see M. Hovell, *The Chartist Movement* (Manchester, 1918); Mather, *op. cit.*, pp. 15–16, 228–31. On the causes and progress of the strike and riots in the Black Country, see *Midland Mining Commission*, pp. cix-cxxiv.

39. Enclosure containing the five resolutions passed at the miners' meeting of 'not less than 15,000 persons' at West Bromwich (PRO: HO 45/260, Dartmouth to Graham, 4th August, 1842). See also reports of speeches by

Chartists, and the attitude of striking miners to the Charter, *S.A.*, 27th August and 3rd September, 1842.

40. Except, perhaps, in a very vague reference; the last resolution ends by saying that the miners 'will no longer suffer ourselves to be treated as slaves in a Country called over the whole world the Land of Freedom'. (PRO: HO 45/260, Dartmouth to Graham, 4th August, 1842.)

41. *Midland Mining Commission*, p. cxii.

42. *Ibid.*, p. cix.

43. *S.A.*, 10th September, 1842. Linney and O'Neill addressed a number of large outdoor meetings of miners during the strike, keeping the grievances before the miners and encouraging them to stay out until the wage cut was restored and their grievances met. (*S.A.*, 20th August, 27th August, 3rd September, 1842).

44. On the Truck system – payment of wages in goods ('tommy') instead of cash – see G. W. Hilton, *The Truck System* (Cambridge, 1960), and *Midland Mining Commission* pp. lxxxvi-cii. The butty system was widespread in the southern and western parts of the Black Country coal-field; instead of working his pits himself, a mine-owner would sub-contract the working of the mine to a 'butty' or 'chartermaster'. The butty would contract to raise the coal, ironstone or limestone at a fixed price per ton, and would himself hire and pay all the miners. Since the butty was always a man of small capital – often an ex-miner himself – and was receiving a fixed sum per ton, it was in his interest to keep his cash outlay on miners' wages as low as possible – hence butties figure prominently in miners' complaints about the exaction of 'buildases', payment of wages at long, irregular intervals, part-payment of wages in tommy or beer, or compulsion to spend part of their wages in public-houses owned by the butties (*Midland Mining Commission*, pp. xxxiiii-xlvii).

45. On the provisions and difficulties of enforcement of this Act, see *Midland Mining Commission* p. xliv, and O. MacDonagh, 'Coal Mines Regulation: the First Decade 1842–1852' in R. Robson (ed.), *Ideas and Institutions of Victorian Britain* (London, 1967), pp. 58–86.

46. See the report of a meeting of magistrates to discuss action to repress those activities of the striking miners which aimed at preventing blacklegs returning to work. Those magistrates who were also coal and iron masters here firmly blocked a resolution proposed by the Lord Lieutenant which would have appealed to the masters to investigate and remove the workmen's valid grievances, and would have pledged the magistrates to enforce the Truck laws; this was opposed as 'an unwarrantable interference between the masters and the men'. (*S.A.*, 10th September, 1842).

47. PRO: HO 45/260, Hunt to HO 2nd August, 1842; *Midland Mining Commission* p. cxiii, xxiv; *S.A.*, 30th July, 6th August, 13th August, 20th August, 27th August, 3rd September, 1842.

48. *S.A.*, 27th August, 3rd September, 1842.

49. See the description of the riot in Hanley in *Life of Thomas Cooper* written by Himself (London, 1872), pp. 188–98.

50. Calendars of Prisoners for Trial: Special Commission of Assize, October 1842 (WSL); Staffordshire Quarter Sessions Michaelmas 1842, Worcestershire Quarter Sessions Michaelmas 1842, Shropshire Quarter Sessions

Michaelmas 1842; *S.A.*, 30th July to 10th September; 1st October, 8th October, 15th October, 22nd October, 1842.

51. Barnsby, M.A. thesis, p. 335; Barnsby, 'Standard of Living', p. 234.

52. SRO D260/M/F/5/6/1, Shipton to Hatherton, 26th and 27th February, 1855; Hatton to Hatherton, 3rd March, 1855.

53. SRO D260/M/F/5/6/1, Hill to Hatherton, 24th March, 1855; Thursfield to Hatherton, 23rd March, 1855 (the enclosed statements); Thorneycroft to Hatherton, 23rd March, 1855; Thursfield to Hatherton, 24th March, 1855.

54. W. L. Burn noted that, by the mid-1850s 'the maintenance of public order had ceased to be a national, though it might still be a local, problem'; he highlighted this by contrasting Peel's action in 1842, in sending arms and ammunition for the defence of his Staffordshire country house against rioters, with the ridicule which such an action would have evoked in London had Palmerston or Derby done the same for their country houses in the very different political climate of the mid-1850s. (W. L. Burn, *The Age of Equipoise* (London, 1968), p. 58.)

55. SRO D260/M/F/5/6/1, Hatton to Hatherton, 3rd March, 1855 and 25th March, 1855.

56. SRO D260/M/F/5/6/1, Collis to Hatherton, 28th March, 1855; Hatherton to Grey, 1st April, 1855; Hatton to Hatherton, 28th March, 1855 and 19th April, 1855. On the police as strike-breakers, see also their role in the 1858 strike – SRO D260/M/F/5/6/2, Hogg (new Chief Constable) to Hatherton, 8th and 31st August, 1858; PRO: HO 45/OS6378 Hogg to HO 24th September, 1858.

57. See, for example, D260/M/F/5/6/2 Matthews to Hatherton 1st October, 1858, which makes explicit this dual role of the employers and their exploitation of this position: Matthews (a large coal and iron master and a magistrate) writes to the Lord Lieutenant that he has just returned from a meeting of ironmasters who are determined to resist the current colliers' strike and its demand for the restoration of a wage cut; '. . . it is the opinion of *most of us* [ironmasters] . . . that the time has arrived when at least steps must be taken to prevent any interference directly or indirectly with the men who are willing to work'. A meeting of magistrates is to be convened, and it is 'my own impression, an impression extensively prevalent *among my brother Magistrates* in this part of the District, that we must no longer remain quiescent under this state of things'. (*Author's italics.*) On this dual role, and the uses of the forces of law and order to break the strike, see also A. B. Cochrane (iron and coal master and magistrate) to Hatherton, 4th October, 1858; Richard Smith to Hatherton, 4th October, 1858; Leigh to Hatherton, 4th October, 1858 (SRO D260/M/F/5/6/2).

58. SRO D260/M/F/5/6/1, Hatton to Hatherton, 25th and 28th March, 1855; Hatherton to Grey, 2nd April, 1855; Loxdale to Hatherton, 26th March, 1855.

59. See the discussion of this point, p. 151 above.

60. Critchley, *op. cit.*, and *The Conquest of Disorder* (London, 1969).

61. Barnsby, 'Standard of Living', p. 235; PRO: HO 45/OS 6378 November to December 1857; SRO: D260/M/F/5/6/2, Williams to Hatherton, 26th January, 1858.

62. PRO: HO 45/OS 6378 August–October 1858; SRO D260/M/F/5/6/1, August – October 1858.

63. See, for instance, PRO: HO 45/260, Baldwin and Foster (magistrates for Bilston) to Graham, 28th January, 1842; Mather, *op. cit.*, pp. 58, 62–3.
64. See PRO: HO 45/OS 6378 Hatherton to Walpole, 13th and 14th August, 1858.
65. One of the printed song-sheets sold is entitled 'The Colliers' Lament on the Shilling Drop'; it appeals for charity to the miners and their families during the strike; the chorus runs:

> '*Oh, the Shilling – oh, the shilling!*
> *The Shilling with a sigh we say;*
> *We would rather starve than go to work,*
> *To be bated one shilling a day.*'

(Enclosure in D260/M/F/5/6/2, Hogg to Hatherton, 31st August, 1858. The 'shilling drop' is the wage cut.)
There is evidence of strong resentment of the police presence by the miners (SRO D260/M/F/5/6/2, Hogg to Hatherton, 8th and 30th August, 1858), and evidence of bitterness of feeling against the masters in one of the printed papers sold, a parody called 'The Miner's Catechism'. In it, a miner, 'Peter Poverty', answers an employee's catechism, which includes the following:

> '*Q.* What did your masters, butties, and doggies do then for you?
> *A.* They did promise and vow three things in my name. First – That I should renounce all opposition to my master's will. Secondly – That I should believe that every word and action of the butties was said and done for my benefit. Thirdly – That I should obey them in all things, work for their benefit alone, and live in poverty and want all the days of my life.'

It sets out the Master's 'Ten Commandments', which include:

> '*IV.* Remember thou workest six days in the week; and be thankful I allow the seventh day to recruit thy exhausted strength; for I thy master want as much work out of thee as possible; . . .
> *VI.* Thou shalt work thyself to death and commit self murder.'

(Enclosure in D260/M/F/5/6/2, Hogg to Hatherton, 24th September, 1858.)
66. Shorthandwriter's report of meeting, in SRO D260/M/F/5/6/2, Hogg to Hatherton, 30th August, 1858.
67. In fact, there was one prosecution arising out of the strike, of three colliers for wounding another collier who went back to work; but the Jury acquitted all three on the grounds that the injuries could have been inflicted accidentally during a struggle to prevent the man leaving the stable in which he was at the time. (PRO: Assizes 5/179 Staffordshire Assizes Spring 1859; and report in *S.A.*, 12th March, 1859.)
68. PRO: HO 45/OS6378. Hatherton to Walpole, 6th October, 1858. (In this same letter, he said: 'The Rights of the Question [in the strike, are] entirely with the masters.') This idea of the control and self-restraint exercised by the miners is reinforced by the comment of a magistrate during the November/December 1857 strike: 'Great crowds of working men unemployed assemble at night at W'Hampton but show no signs of

disturbance' (SRO D260/M/F/5/6/2, Leigh to Hatherton). This was unlikely to have happened twenty years earlier.

69. See R. M. Hartwell, *The Industrial Revolution and Economic Growth* (London, 1971), pp. 243–4.

70. Allen, *op. cit.*, pp. 171–2.

71. SRO D260/M/F/5/6/1 and 2 – letters and reports of Staffs. Chief Constable to Hatherton, 2nd November, 1855–19th, February, 1856.

72. Allen, *op. cit.*, pp. 39, 75–7, 125–8; *Midland Mining Commission*, p. vi.

73. Barnsby, M.A. thesis, p. 347; Allen, *op. cit.*, p. 171.

74. See PRO: Assizes 5 Worcestershire Assizes Spring 1860; Barnsby, M.A. thesis, p. 348.

75. PRO: Assizes 5/179 Staffordshire Assizes Summer 1859, Worcestershire Assizes Spring and Winter 1860; Staffordshire Assizes Spring and Summer 1860 (WSL).

76. *Worcester Chronicle*, 14th March, 1860, report of the Spring Assizes.

77. E. Hobsbawm, *Labouring Men* (London, 1964), p. 7.

78. On the Murphy riot in the Black Country, see H. J. Hanham, *Elections and Party Management: Politics in the Time of Disraeli and Gladstone* (London, 1959), pp. 304–5. Such public anti-Catholic lecturers were a common feature in the 1850s and 1860s – see G. Best, 'Popular Protestantism' in R. Robson (ed.), *Ideas and Institutions of Victorian Britain* (London, 1967), pp. 113–42, at p. 140; see also E. R. Norman, *Anti-Catholicism in Victorian England* (London, 1968), pp. 16–18.

79. PRO: Assizes 5/178 Staffordshire Assizes Summer 1858; SRO D260/M/F/6/2, Mayor of Wolverhampton to Hatherton, 5th July, 1858; PRO: HO 41/20, Walpole to Mayor of Wolverhampton, 2nd and 6th July, 1858; *S.A.*, 3rd July 1858.

80. See pp. 8–10 above.

81. R. Lane, 'Urbanisation and Criminal Violence in the Nineteenth Century: Massachusetts as a Test Case', in H. D. Graham and T. R. Gurr (eds), *The History of Violence in America* (London, 1969), pp. 468–84, on the towns of Massachusetts, especially Boston; K. K. Macnab, 'Aspects of the History of Crime in England and Wales between 1805 and 1860' (D.Phil. thesis, University of Sussex, 1965), pp. 226–9, 243, 264–5, on the introduction of the police into London and Leeds.

82. On these recreations and animal 'sports', see M. and J. Raven (eds), *Folklore and Songs of the Black Country*, 2 vols (Wolverhampton 1965–6). For the police crackdown, see Report of Staffordshire Chief Constable to Quarter Sessions (SRO Q/SB M.1843).

83. See reports of Staffordshire Chief Constable to Quarter Sessions, SRO Q/SB A.1846, M.1846, A.1848.

84. See *Second Report from the Select Committee on Police, Parl. Papers 1853*, XXXVI, pp. 178–84, evidence of Staffordshire magistrate Hon and Rev A. Talbot – the introduction of the Staffordshire Force has led to the complete cessation of all bull baiting and cock fights, though not yet of all prize fights. And 'the opposition to the force has completely died away' (*ibid.*, p. 182).

5

The Warwickshire County Magistracy and Public Order, c.1830–1870

R. QUINAULT

Modern studies of popular disturbances in Britain have tended to focus attention on the people who create disorder rather than on the people responsible for restraining and suppressing it. There has been much interest in the anatomy of the mob and the environmental conditions which provoke disorder, but the counteracting role of the authorities – particularly the local authorities – has received little attention. Superficially, the motives of the authorities appear so transparent – the desire to preserve the status quo – that consideration of their involvement is largely confined to a recital of their formal activities to curtail disorder. This is an unfortunate neglect since we know surprisingly little about the group of men primarily responsible for maintaining order in mid-nineteenth-century Britain – the magistracy.

It is easy to overlook the elementary point that the prime function of the justice of the peace was to maintain public order. But from either a nineteenth or a twentieth-century perspective the magistracy are often thought of in a different context. Until 1888, the magistrates, assembling at quarter sessions, formed the executive government of the counties. But for the great majority of justices the real orbit of their professional duties was not the county but the petty sessional division – which, in practice, was the immediate locality in which they resided. Within this district they maintained order by judicial proceedings within doors in quiet times and by personal supervision out of doors in times of disturbance. But in the twentieth century the extra-mural role of the magistracy in preserving the peace has been largely delegated to the police. The latter, under the supervision of the Home Secretary, are primarily responsible for public order.

Both the police and the Home Secretary played an important role in preserving public order in the mid-nineteenth century, but the former (outside the metropolis) were the agents of the magistrates while the Home Secretary, in most cases, did little more than advise and reimburse the local justices during outbreaks of disorder. With the important exception of London and a very few provincial disturbances (such as the Birmingham Chartist riots of 1839), the role of the Home Secretary in combating disorder was a largely passive one. Despite this limited role, historians have paid considerable attention to the character and correspondence of successive Home Secretaries in relation to public order in the Chartist period.[1] In part, this may reflect some misunderstanding of the machinery of government at the time, but it also reflects an undeniable evidential problem. The reaction of the various Home Secretaries to popular disorders is amply illustrated by government records and private papers. But, with the exception of occasional reports to the Home Secretary, few magistrates appear to have written accounts of their role in the maintenance of public order. Reports to the Home Secretary, although often informative, imply a national significance or direct government involvement not always substantiated by the course of a particular disturbance. Reports in the press provide additional information, but these are sometimes coloured by obvious political bias, particularly if the restoration of order was somewhat ineptly organised.

It is necessary to get away from a stereotyped view of popular disturbances conceived of in terms of a simple confrontation between local grass roots feeling and national government reaction. In most cases local disorders were controlled by the local justices operating either individually or in small groups. Exclusive attention on major disturbances gives us an exaggerated view of the involvement of the national government in the maintenance of order. But even in such major disorders as those in Birmingham in 1839 and Lancashire in 1842, the attitude of the local justices was a crucial determinant of the course which the disorders took. Nor should it be forgotten that the removal of Frost from the Newport magistracy in 1839, precipitated the abortive rising.[2]

Since the maintenance of public order was largely a local responsibility, it is not surprising that the national Parliament debated the problem indirectly, if at all. Controversy at Westminster was largely confined to the political and social character of the magistracy in sensitive districts and not to the motives and actions of the rioters on one hand, or the responsibility of the Home Secretary on the other.[3] Only one Home Secretary lost his job for failing to preserve the peace – Spencer Walpole after the Hyde Park Reform riots of 1867. The London venue was significant because it meant that the Home Secretary was directly responsible for what occurred and thus had to shoulder the blame. Outside the metropolitan area the Home Secretary's position was not at risk in the same direct way. Thus to understand the problem of public order in most parts of the country in this period we have to consider the situation primarily at the local level and – as far as the authorities are concerned – principally from the perspective of the local acting magistrate.

In what follows I will consider the character and public order record of the magistracy in one county – Warwickshire. This study is confined to the county magistracy and does not therefore directly involve the serious threats to public order posed by those Warwickshire boroughs with their own magistrates. Coventry, in which there was a series of riots in the early nineteenth century, had enjoyed autonomous borough status since the medieval period. Birming-

ham was incorporated in 1838, so that the main Chartist
disorders had to be faced by a newly appointed borough
magistracy as yet unschooled in the maintenance of public
order. What disorders there were within the jurisdiction of
the Warwickshire magistracy were smaller and less dangerous. But the very fact that the county was somewhat removed
from the epicentres of popular protest makes it, in some ways,
a more typical area to study than say Coventry, when an
election was held and the textile trade was depressed, or
Birmingham when it was the headquarters of the Chartist
National Convention. Moreover, it was often the county
authorities who helped to check disorders in the industrial
boroughs – both by limiting the spread of disturbance and
by assisting the borough authorities in various ways.

Co-operation between county and borough magistrates
reflected the fact that disturbances in both jurisdictions were
largely restricted to the manufacturing and mining classes.
There was no real problem of rural disorder in Warwickshire. The agricultural incendiarism and machine-breaking
known as the Swing Riots hardly affected the county, which
was on the borders between the low wage arable area of
south-east England and the higher wage zone of the industrial north. But the industrial areas of north Warwickshire were far more volatile in their social behaviour than the
agricultural districts. This was particularly true of the
industrial area which stretched between Atherstone and
Coventry and in which coal mining and textile (largely
silk) weaving were concentrated. The marked contrast
between the social tempo of this region and the agricultural
area which surrounded it was noticed by the novelist
George Eliot who was brought up in the locality:

'In these Midland districts the traveller passed rapidly from
one phase of English life to another: after looking down on a
village dingy with coal-dust, noisy with the shaking of
looms, he might skirt a parish all of fields, high hedges, and
deep-rutted lanes! After the coach had rattled over the
pavement of a manufacturing town, the scene of riots and

trades-union meetings, it would take him in another ten minutes into a rural region, where the neighbourhood of the town was only felt in the advantages of the near market for corn, cheese and hay and where men with a considerable banking account were accustomed to say that "They never meddled with politics themselves." . . . it was easy for the traveller to conceive that town and country had no pulse in common . . .'[4]

This impression of an agricultural ocean with an archipelago of industrial islands provides the general setting in which the work of the magistracy was performed.

The qualifications for admission to the county bench in England and Wales had been laid down in Acts of Parliaments of 1731 and 1744. All candidates had to own real property to the value of £100 freehold per annum, or the reversion to property worth annually over £300. This qualification ensured that J.P.s were men with some property, but the value fixed was low enough to allow quite minor land-owners to sit on the bench. Since it was the large landowners who largely engrossed parliamentary representation at that period it is unlikely that such local government legislation was inimicable to their interests. On the contrary, the nature of the qualification was probably not unrelated to the general reluctance of the peerage and greater landed gentry to act as J.P.s throughout the eighteenth century.[5] The property qualification was never intended to reserve the magistracy for the broad-acred aristocracy and squire-archy. Rather it made eligible for admission to the bench men who, although attached to the propertied class, were in no sense county magnates.

In Warwickshire, the reluctance of the leading county families to involve themselves in the work of the bench persisted into the 1830s. Of the fifty-four acting magistrates in Warwickshire in 1830, only one – Lord Aylesford – was a peer.[6] Yet there were at least ten peers with country seats in the county in 1825.[7] It is true that of these men, one, the Earl of Warwick, was Lord Lieutenant, while one was a catholic and others were not normally resident, but, for whatever reason, there was only one peer who was an acting J.P. Lord Aylesford was probably included because, as Colonel-in-Chief of the Warwickshire Yeomanry Cavalry, he might have to lead out his men in aid of the civil power in the event of disturbance. In such circumstances he needed the judicial authority of a magistrate to be able to act effectively.[8] Nor were the more substantial and established landed gentry much better represented on the bench. The latter included four baronets in 1830, one of whom, Sir J. E. Eardley-Wilmot Bt., was the Chairman of the Warwickshire Quarter Sessions. Although an important man, who later became one of the M.P.s for the northern division of the county, Eardley-Wilmot did not spring from an old Warwickshire family and had been created a Baronet as recently as 1821. Many famous Warwickshire families – with broad acres and ancient county pedigrees – had no representative as an acting J.P. Such names as Newdigate, Lucy, Mordaunt and Shirley are conspicuous only by their absence from the list. Clearly the leaders of county society in Warwickshire were not, *ex officio*, county magistrates.

The relative absence of the 'bigwigs' from the bench is a matter of some significance since it questions the generalisation made by Sidney and Beatrice Webb in their standard work on English local government. They asserted that the reluctance of the aristocracy to act as magistrates – characteristic of the eighteenth century – had been overcome by 1835 so that the bench was '. . . composed almost exclusively of the principal landed proprietors within the county, whose fathers and grandfathers had held their estates before them; nearly all men of high standing and personal honour according to their own social code, but narrowly conventional in opinions and prejudices . . .'[9] This verdict has been accepted uncritically by the leading modern authority on public order in the Chartist period.[10] But the accuracy of this generalisation is questioned not only by the evidence for Warwickshire but also by other information supplied by the Webbs. For in England and Wales in 1832 more than a quarter of the acting J.P.s were clergymen.[11]

The importance of the clergy in manning the county bench was quite evident in Warwickshire in 1830 where they accounted for twenty-one out of the fifty-four acting magistrates. Nevertheless, Warwickshire did not have an exceptionally high proportion of clerical J.P.s. In 1832 eight English and Welsh counties had a majority of clerical justices on their benches.[12] As in many other counties the clerical justices of Warwickshire appear to have been exceptionally diligent in the performance of their official duties. A Coventry Churchman in 1827 deplored the fact that three-fourths of the acting magistrates of the county were clergy.[13] In the context of the maintenance of public order the clerical J.P.s were also particularly important and active. This was probably simply for obvious geographical reasons. Those members of the landed gentry who were in the commission of the peace tended to live in country seats surrounded by an agricultural community. Since the rural villages presented no significant threat to public order, the country gentleman J.P. was unlikely to have to deal with major disorders. But many of the clerical justices held livings in the industrial areas where trouble sometimes occurred. Indeed, they were often included in the commission of the peace because they were the only men with sufficient leisure, property and gentility to be able to act in such localities. Thus in 1827, for example, the most active J.P.s in the industrial suburbs of Coventry (outside the borough jurisdiction) were the Revs T. C. Adams, F. D. Perkins and T. C. Roberts, who all held livings in the vicinity. These men were far from being retiring country parsons. Adams managed the National Central School; the County Asylum; the lucrative charity estate at Bedworth and was secretary to the Foresters of Arden. Perkins was one of the King's Chaplains and active in Coventry parliamentary politics. Roberts often travelled over much of the county on judicial business.[14] Some had other kinds of experience which may have helped them when trying to suppress disorder. The Rev Henry Bellairs, who was Rector of Bedworth, during the 1842 disturbances there, had served in the navy at the battle of Trafalgar and also in the Fifteenth Hussars.

The preponderance of clerical justices on the bench was strongly opposed by various groups. Conscientious Anglicans objected to a system which gave the clergy little time for pastoral care while dissenters opposed the religious (and political) exclusiveness of a policy which enrolled Anglican clergy on the bench while excluding nonconformist ministers. The triumph of parliamentary reform and Whiggism in 1832 inaugurated a period in which the numerical strength of the clergy on the county benches was slowly, but steadily, eroded. The Whig government was anxious both to please its nonconformist allies and to reduce the Tory predominance in the county magistracies. This new climate of opinion was soon felt in Warwickshire. In 1837, Sir J. E. Eardley-Wilmot, the Chairman of the county quarter sessions, opposed the appointment of clerical magistrates in principle, but thought it would be impossible to obtain sufficient justices if they were excluded.[15] Joseph Parkes, the radical attorney, attributed the strength of the clergy on the Warwickshire bench to political rather than practical expediency. He believed they were enrolled simply to enforce the Tory ascendancy, while their unpopularity and misconduct on the bench brought the clergy generally into contempt.[16] However, there is no firm evidence that clerical J.P.s were any more unpopular in general than other justices. In reply to these criticisms, the Lord Lieutenant of Warwickshire, the Earl of Warwick, pointed out that over a period of seventeen years he had nominated only twelve clergymen to the bench. Half of these had been appointed in the first year of his lieutenancy, while in his last commission (c. 1839) only one parson had been selected. His reluctance to appoint more clergy was criticised in some quarters as injurious since there was a lack of alternative candidates with the necessary qualifications.[17] Nevertheless, he appointed hardly any more clergy to the bench before his death in 1853.

As a result of Lord Warwick's policy – doubtless stimulated

by the Whig government's hostility to parson justice – the proportion of clergymen on the Warwickshire bench fell from about 40 per cent in 1830 to 7 per cent in 1868. The reduction took some time to show itself since appointments to the bench were for life. The absolute number of clergy on the bench only fell markedly after 1850, but by the end of the century there were only four clergymen acting as justices. But although the clergy were a declining force on the bench they remained an important group throughout the period when there was a serious threat to public order in the county. It is hardly an exaggeration to say that the demise of the parson magistrate was coterminous with the demise of popular disturbances as a frequent threat to public order. Any model of the suppression of rioting in Warwickshire, therefore, would have to include the clergyman justice as a permanent variable.

With the steady increase in the population of the county in the early Victorian period it was found necessary to increase the number of acting J.P.s. New recruits to the bench were found largely by enlisting the services of the resident aristocracy and landed gentry in a hitherto novel fashion. The aristocratic (peers and baronets) group rose from five in 1830 to nineteen in 1850 and in 1868. By 1850 they were as numerous a group as the clergy; by 1868 the aristocrats were half as numerous again as the clergy. The landed gentry became easily the largest group on the bench. In 1868, seventy out of the 171 acting J.P.s owned (or had close relatives who owned) over 500 acres in the county. A further group of twenty-three were similarly circumstanced with respect to land from 100 to 500 acres. By the later Victorian period the county magistracy was accurately described as the 'close preserve of the squirearchy.'[18] There was hardly a county family which did not have a representative on the commission of the peace. The time had arrived when the title of J.P. was regarded as an indispensable aid to social respectability and gentlemanly status.[19]

The change in the composition of the bench after 1830

was, to a degree, the result of certain political pressures. The Warwickshire magistrates – like those in most rural southern counties – were traditionally and predominantly Conservative. This was largely a reflection of the fact that Warwickshire landed society was largely Tory. In 1839, Joseph Parkes, the radical attorney, accused the Earl of Warwick of political bias in his selection of candidates for the county bench. He claimed that a Tory monopoly had only been broken when a Whig government came to power and questioned the Lord Lieutenant's nominations:

'Before Lord Grey came into office, I believe I am correct in saying that you had not a dozen Liberals in the county magistracy, and only one dissenter . . . five or six Liberals were added in March 1831. In July 1833, about seventeen further Liberals were added . . . most of them were forced on you by Lord Brougham . . .'[20]

This accusation was denied by the Earl in the House of Lords:

'. . . not one individual in the county of Warwick had been recommended by him to be placed in the commission of the peace because his politics agreed with his own, nor had he ever refrained from recommending a person because he differed from him in politics.'[21]

He had made the same assertion in a private letter to the Whig Home Secretary, seven months earlier.[22]

There are reasons for accepting Lord Warwick's assertion. After his death, Warwickshire had a Liberal Lord Lieutenant, in the person of the second Lord Leigh, from 1856 to 1905. Yet the Tory preponderance on the county bench remained as large as ever. In 1893, for example, it was claimed that nine-tenths of the magistrates were Conservatives.[23] In 1877, Charles Newdegate (who was both a county magistrate and M.P. for the northern division of the county) denied that magistrates were appointed for political reasons.[24] By that time, however, the controversy over the selection of justices had died down.

For most Warwickshire J.P.s–like their colleagues in other counties–sitting on the bench meant attending the local petty sessions rather than taking an active part in the work of quarter sessions. In 1837, Eardley-Wilmot, the Chairman of the Warwickshire quarter sessions and one of the county M.P.s reproved a colleague in the Commons for failing to realise this point:

'The hon. Member seemed to suppose that the chief and most important duties of the magistrates consisted of trying prisoners. He totally forgot how they were employed when they did not sit at quarter sessions. The most important of their duties was their residence in the various places in the county where they lived and where they were enabled to act as friends of the poor and heal disputes as arbitrators and referees. In cases of assault, differences between masters and servants, and cases of trespass their interposition was most constant and useful. They formed a link in the social chain which bound the poor and the middle class together . . .'[25]

In the eighteenth century much of the J.P.s duties had been dispensed in his own home, but from the early nineteenth century more of their work was enacted at petty sessions. The latter were, in origin, nothing more than two or more justices acting out of sessions. In more populous villages and towns petty sessions had long been held, often in a convenient pub. In the 1820s, Warwickshire was formally divided up into sixteen petty sessional districts each of which had its own clerk, though apparently few minutes of such meetings were kept.[26] Some of the petty sessional districts covered large and troublesome suburban industrial areas. An example was the Ansty division which covered the mining and weaving district north-west of Coventry. The pressure on the few resident justices inevitably created considerable delays in hearing cases. The chairman of the Ansty bench wrote to a neighbouring justice about the proposal for creating a new petty sessions in 1842:

'In my humble judgement nothing can be more injurious to the public interest than that of holding different petty sessions for the same district. It cripples the power of the magistracy by division. It excites discontent by the hopes of appeal to another tribunal. It creates unwholesome competition amongst the officers and subordinates; it prevents that unity of action by which submission to authority is chiefly gained and above all it is apt to sully the seat of justice by the contaminating prevalence of local and personal influence and interest. On principle therefore I object to such divisions and I am sure the trifling inconvenience of walking a mile or two more (and which by the bye often prevents that love of petty litigation which too much predominates) is amply repaid by the *security* of having business transacted and by obtaining the united judgement of all the magistrates of the district.'[27]

It was significant that both Adams and another J.P. objected to holding petty sessions in their own parishes. Justices were anxious to keep at some remove from those on whom they sat in judgement. Adams' remarks are also interesting in the context of public order inasmuch as they were made shortly after the disturbances of 1842 which had been largely in the Ansty petty sessional district. His emphasis on security and unity partly reflect the magistrate's exposed position in face of a major disturbance. Co-operation in fairly extensive petty sessional districts reduced the personal responsibility and possible unpopularity of the individual justice in times of disorder. In this sense, the organisation of the petty sessional districts in the 1820s in Warwickshire may have reflected, in part, considerations of collective security.

Throughout the period from 1830 to 1870, the Warwickshire magistrates – like those in many other counties – always had to guard against the possibility of riots during parliamentary elections. One of the most serious election disturbances was at Nuneaton in 1832. There was much controversy at the time about the handling of the riot by the magistrates and the wisdom of calling in the military who restored order in a heavy-handed fashion. Some questioned whether there had been a riot at all. The event had some literary significance since its main features were incorporated by George Eliot into her novel *Felix Holt, The Radical*. The author had first-hand knowledge of the riot since she had been a school-girl in Nuneaton at the time.[28] Her account (without its fictional trappings) is a useful complement to contemporary reports.

Nuneaton was the scene of disturbances before the 1832 election. The depressed state of the ribbon trade in November 1831 provoked the weavers to attack the property of the manufacturers. Further violence was only averted by the creation of some 250 special constables.[29] Elections had also threatened to disturb the peace. In 1820, for example, popular feeling in the town against Lawley, the successful candidate in the county election, ran so high that his supporters were prevented from celebrating his return and their shops were boycotted.[30] But disorders directly associated with polling could not occur since voting took place at Warwick. This was changed by the Reform Act which split Warwickshire into two divisions and created a plurality of polling places. In March 1832, a public meeting in the town hall in Nuneaton considered how the town could be made a polling centre for the northern county division.[31] In due course the town was made a polling centre so that the magistrates were faced with the novel task of ensuring order round the polling booths.

The majority of Nuneaton inhabitants – whether or not they were entitled to vote – supported the radical candidate Dempster Heming. His triumphal reception in the town contrasted with the hurried exit from the place of Eardley-Wilmot, one of the Tory candidates. The latter left a barrel of beer behind to overcome opposition but this provoked 'Scenes of tumult'.[32] George Eliot's description of the mood of the town before the election would appear to be accurate:

'. . . prices had fallen, poor-rates had risen, rents and tithes were not elastic enough . . . Thus, when political agitation swept in a great current through the country, Treby Magna [Nuneaton] was prepared to vibrate.'[33]

The high state of party feeling in Nuneaton was fairly general throughout Warwickshire. Just before the election, the Earl of Warwick, who, as Lord Lieutenant, was responsible for the preservation of order in the county, wrote to Melbourne, the Home Secretary, voicing his concern that measures to prevent disruption should be supported by the government. Melbourne replied that he hoped that the exertions of the magistrates and the arrangements of the local military commander should prove sufficient.[34] At the nomination for the county election, at Coleshill, special constables were sworn in and a party of Scots Greys stationed in the vicinity but their services were not required.[35]

At Nuneaton the commencement of polling was followed by some disorder: 'Some election outrages were committed upon those opponents of Heming who had made themselves obnoxious to the people by their false accusations against Dempster Heming . . . and the windows were broken in several houses.'[36]

The extent of the disorder was variously estimated in the press according to the political complexion of each journal. The radical-inclined *Birmingham Journal* claimed that the disturbance was started by supporters of the Tory candidates and that, in any case, 'Nothing occurred calculated to excite alarm in the breast of any rational and unprejudiced person.'[37] But the disorder was serious enough to demand action from the local magistrates. Confusion arose, however, from the divided nature of judicial authority in the town. Four magistrates were in the town – all of whom had close political affiliations with the various candidates. The two acting magistrates for the division who were present were the Rev Samuel R. Heming (brother of the radical candidate) and C. H. Bracebridge (the official proposer of Eardley-Wilmot, a Liberal-inclined Tory candidate). But the assistance of the military was called for by two non-acting magistrates for the division. These men were Mr Inge (the proposer of Dugdale, the other Tory candidate) and Colonel Newdigate (who also supported Dugdale).[38] The propriety and motives of Inge and Newdigate in sending for the military without consulting the acting magistrates was strongly condemned in the radical press. But Newdigate, at least, had been involved in restoring order in the town during the weavers' disturbances in the previous year.[39] The two magistrates had read the Riot Act before summoning the soldiers but many had apparently not heard it above the hubbub of the election.[40]

The arrival of the Scots Greys took many of the inhabitants by surprise. The cavalry had apparently been ordered to clear the streets and their somewhat brutal way of doing so resulted in the death of one elector and injuries to several others. The Rev Heming, appalled by the excesses of the soldiers, ordered them to leave the town which they did eventually.[41] The soldiers returned next day when the poll was re-opened and the radicals later claimed that they had been prevented from polling – though, in fact, they appear to have abstained from polling as a protest against the presence of the military.[42] There is no clear evidence that the presence of the military was the reason for the defeat of the radical candidate and the return of the two Tories.[43] After the election, the radical *Morning Chronicle* attributed the defeat of Heming not to the use of the military (Nuneaton was only one of several polling places and Heming polled a majority there) but to the Tories' superior financial resources and their control of the tenant vote.[44]

Certainly the Home Secretary did not endorse the radical version of events. After the riot he wrote to Lord Warwick: 'I beg to express my approval of the measures taken by the magistrates on this occasion and my great satisfaction at the account given by your Lordship of the conduct of the military.'[45]

Melbourne also wrote to Colonel Newdigate telling him that he did not 'Impute the least blame to you and Mr Inge'.[46] In a second letter, Melbourne wrote that the magistrates had been fully justified in calling in the military.[47] Rather ironically, it was the Rev Heming who was called to account for his actions. The Home Secretary was concerned with a report that after Heming had ordered the military to leave the town there had been a renewal of rioting. He had also been told that the soldiers had been ill-treated by the Nuneaton populace (including some of the special constables) in the presence of the Rev Heming.[48] But the latter's version of events was later accepted by Melbourne.[49] Nevertheless, Heming had to face a criminal proceeding accusing him of encouraging the riot. The charge was dismissed in November 1833, but the defendant had to find his own costs, a ruling which provoked some display of feeling on the part of his supporters.[50]

Several Nuneaton rioters were fined for the minor charge of misdemeanour but the more serious charge of riot against two men was rejected by a jury at Warwick Assizes.[51] But if the authorities failed to prove the case against the rioters, the case brought against the military for undue severity was also unsuccessful. The inquest on the man killed by the soldiers returned a verdict of accidental death. *The Birmingham Journal* pointed out, by way of explanation, that the jurors were mostly Tory tenants-at-will, while several of them were the tenants of Mr Inge – who brought the military into Nuneaton.[52]

Liberal public opinion in the country did not approve of the widespread use of the military during the elections. *The Times* listed several incidents where the soldiers were alleged to have restricted electoral freedom, while the Chairman of the Bank of Birmingham wrote to Melbourne to protest over the deployment of the Scots Greys at Nuneaton. He stressed that few of the inhabitants had heard the Riot Act read since the magistrate who made the announcement had a very feeble voice. He finished on a note of general disillusionment with the Whig government: 'The Tories in the zenith of their power never suffered the military to be employed at elections but always ordered them away from the towns . . .'[53] George Eliot's account of the riot, in keeping with her Tory family background, emphasised the threat to order and property and did not accuse the magistrates of hiding political objectives behind a facade of concern for public order. She emphasised the difficulty faced by the magistrate in trying to make himself heard to the mob when reading out the Riot Act. The use of special constables to check the disorder was described as wholly ineffective since, 'Once mischief began, the mob was past caring for constables.'[54] But the use of the military, on the contrary, was seen as an effective way of speedily restoring order against a mob more intent on looting than political protest:

'. . . with this sort of mob, which was animated by no real political passion or fury against social distinctions, it was in the highest degree unlikely that there would be any resistance to military force. The presence of fifty soldiers would probably be enough to scatter the rioting hundreds. How numerous the mob was, no one ever knew . . .'[55]

The 1832 Nuneaton election riots illustrated the difficulties facing the magistrates. They were dealing with a novel situation – polling in their town – while their differing political loyalties if they did not actually determine their attitude to the disorders probably prevented them acting cordially together. The absence of a senior magistrate to whom the others automatically deferred was an obvious problem in determining who was responsible for what. The physical difficulties of controlling a riot either by public warnings or by using special constables were obviously formidable. But the history of elections at Nuneaton after 1832 shows that the local magistrates did at least learn some important lessons. At the next election in 1835, the polling booths were erected in three different parts of the town, thus minimising the chances of a large crowd collecting in one place. No less than 300 special constables were sworn in but they were not required since 'All was peaceable throughout.'[56] There was no major disturbance at the 1837 election either, but the preventive measures taken put a considerable burden on the rates. The cost of holding in readiness 174

special constables during the three days of polling came to
£108.[57]

But if the danger of disorder had been checked at elections
it had not been entirely removed. This was shown by the
course of the 1852 election for North Warwickshire. Nominations of candidates for the division at Coleshill tended to
be fairly rowdy occasions. At the previous election in 1847
it was alleged that the Conservative candidates, Newdegate and Spooner, entered the town 'Supported by a pugil-
istic bodyguard'.[58] Nor did they want to take any chances
when they stood again in 1852. Newdegate wrote to a friend:
'I hope we shall have a strong muster at Coleshill on Monday
and that our friends who ride will meet us at Blyth Bridge an
hour before time.'[59] But such support proved quite incapable
of dealing with the situation amongst the crowd assembled to
support the nomination of the rival candidates: 'Thousands of persons were present from Birmingham, Coventry
and all the surrounding districts, and the place presented an
extraordinary scene of excitement, even beyond that usually
witnessed at elections where party spirit was high.'[60] A large
group of men from Coventry and Nuneaton, who were
opposed to the Conservative candidates, were described in
the press as 'The genuine descendants of the old "Jeffrey and
Barlow" mob'.[61] Given the character of the crowd it was not
surprising that at least a dozen fights broke out in which a
carpenter's bench in front of the hustings was smashed to
atoms. One or two farmers were seriously injured and it
proved quite impossible to hear the nomination speeches.[62]

The disorder at Coleshill naturally made the county
magistrates highly apprehensive about the threat to public
order posed by the commencement of polling three days after
the nomination. At Bedworth, a mining and weaving centre
where serious disturbances had occurred in 1842, the local
magistrates were not keen to take any chances. But Henry
Bellairs, the Rector of Bedworth and a leading county J.P.,
had his own views on how to cope with the situation. He
wrote to the magistrate responsible for concerting measures
to maintain order in the district:

'A Lieutenant Trafford reported to me today that he with twenty men of the first Royal Irish Dragoons were quartered in Bedworth. Their coming here I am given to understand is the result of an order from yourself and some other magistrate and I presume the order is in anticipation of riots in the approaching election . . . I venture to express a hope that the soldiers will not be sent for, unless necessity demands it, but if sent for that they act immediately; and not be subjected to the merciless pelting of a mob. I see order has been kept in and about London by the construction of approaches to the polling booths. Can anything be done in this way at Nuneaton? I hope to escape being called upon to act as a magistrate but if called upon I shall be for very energetic measures so as at once to suppress any direct breach of the peace.'[63]

In fact, the election passed off quietly at Bedworth, but further measures to ensure the peace were criticised as a breach of etiquette by Bellairs:

'I feel a want of courtesy has been evinced towards me . . . I allude to the fact of special constables in my parish being sworn in by the Rev F. D. Perkins, without the slightest intimation being given me of either the necessity or the wish for such a course to be adopted.'[64]

The recurrent problem of which magistrate was responsible for what place and which action lay behind Bellairs' somewhat testy correspondence. In a more serious situation – as in Nuneaton in 1832 – such divided authority often acted inefficiently or in contradictory ways.

Throughout the country the 1852 election was fought largely over the two issues of free trade or protection and the question of alleged concessions to the Roman Catholic Church. Both Newdegate and Spooner, the Tory candidates for North Warwickshire, were strong opponents of concessions to Rome and their hostility seems to have provoked an attack on their supporters at Nuneaton by a Catholic Irish mob. Newdegate took, not surprisingly, a strong view on this attack on his supporters. He wrote to the local Nuneaton magistrate:

'. . . it is very important that this case should be properly investigated and dealt with . . . not only on account of the injustice of allowing men to be half murdered in the streets of Nuneaton, but because our policy has been, and I trust, always will be, strictly defensive . . . if . . . those who violate the law . . . are allowed to escape with impugnity we shall have mob law predominant at the next election . . . I hope that Mr Jee and Sir John Chetwode will be on the Bench when it is tried, or it might be more prudent to take it to the County Court . . . it is indispensable to shew these "Irish Neds" that Nuneaton is not Ireland.'[65]

No further disorders marred the course of the election. After the second day's polling the Liberal candidates retired from the contest ensuring the comfortable victory of their opponents. The declaration of the poll at Coleshill was attended by none of the disorder which had marked the nomination, but a detachment of Birmingham police and a troop of dragoons were there to ensure order.[66]

At the two subsequent elections for North Warwickshire – in 1857 and 1859 – the sitting members were returned without a contest. But the contested elections for both divisions of the county in 1865 saw the last serious outbreak of disorder at a Warwickshire election. The nomination of the candidates for the northern division of the county passed off reasonably peacefully, thanks to the presence of a large number of policemen. But there were disorderly scenes during the polling at other places:

'At Nuneaton, about ten minutes before the poll commenced, fifty or sixty men, well primed with beer, marched down and placed themselves in front of each booth, ready to do battle in the Conservative interest, but as the Liberals were less demonstrative than their opponents, the voting passed off quieter than might have been anticipated.'[67]

There was a more serious disturbance at Atherstone, where some of the special constables were roughly handled by the mob.[68] There was also disorder during the elections for the southern division. In Leamington a Liberal mob smashed the windows of the two principal Tory hotels and the police superintendent and sixty special constables proved unable to prevent further violence on the following day. In Warwick, one of the Tory candidates Sir Charles Mordaunt, was pelted with mud by a Liberal mob before being rescued by the chief constable. A fight between the rival factions led to one man being seriously wounded.[69]

The disorders during the 1865 elections provide a strong contrast with the peaceful character of the contest three years later. There were no serious disorders in either division in 1868. The local newspaper remarked of the declaration for the northern division at Coleshill: 'The proceedings were entirely bereft of any of their ancient excitement and the audience around the hustings was very small and not at all demonstrative.'[70]

One of the successful Tory candidates, Charles Newdegate, referred to the peaceful character of the election in his speech:

'I congratulate you Mr Sheriff, upon the fact that in this populous district there has been no manifestation of disrespect to the great principle of freedom of election, and I rejoice to find that when there was a fear on that account there was a promptitude among the electors to be sworn as special constables.'[71]

After 1868 elections in Warwickshire for the county divisions were no longer a serious threat to public order.

It is not entirely clear why the elections ceased to occasion disorder. In 1868 there were bad election riots in several places such as Blackburn and Newport, but it is difficult to avoid the conclusion that the creation of a much larger electorate as a result of the passing of the Second Reform Act of 1867, contributed directly to more peaceful electoral conditions. The very size of the new electorates put most constituencies beyond the reach of attempts at intimidation of voters or extensive treating. Candidates could no longer afford to indulge voters' thirsts and thus provoke the disorders associated with drink. Moreover, the introduction of the ballot in 1872 further shielded the individual voter, while the Corrupt and Illegal Practices Act of 1883 laid down tight restrictions on expenditure at elections. Thus electoral reform sapped the sources of electoral disorders.

The record of the county magistracy in combating electoral disorder is harder to assess. Obviously, the vigilance or laxity of the individual J.P. could count for much, but it was not enough just to keep a cool head in a critical situation. Preservation of the peace largely depended on the number and quality of the policing agents which the justice could call upon. In most cases of serious disorder special constables – however numerous – were insufficiently trained and equipped to quell a riot although they might retard its growth. The military – particularly cavalry – were far more effective. Far better trained and equipped and operating in much smaller groups than the specials, they provided a disciplined force which could quickly restore order. But their relative ruthlessness made many magistrates reluctant to call on their services. Moreover, they were always held in reserve so that much disorder might occur before they arrived on the scene. By contrast with these groups, the regular police were the best force for dealing with such disturbances. But there were insufficient county police available to effectively police elections since polling and the disorders associated with it could occur simultaneously in several places. Thus the Birmingham police were called upon to maintain order at Coleshill during the nominations and declaration of the poll. The holding of the county elections after the borough elections thus provided the county magistrates with a welcome addition of police from the neighbouring towns for the duration of the poll.

Election riots were only one type of threat to public order faced by the Warwickshire magistracy in this period. Although the most frequent of such disorders they were, in an obvious sense, predictable. Thus the justices usually had time to take some precautionary measures beforehand. This was not the case with disturbances associated with industrial strikes which occurred without warning. In Warwickshire, the most potentially serious of such strikes was that centred amongst the Bedworth colliers in 1842. Since this was part of a much wider national movement known as the Plug Plot disturbances, the Warwickshire strike (although a relatively minor affair) appeared to the authorities to be invested with a semi-revolutionary character.

In July 1842 the Staffordshire colliers struck in protest about their pay and conditions of employment (particularly the widespread 'truck' system of remuneration in lieu of cash). In August the strike spread to other trades and districts, notably the East Lancashire cotton industry. In the middle of that month delegations from Lancashire and Staffordshire arrived in Bedworth (the centre of the relatively small Warwickshire coalfield) to persuade the local miners to join what appeared to be assuming the character of a national strike. Consequently, all the miners from three of the Bedworth pits immediately went on strike. No scenes of disorder occurred, but it was announced that O'Neil, a Chartist lecturer, would address the strikers in Bedworth. This attempt to politicise the strike was assessed by an observer in the local newspaper:

'I do not think that chartism is much understood among the miners of Warwickshire, neither do I think it will be possible to give the turn-out any political cast in this district; but whether it will terminate without bloodshed is quite another question.'[72]

Measures to prevent the outbreak of any disorder were concerted by the local magistrates, Lord Aylesford, Lord Lifford, Sir Charles Newdegate and George Whieldon. The latter two were both proprietors of coal mines, but it was largely Lord Aylesford who was responsible for directing the precautionary measures. The fifth Earl of Aylesford had considerable stature within the county. He was the brother-in-law of the Earl of Warwick, Lord Lieutenant of the county, and for twenty-eight years had been Colonel of the Warwickshire Yeomanry Cavalry. His combined official position, both as magistrate and commander of the yeomanry, together with his high social status, gave him a precedence amongst the local justices which largely allowed him to determine the measures adopted by the magistrates for the preservation of the peace.

As soon as the authorities had been informed of the colliers' strike and their intention to hold meetings to consider further action, the magistrates called for the assistance of the regular army. But since the Warwickshire disturbance was only a small part of a much wider disorder, only nineteen soldiers could be spared to assist the civil authorities. This was considered by the magistrates insufficient to ensure the maintenance of public order, whereupon Lord Aylesford called out the yeomanry to assist the civil power. Two troops were sent to Bedworth and two to Coventry where the miners intended to hold a meeting and persuade the distressed ribbon-weavers to join the strike.[73] At Bedworth the presence of the yeomanry helped prevent any disorder and Aylesford caused the proclamation: 'For the suppression of tumultuous assemblies', to be read out as a caution.[74] Coventry, however, reacted much more sharply to the arrival of the yeomanry, who (as in many other towns), were disliked on principle by the population:

'The Warwickshire Yeomanry Cavalry have just rode into the city. Their appearance has been the signal for agitation. As they passed along the street they were shouted, groaned and hissed at in the most violent manner. Whoever have advised their appearance have acted most unwisely. The main street is now crowded with persons anxiously inquiring what this means.'[75]

The deployment of the yeomanry in Coventry might have precipitated a 'Peterloo' style encounter with the mob, but the force did provide some support for the worried municipal authorities. The latter had only seventeen regular police (including the Chief Constable) in their employ in 1842.[76] Moreover, the city authorities were anxious to co-operate with the county magistracy – particularly those justices who lived in the suburban districts of Coventry. For when the miners and weavers met to discuss their grievances they often left the city boundaries and passed into the county so as to avoid the presence of the Coventry constabulary.[77]

The continuance of quiet at Bedworth depended, to a considerable extent, on the progress of the talks between the miners and the coal-owners. On August 15th, the men of one or two collieries returned to work under a promise of protection given them by the magistrates. But Lord Aylesford thought it unlikely that the men would generally return to work till they had received further news from the strikers in Staffordshire.[78] A meeting between masters and colliers was held to attempt an agreed settlement. The two principal masters (both J.P.s) – Whieldon and Newdegate – addressed the men but apparently made no attempt to present a common front:

'Mr Whieldon declared that he could not give more wages and sooner than he would be coerced to promise to do that which would not be generally carried out, he would close his pits altogether. Sir Charles Newdegate seemed astonished at the exposure made in relation to the management of his pits and declared that he would cause a searching enquiry to be made into the conduct of the whole of those who had been charged with insult and oppression to the working men.'[79]

Lord Aylesford thought that the terms offered by the masters would remove just complaints and informed the Home Secretary that many of the miners had expressed a wish to return to work. But although Aylesford addressed the men to counsel them to remain orderly, he made no attempt to arbitrate or interfere in any way between the negotiations of masters and men.[80] The men were urged to stick to their demands by a Chartist named Holmes, but Aylesford did not think the men would be drawn into supporting the Charter.[81] Sensing that the danger was largely over, he withdrew all the yeomanry save for detachments of thirty at Coventry and twenty at Bedworth. At the latter place the quarters were very bad and could not cater for a large number of men.[82]

The only real disturbance occurred when the Bedworth strikers attempted to spread the stoppage to all the pits on the Warwickshire coalfield. The pits at Chilvers Coton, a few miles from Bedworth (and including Charles Newdegate's mine) remained in operation during the disturbances. When the Bedworth miners decided to enforce a stoppage at Coton a magistrate with a party of constabulary forced them away. In Nuneaton 130 special constables were sworn in to keep the peace by C. H. Bracebridge and R. Jee, the local acting J.P.s. The latter informed the Home Secretary of the situation and appended a sympathetic comment on the conditions which provoked the strike: 'We have no immediate reason to apprehend any disturbance, though large meetings may of course be held at any moment amidst this large and distressed population, partially employed and very inadequately paid for their labour in the pit and at the loom.[83] By the end of August all the men had returned to work and quiet was restored in the locality.[84]

The peaceful conclusion of the Bedworth disorders was largely attributed to the firm, but cautious, maintenance of order by Lord Aylesford and the yeomanry. The Prime Minister, Sir Robert Peel, thought that Aylesford had behaved 'With great good sense and resolution.'[85] Graham, the Home Secretary, approved highly of Aylesford's activity and energy.[86] Certainly the Home Secretary had played no significant part in coping with the disorder, his main concern being that the men should not advance towards London.[87] The other magistrates and inhabitants of the Bedworth district certainly regarded Aylesford as their saviour. They presented him with a testimonial of thanks, but in his reply, the peer stressed that the maintenance of order was a co-operative effort:

'I have to acknowledge the approbation they have so handsomely expressed of my conduct . . . at the same time I am sensible that it was entirely owing to the cordial co-operation of the magistrates; to the very efficient manner in which their directions were obeyed by the Superintendent of the police of the Hundred, and to the men under his command; and to the inhabitants themselves, who so readily came forward to act as special constables, that the suppression of these unfortunate disturbances was so satisfactorily effected.'[88]

Throughout the strike the chief part of the Knightlow Hundred Police – some 45 men – were stationed at Bedworth. They were commanded by superintendent Isaacs and his effective management of his men was remembered by the county magistrates 14 years later when he was a candidate for the post of Chief Constable of Warwickshire under the new Police Act.[89]

Unlike in the Black Country, where many of the magistrates were mine owners, only Whieldon and Newdegate were both J.P.s and coal masters. Since only Whieldon's pits were involved in the disturbances it is not meaningful to talk of an economic confrontation which underlay the magistrates' desire to preserve the peace. But the fact that most of the justices had no direct interest in the strike may help to account for the absence of disorder or bitterness on the part of the men. The sympathetic attitude of the Nuneaton J.P.s to the strikers is in marked contrast to the harsher attitude of Whieldon who, even though the strike was peacefully concluded, wrote to the Home Secretary calling for the re-enactment of the Combination Laws.[90] But Newdegate's conciliatory attitude towards the miners manifested at the Bedworth meeting appears to have been sincere and thereafter he was on excellent terms with his men. By 1852 he was offering their services as special constables to preserve the peace during polling at Nuneaton and inviting a neighbouring magistrate to take tea with them.[91]

During the 1842 emergency the special constables created to help preserve the peace were commanded by Newdegate

who, many years later, recorded his memories of attempting
to turn such a scratch group into a disciplined force:

'I remember being in command of eight hundred special
constables, and anything more like a mob I never had to do
with. Before I could do anything with them I had to break
them into tens. After I got the tens under the command of
their own parish neighbours, I was ready to fight in about
four-and-twenty hours . . . Lord Aylesford came to me . . . I
said "I do not know who to swear in as special constables,
but we will take every man who comes out of evening
Church, and we shall probably make these men captains of
tens." Lord Aylesford consented, for he thought these men
would, in all probability, be trusty fellows – persons who
might be trusted at a pinch, and fit to lead their own parish
neighbours; and I was pretty sure that if they had the inclination to run away, they would be ashamed to do so.'[92]

The *ad hoc* nature of the specials' selection and training
underlines their questionable utility in coping with disturbances. With the possible exception of their being used to
deal with rioting on a large scale, the very number of them
was more of a hindrance than a help to the authorities.

It was inevitable that the problem of public order in
Warwickshire was overshadowed by the prime necessity to
keep the peace in Birmingham. The latter was, by 1850, the
third largest provincial city in England. When it received its
Charter of Incorporation in November 1838, it accounted
for about half the population of Warwickshire. The incorporation of the city created problems about the relationship
of the city government to that of the county. In part, this
reflected the inevitable difference of attitude between a
radically inclined manufacturing city and a largely Conservative country area. In the context of public order this
dispute became most intense in 1839 during the Chartist
disturbances in Birmingham, but it had commenced with
the creation of a separate borough magistracy.

In July 1838, the Earl of Warwick, the Tory Lord Lieutenant of Warwickshire, complained in the House of Lords

that the appointment of magistrates for the Warwickshire boroughs appeared to be controlled by Joseph Parkes, the radical attorney. He thought the entire borough patronage was dispensed 'With an entire regard to party feeling'.[93] In the following year, Warwick supported a petition from the county magistrates acting in Birmingham to become borough justices under the new charter. He pointed out to the Whig Home Secretary: '. . . these gentlemen collectively form no political party for I have always taken especial care in my recommendations to select the most respectable individuals from all parties who I thought likely to act and give the most *general* satisfaction'.[94]

His fear that the Birmingham magistrates should belong to the radical party only, seemed to be borne out when, a few months later, the city was beset by the disorders that followed the assembly of the Chartist National Convention there. The ineffectiveness of the local J.P.s was regarded by Warwick and others as a sign of secret political sympathy for the Chartists which threatened the fabric of public order. Warwick felt angry that the city justices had not informed him of the situation in the town:

'Standing in the situation of lord-lieutenant of the county, still he had received not one word of communication on the subject from the magistrates or any other authorities of the town, or even from the Home Office. Had it been so, he should have been very glad to give immediate assistance, for the purpose of securing the public peace.'[95]

The reason for this neglect the Earl attributed to political jobbery. He claimed that thirteen of the new borough J.P.s were connected with the political union and that there were only four Tories on the bench.[96]

In fact the county authorities were not entirely ignorant of the disorders in Birmingham since, on July 6th, they allowed the Warwickshire Yeomanry to be sent to the city to help to maintain order. The force was stationed at Edgbaston (with a troop at Handsworth) throughout the disorders, although this meant considerable inconvenience to the many farmers in the ranks who would otherwise have been engaged on the harvest[97] The deployment of the yeomanry to maintain order in the city was not a novel procedure since they had previously aided the civil power in the city in 1795 and 1816. The last time they were called out to aid the civil power – in 1848 – was also to guard against possible disturbances in Birmingham.[98] But the use of the yeomanry for such work was not popular in some circles. The local county paper commented in 1839: 'We deeply regret the necessity for this step, as we are of the opinion that the appearance of the yeomanry on the scene of action may produce an increase of irritation in the excited people, while the latter might be kept in subjection by regular troops.'[99] The reception accorded the yeomanry by the mob was decidedly hostile but they were given much hospitality by the respectable inhabitants of the town whose property they were protecting.[100] It seems likely that many Birmingham people, however, resented the use of a county force in what was now an autonomous borough. Some years later a squib published in the city welcomed the proposal to form a Birmingham Volunteer Rifle Corps on the grounds that it would be 'Free from county and club influence'.[101]

But the county also had a bone of contention in relation to the Chartist disorders. The riots had occasioned widespread damage to property and compensation for the losses involved was obtained by levying a rate on the rural districts of Warwickshire nearest to Birmingham, as well as on the borough itself. This brought forth strong protests from the people of the district which was expressed in Parliament by the Earl of Warwick and Sir Robert Peel who owned agricultural land in the region.[102] Another problem related to the trial of Birmingham offenders at Warwick. Although Birmingham accounted for the great majority of the prisoners who were tried at Warwick Assizes no criminal Assize was established at Birmingham until 1884. Indeed, it was only in 1854 that civil cases from the Warwick division could be heard at Birmingham. In 1839, the men arrested in relation to the Chartist Birmingham disorders were committed to

Warwick gaol before trial since the Charter of Birmingham was in course of litigation. The result was that Warwick gaol became greatly overcrowded and in the words of the Chairman of the quarter sessions: 'The magistrates hardly knew what to do.'[103] Moreover, the arrangement for the Birmingham authorities to pay for their prisoners at Warwick was upset by the refusal of the overseers to levy a rate. Thus in November 1839, the county authorities had delivered a bill of £1,000 for the city's prisoners which was only met with the assistance of a government loan. It was not until 1841 that the city authorities succeeded in raising the necessary rate.[104]

The Warwickshire county magistrates faced a variety of problems in attempting to preserve the peace in the mid-nineteenth century. After 1870 these problems were far less acute or frequent. There were serious strikes in the county, such as the agricultural labourers 'revolt of the Field' in 1872 and the strike of the colliers in 1874, but they passed off with very little actual violence or even the threat of it. By the 1870s the changing conditions were reflected in the measures which the magistrates took to preserve order. The military were not called upon after the 1850s and the use of special constables apparently lapsed in the 1860s. The formation of the new county police force in 1857 thus marked something of a watershed in the history of public order in the county.

But too much attention should not be given to the novel features of maintaining order. The disturbances between 1830 and 1870 were effectively dealt with largely by the J.P.s acting on their own initiative and with little help from the national government. The forces at their disposal were none of them ideal for maintaining order and not primarily intended to do so. Criticism of the record of the magistrates for displaying a 'Lack of self-reliance', an 'incapacity for taking a large view' or a 'predisposition to excesses' in coping with disorders must be considered within the limited context of the resources and information available to the individual justice. In retrospect, it appears rather remarkable that their record was as successful and achieved at as little cost as it was. In the making of a peaceful modern society the magistrate deserves to rank with the police constable as one of the principal agents of order.[105]

Notes

1. F. C. Mather, *Public Order in the Age of the Chartists* (Manchester, 1659), pp. 36–45. See also Asa Briggs, *The Age of Improvement* (London, 1959), pp. 249–50 and 333.
2. *Ibid.*, p. 41.
3. *Ibid.*, p. 29.
4. George Eliot, *Felix Holt, The Radical* (London, 1866; 1967 Everyman Edition), pp. 4–5.
5. Sidney and Beatrice Webb, *English Local Government from the Revolution to the Municipal Corporations Act: The Parish and the County* (London, 1906), pp. 378–9.
6. William West, *History, Topography and Directory of Warwickshire* (Birmingham, 1830), p. 669.
7. William Reader of Coventry, 'A Chronicle of the Times' (MSS collection in the Bodleian Library, Oxford), no. 1074.
8. The fifth Earl of Aylesford was Colonel of the Warwickshire Yeomanry Cavalry from 1814 to 1848.
9. Webbs, *op. cit.*, p. 386.
10. Mather, *op. cit.*, pp. 54–5.
11. Webbs, *op. cit.*, p. 384, note 2.
12. *Ibid.*
13. William Reader, 'A Chronicle of the Times', *op. cit.*; 'A Churchman' to the Editor of the *Coventry Herald*, 29th May, 1827.
14. *Ibid.*
15. *Parl. Debates*, third series, vol. XXXVI, 10th February, 1837, 420.
16. Warwickshire County Record Office: CR 1097/330, Joseph Parkes to the Earl of Warwick, 28th July, 1839.
17. *Parl. Debates*, third series, vol. XLIX, 2nd August, 1839, 1139–40.
18. *The Warwick & Warwickshire Advertiser*, 1st October, 1892.
19. For the social prestige attached to the magistracy see, for example, Francis Cross, *Landed Property: Its Sale, Purchase, Improvement and General Management* (London, 1857), p. 10.
20. Joseph Parkes, *op. cit.*
21. *Parl. Debates*, third series, vol. XLIX, 2nd August, 1839, 1139.
22. Public Record Office: HO 52/43, Earl of Warwick to the Home Secretary, 9th January, 1839.
23. *The Warwick & Warwickshire Advertiser*, 13th May, 1893.
24. *Parl. Debates*, third series, vol. CCXXXII, 15th February, 1877, 428–9.
25. *Ibid.*, vol. XXXVI, 10th February, 1837, 419.
26. *Dugdale Society Occasional Papers*, no. 4 (Warwick, 1934), Philip Styles,

'The Development of County Administration in the late eighteenth and early nineteenth centuries illustrated by records of the Warwickshire Court of Quarter Sessions, 1773–1837', p. 28.

27. Northamptonshire Record Office: Harpur of Burton Latimer Collection no. 424; T. Coker Adams to H. R. Harpur, 29th August, 1842.
28. J. W. Cross, *George Eliot's Life As Related in her Letters and Journals* (London, 1902), vol. I, pp. 22–3.
29. MSS Memorandum Book of Occurrences at Nuneaton, pp. 51–2.
30. *Ibid.*, pp. 42–3.
31. *Ibid.*, p. 58.
32. *Ibid.*, pp. 65–6.
33. *Felix Holt, op. cit.*, p. 43.
34. PRO HO 41/11, pp. 337–8, Melbourne to Lord Warwick, 20th December, 1832.
35. *The Warwick & Warwickshire Advertiser*, 22nd December, 1832.
36. 'Occurrences at Nuneaton', *op. cit.*, p. 68.
37. Account quoted in *The Warwick & Warwickshire Advertiser*, 5th January, 1833.
38. *Ibid.*
39. 'Occurrences at Nuneaton', *op. cit.*, p. 52.
40. *The Warwick & Warwickshire Advertiser*, 5th January, 1833.
41. *Ibid.*
42. 'Occurrences at Nuneaton', pp. 69–70.
43. Cf. G. S. Haight, *George Eliot: A Biography* (London, 1969), pp. 381–2.
44. *The Warwick & Warwickshire Advertiser*, 5th January, 1833.
45. PRO: HO 41/11, p. 341; Melbourne to the Earl of Warwick, 24th December, 1832.
46. *Ibid.*, pp. 345–6, Melbourne to F. Newdigate, 29th December, 1832.
47. *Ibid.*, p. 350, Melbourne to F. Newdigate, 3rd January, 1833.
48. *Ibid.*, pp. 347–8, Melbourne to Heming, 29th December, 1832.
49. *Ibid.*, pp. 354–5, Melbourne to Heming, 8th January, 1832.
50. Occurrences at Nuneaton, *op. cit.*, pp. 72, 79.
51. *Ibid.*, pp. 73, 79.
52. Quoted in *The Warwick & Warwickshire Advertiser*, 5th January, 1833.
53. PRO: HO 40/31, f. 135–6; John Greene to Melbourne, 2nd January, 1833.
54. *Felix Holt, op. cit.*, pp. 290–1.
55. *Ibid.*, p. 296.
56. 'Occurrences at Nuneaton', *op. cit.*, pp. 97–8.
57. *Ibid.*, pp. 125–6.
58. *The Warwick & Warwickshire Advertiser*, 28th August, 1847.
59. Harpur of Burton Latimer, *op. cit.*, no. 461; C. N. Newdegate to H. R. Harpur, 6th July, 1852.
60. *The Times*, 13th July, 1852.
61. *Ibid.*
62. *Ibid.*
63. Harpur of Burton Latimer Coll., *op. cit.*, no. 463; H. Bellairs to H. R. Harpur, 13th July, 1852.
64. *Ibid.*, no. 465, Bellairs to Harpur, 16th July, 1852.
65. *Ibid.*, no. 471, Charles Newdegate to Harpur, 4th August, 1852.
66. *The Leamington Spa Courier*, 24th July, 1852.

67. *The Warwick & Warwickshire Advertiser*, 22nd July, 1865.
68. *Ibid.*
69. *Ibid.*
70. *The Warwick & Warwickshire Advertiser*, 28th November, 1868.
71. *Ibid.*
72. *The Warwick & Warwickshire Advertiser*, 22nd August, 1842.
73. *Ibid.* See also *Parl. Debates*, third series, vol. CCLVI, 3rd September, 1880, 1223 (Charles Newdegate's reminiscences of 1842 disturbances).
74. Hon H. A. Adderley, *History of the Warwickshire Yeomanry Cavalry* (Warwick, n.d.) pp. 63–4.
75. *The Warwick & Warwickshire Advertiser*, 22nd August, 1842.
76. PRO: HO 45/261A, Mayor of Coventry to the Home Secretary, 22nd August, 1842.
77. *Ibid.*, Mayor of Coventry to Home Secretary, 17th August, 1842.
78. *Ibid.*, Lord Aylesford to Home Secretary, 15th August, 1842.
79. *The Warwick & Warwickshire Advertiser*, 22nd August, 1842.
80. HO 45/261A, Lord Aylesford to Home Secretary, 16th August, 1842. Cf. Mather, *op. cit.*, p. 52, where it is stated that Aylesford headed the coalowners in their negotiations with the men.
81. *Ibid.*, Aylesford to Home Secretary, 16th, 17th August, 1842.
82. *Ibid.*, 18th August, 1842.
83. *Ibid.*, C. H. Bracebridge and R. Jee to Home Secretary, 20th August, 1842.
84. *The Warwick & Warwickshire Advertiser*, 3rd September, 1842.
85. *The Private Letters of Sir Robert Peel*, edited by George Peel (London, 1920), p. 202.
86. HO 45/261A, Graham's endorsement of letter from Aylesford.
87. *Ibid.*
88. *The Warwick & Warwickshire Advertiser*, 24th September, 1842.
89. Harpur of Burton Latimer Coll., *op. cit.*, no. 495, C. N. Newdegate to H. R. Harpur, 15th July, 1856.
90. HO 45/261A, G. Whieldon to Home Secretary, 26th August, 1842.
91. Harpur Coll., *op. cit.*, M. N. Newdegate to Harpur, 14th July, 1852 (no. 464) and no 474, C. N. Newdegate to Harpur, 13th August, 1852.
92. *The Nuneaton Chronicle*, 26th September, 1874: speech of C. N. Newdegate at Astley Harvest Festival.
93. *Parl. Debates*, third series, vol. XLIV, Lords, 17th July, 1838, 275.
94. PRO: HO 52/43; Earl of Warwick to Home Secretary, 9th January, 1839.
95. *Parl. Debates*, third series, vol. XLIX, Lords, 16th July, 1839, 370.
96. *Ibid.*, 18th July, 1839, 444.
97. *Adderley*, History of Warwickshire Yeomanry Cavalry, *op. cit.*, pp. 56, 60.
98. *Ibid.*, pp. 74–5.
99. *The Warwick & Warwickshire Advertiser*, 6th July, 1839.
100. *Ibid.*, 27th July, 1839.
101. J. A. Langford, *Modern Birmingham and Its Institutions* (Birmingham, 1877), vol. II, p. 81.
102. *Parl. Debates*, third series, vol. LVII, 22nd April, 1841, 969–70 and vol. LIV, 18th June, 1840, 1268–9.
103. *Ibid.*, vol. LIII, 15th April, 1840, pp. 115–16.
104. Conrad Gill, *History of Birmingham to 1865* (Oxford, 1952), pp. 261–5.
105. Cf. Mather, *op. cit.*, pp. 62–3.

6

Popular Protest and Public Order

Red Clydeside, 1915–1919

Iain McLEAN

'*During the first three months of 1919 unrest touched its high-water mark. I do not think that at any time in history since the Bristol Riots we have been so near revolution* . . . *On the 27th of January there were extensive strikes on the Clyde of a revolutionary rather than an economic character*'.
(Sir) Basil Thomson[1]

'*A rising was expected. A rising should have taken place. The workers were ready and able to effect it;* the leadership had never thought of it'.
William Gallacher[2]

Many observers, both at the time and later, thought that 1919 marked the high point for the prospects of the British revolution; and the Clyde, or more precisely the Glasgow munitions area, had gained during the war a reputation which events in the first two months of 1919 seemed to confirm. Labour unrest on the Clyde first attracted government attention early in 1915, and on several occasions the apparent threat to public order was discussed at Cabinet level. The two most important were the 'dilution' crisis from January to March 1916, and the Forty Hours' Strike in January 1919, and it is to these that I intend to devote most attention.

The background to the dilution crisis has been examined

215

elsewhere,[3] and I wish to mention only essential details here. 'Dilution' meant the substitution of unskilled or female labour for skilled labour in engineering, and particularly in munitions. The craftsman's job was to be split up, with those components which could be done by less-trained workmen, or women, being given to 'dilutees', and the craftsman being restricted to the tasks which could only be done by a fully-skilled man. From March 1915 until the end of the war, the government was continually pressing for more dilution as an essential means of increasing the production of war materials. The 'Treasury Agreement' of March 1915 was signed between Lloyd George and the leaders of most of the craft unions, who agreed to suspend for the duration of the war their customary trade practices reserving certain jobs to craftsmen, in return for a promise that the government would legislate to restore them after the end of the war. This agreement was given the force of law in the Munitions of War Act in July 1915, by which time the Ministry of Munitions had come into existence. One of the chief functions of its Labour Department was to impose dilution, a task in which it faced several opponents. Within Whitehall, other departments resented the fact that an upstart new ministry, created from scratch by Lloyd George, had taken over their responsibilities for industrial relations. In the munitions industry, neither the employers nor the unions were keen on dilution. The employers were unwilling to dilute for two reasons, one of which was sheer conservatism or incompetence. Dilution placed a heavy demand on line management at a time when many engineering employers had still not adapted to the rapid technical changes involved in mass production. Therefore, many employers were reluctant to initiate dilution schemes; 'some', according to a Ministry report, 'were frankly of opinion that women were unsuitable for engineering'. And, in the second place, employers knew very well that the agreement to dilution given by the craft unions, especially the Amalgamated Society of Engineers (A.S.E.) was at best very grudging. They regarded it as the Ministry's job, not theirs, to impose dilution. They were not prepared to pull Lloyd George's chestnuts out of the fire, and find themselves with strikes on their hands which could be avoided if dilution were quietly ignored. Ministry officials in Glasgow soon found out that merely issuing instructions to employers to introduce dilution was fruitless: 'It was hopeless to expect employers to take any action in the direction suggested until the Ministry of Munitions had brought the necessary pressure to bear on Trade Unions to secure the waiving in actual practice – and not merely on paper – of their restrictions'.[4]

As this indicates, the A.S.E. fought a long and dogged rearguard action to protect its craftsmen members against the effects of dilution. The position of the craftsman was being threatened by technological change, change which was rapidly accelerating under war conditions. As one of the shrewdest Ministry observers saw, the men's gut suspicion was that by the end of the war 'women will . . . have become so proficient that Employers will after the Munitions Act has ceased to operate employ them at a lower wage than and to the exclusion of the skilled men. This is the real difficulty in the case, and at the bottom of much objection to dilution.'[5]

The A.S.E.'s unwillingness to co-operate was a serious threat to the Ministry, both on its own account and because of the truculence it induced among employers, and it took more than a year from the signing of the Treasury Agreement for the Ministry to arrive at what it regarded as a satisfactory settlement. For a short part of this period, other bodies appeared on the union's left flank which posed a far more explicit threat to public order. Most celebrated of these was the Clyde Workers' Committee (C.W.C.), whose heyday was from October 1915 to March 1916. Its declared objects were:

'1. To obtain an ever-increasing control over workshop conditions.
2. To regulate the terms upon which the workers shall be employed.

3. To organise the workers upon a class basis and to maintain the Class Struggle, until the overthrow of the Wages
System, the Freedom of the Workers, and the establishment of Industrial Democracy have been obtained.'[6]

The committee's leaders were mostly revolutionary syndi-
calists of one kind or another, although it also featured
opportunists who were 'determined to use the Munitions
Act as a means for their own advancement . . . [and] came
forward as champions of Trade Unionism to oppose the
Act.'[7] Grassroots support for the C.W.C. came almost
entirely from skilled engineering workers. What drew these
groups together was condemnation of the unions for their
'act of Treachery' in assenting to the Munitions Act. Rank-
and-file members did not know how hard the A.S.E. was in
fact fighting behind the scenes against dilution; all they
could see was that their officials were failing to protect their
interests – their craft interests – in public. The C.W.C. was
an uneasy coalition between revolutionary syndicalism and
craft conservatism. By failing to realise that it was the latter
which was its real driving force, the authorities (like many
subsequent writers) were misled into seeing it as a
much more severe threat to public order than it actually
was.

The C.W.C. was the body which organised opposition to
Lloyd George when he came to Glasgow at Christmas 1915
to encourage dilution. The visit spectacularly misfired. On
Christmas Day, an impatient audience of shop stewards
listened to Arthur Henderson explaining at some length the
justice of the war on behalf of the 'brave and independent'
Belgians ('Oh heavens! How long have we to suffer this?')
and to Lloyd George asserting with passion that the responsibility of a Minister of the Crown in a great war was not
a light one ('The money's good', and laughter). The socialist
weekly *Forward* printed an accurate and unflattering account
of the meeting, from which these comments are taken. In
view of the damage the report might do to the dilution
campaign, the Ministry suppressed the paper – certainly a

mistake, which only highlighted Lloyd George's failure to impress the Glasgow munitions workers.

Nevertheless, after the *Forward* incident[8] the C.W.C. faded from the centre of interest for a couple of months. The Ministry of Munitions' immediate task was to break the A.S.E.'s opposition to dilution; its weapons were the three Dilution Commissioners who were sent to the Clyde in the middle of January. The obduracy of the union and the incompetence of the employers were their principal headaches, but from early February they began to become concerned about the C.W.C. They discovered that it was 'ostensibly a Socialist Organisation, if indeed it is not something worse. Its primary object is to overthrow all official Trade Unions on the Clyde and to supplant such effete organisations by a revolutionary propaganda of the international Anarchist type.'[9] Thereafter, two of the Commissioners sought a confrontation with the C.W.C. The third, a former union official and a professional arbitrator, sent a memorandum of dissent in which he argued that the Commissioners should attack the ' "old trade-union" bitterness, narrow and selfish'[10] of the pure craft conservatives rather than the C.W.C. But he was over-ruled, and the dramatic confrontation came in late March. On the 17th, men at the giant Parkhead Forge, in the East End of Glasgow, struck in protest at restrictions on the rights of David Kirkwood, their chief shop steward. They appealed to workers in other plants to join them:

'Unite with us in demanding that during the present crisis our shop stewards in every workshop where dilution is in force shall have the fullest liberty to investigate the conditions under which the new class of labour is employed, so that this may not be used to reduce us all to a lower standard of life.'[11]

The response was lukewarm, largely because C.W.C. leaders in other factories were suspicious of Kirkwood for having co-operated with the Dilution Commissioners. (He had produced a scheme of dilution for Parkhead which they approved without alteration.) Therefore, when Kirkwood's employer turned against him, C.W.C. supporters in other plants observed, somewhat smugly, that he had got his due reward. So only a few factories struck in sympathy. This did not stop the Commissioners from sending 'frenzied telegrams'[12] to the Ministry demanding action against the C.W.C. The Committee, according to them, had decided to cripple the war effort by bringing out on strike those of their supporters who worked in factories where howitzers essential for the Western Front or barges for the Mesopotamia campaign were being built.[13] The Ministry chiefs decided that 'We have been patient long enough,'[14] and deported ten of the leaders of the C.W.C., including Kirkwood, out of the Clyde munitions area. They were sent in the first instance to Edinburgh, where the workers were presumably regarded as impervious to revolutionary sedition-mongering.

Shortly afterwards, on March 30th, the Cabinet discussed the deportations:

'It was shown that the principal danger of the situation depends not so much on the proceedings of the small (by comparison) number of workmen holding syndicalist views and revolutionary aims, as on the fear that the vastly larger body of patriotic and loyal trade unionists may be deluded by misrepresentation of the facts into expressing sympathy with the violent minority, believing them to be unjustly treated.'[15]

By April 4th, the men on strike, including those who had joined out of sympathy for the deportees, were almost all back at work, and members of the Cabinet were congratulating each other that they had averted a major crisis.[16] It is not obvious, however, that one was ever in prospect. The Commissioners' claim that the C.W.C. was plotting to disrupt the war effort was sheer nonsense, and was painstakingly shown to be so by a Labour Party committee which later investigated the case.[17] It is possible that they decided to fabricate the story in order to force the government to get rid of the C.W.C. It is much more likely that they simply took fright, and believed one of the scare stories which were constantly being passed on to them by agitated employers and self-appointed sniffers-out of German spies. At any rate, the government took the Commissioners at their word. They took dramatic action against the deportees as they had against the *Forward*; the *dénouement* appeared to be the government's success in scattering the members of a dangerous revolutionary organisation, the C.W.C. But, like many later commentators, they grossly overestimated the C.W.C. by taking it at its own valuation. The Clyde Workers' Committee was not the harbinger of the revolution; it was a loose coalition of revolutionary socialists and craft conservatives. And it could thrive only when the craftsmen felt their position was at stake. Unlike (say) the Bolsheviks, the C.W.C. could make no effective appeal to the rest of the working class outside its own constituency. Its immediate appeal was to a group of craftsmen, and the threat to their status which they perceived came from women and unskilled men just as much as from 'the bosses' or 'the government'. They never received the support of the unskilled in their campaign; indeed, there is no reason at all why they should have done. Moreover, there is no way of knowing to what extent the C.W.C. leaders represented opinion even among the munitions workers from whom their strength was drawn. A supporter of the committee explained the position candidly to the Labour Party inquiry:

'The Clyde Workers' Committee was a heterogeneous crowd which had practically no constitution. It was more a collection of angry Trade Unionists than anything else, which had sprung into existence because of the trouble which was going on on the Clyde. The Clyde Workers' Committee was the result of the trouble, the outcome of the trouble . . .

You must remember that it was not absolutely necessary for your Shop to send you; you could represent a minority in the Shop just the same as a majority, even though the minority was one.'[18]

In spite of these drawbacks, the Committee seemed to have presented the government with a revolutionary threat, and when it once again became involved in a major industrial upheaval, in 1919, the government was again to make the mistake of taking it too seriously. In the intervening period, the reputation 'Red Clydeside' had acquired was enough to make the Cabinet jittery on several occasions. In August 1917, for instance, the Secretary for Scotland took fright at the notion of a Workers' and Soldiers' Council being formed in Glasgow as a result of the Leeds Conference in June, which had been called by the I.L.P. and the British Socialist Party in order to welcome the Russian Revolution and encourage the formation of local soviets. He brought the matter to the War Cabinet, which authorised him to ban the meeting, and announced that 'the Cabinet regarded the objects of such meetings as illegal, and would not permit them to be held'.[19]

Once again, Red Clydeside's bark was shown to be worse than its bite. When the government announced the ban, the meeting of the Glasgow Soviet was transformed into a demonstration of protest at its prohibition. The Glasgow Trades Council, which had been in charge of the plans for a Workmen's and Soldiers' Council, recorded with pride that although 'quite 4,000' had attended for the meeting, there was 'not the slightest semblance of disorder', so that fifty plainclothes police who had been drafted in had had a 'holiday with pay'.[20] After two more months of abortive attempts to find a meeting-place for the Soviet which would be permitted by the Glasgow magistrates, the affair faded away. The revolution was postponed *sine die* because of the disapproval of the magistrates and the Secretary for Scotland.

The Leeds Convention and the outburst of enthusiasm for Workers' and Soldiers' Councils were perhaps untypical of wartime Labour politics, and normally cautious and bureaucratic bodies like the Glasgow Trades Council soon recovered from the burst of anarchic romanticism which had affected them. But there were individuals whose pursuit of the revolution was both more wholehearted and more consistent. Such a person was John Maclean, a Glasgow schoolteacher turned Marxist propagandist who had been sentenced to three years' imprisonment for sedition in 1916. He had been released on a ticket-of-leave in 1917 because his health, both physical and mental, had been deteriorating in prison. Far from ceasing his activities, however, he had stepped them up; after the October Revolution the Russians appointed him Soviet Consul in Glasgow. Munro, the Secretary for Scotland, was urged by several of his advisers to take action against Maclean. The Army's General Officer Commanding in Scotland, for example, expressed his annoyance with Munro for so much as raising the matter in the War Cabinet rather than simply imprisoning Maclean without further ado.[21] Less impetuously, the Lord Advocate suggested that there would be little point in doing anything beyond prosecuting Maclean and deporting his Russian secretary, Louis Shammes. But in the War Cabinet the note of alarm was sounded by H. A. L. Fisher: 'He learned from a reliable French source that there was an intimate connection between the more extreme Labour leaders in Glasgow and similar Labour leaders at S. Etienne. The latter were taking instructions from Glasgow.'[22] Rumours of close connections between Red Clydeside and unsavoury revolutionaries elsewhere were to disturb the Cabinet a good deal more in 1919, when served up more spicily by Basil Thomson and the Special Branch; but here they had at least a foretaste. The Lord Advocate was authorised to take proceedings against Maclean, as a result of which he was again tried and sentenced to five years' imprisonment with hard labour for breaches of the Defence of the Realm Acts.

Towards the end of the war, his supporters stridently took up the appeal to release him. Their efforts impressed George Barnes, the Labour member of the War Cabinet, and himself M.P. for the Gorbals district of Glasgow. 'Mr Barnes said he thought the continual agitation about this man constituted a serious danger for the government, and no good purpose was served by keeping him in prison. Maclean's supporters were threatening to take very drastic steps, e.g.

cutting off the light on the Clyde, if his release were not brought about.'[23] The matter had been referred to the Imperial War Cabinet, which agreed to Maclean's release with only one dissenting voice, that of Cave, the Home Secretary, who thought it would be an undesirable encouragement to the revolutionaries of South Wales and London.

How justified was Barnes's alarm at Maclean's capacity for revolutionary disruption? There is no doubt that Maclean's prison terms made him a martyr in the eyes of many Clydeside sympathisers. The press, although totally hostile to his views, gave ample evidence of his popularity; the tumultuous welcome he received on 3rd December, 1918, on his return from prison, was prominently featured on the picture page of the leading popular daily.[24] But it is not at all clear that Maclean could have started a revolution. His aims sometimes (although not always) coincided with those of the C.W.C. But it is an exaggeration to claim that 'his agitation constituted the elemental driving force behind the whole revolutionary movement on the Clyde'.[25] A truer view of the relationship between the schoolteacher Maclean and his working-class audiences is that of another middle-class Marxist, Walton Newbold,[26] who said of him:

'That forceful exponent of a fanatic evangel of revolutionary purpose could never take kindly to the thought that his audiences were motivated by material conditions rather than by the logic and urgency of his personal appeal . . . he was external to the life of the working class by reason of his professional work as a school-teacher of considerable academic distinction . . .'[27]

In its assessment of Maclean, as with the C.W.C. in 1916, the government was unduly impressionable. There is no solid evidence that either Maclean or the C.W.C. posed a real revolutionary threat. Both of these incidents, however, had been overshadowed by a much more spectacular affair, the Forty Hours' Strike of January 1919, which contributed more than any earlier incident to Red Clydeside's revolutionary reputation.

The origins of the strike lay in events which took place long before the end of the war. In 1917 and 1918, many labour leaders on Clydeside (and elsewhere) became concerned about the possibility of widespread disruption and unemployment at the end of the war, when demobilisation and the end of munitions production were expected to throw millions of men and women into the labour market. They advocated reducing the length of the working week and spreading the available work around to ensure that everybody had some – a solution traditionally favoured by trade unionists and equally traditionally condemned as economically unsound by employers, newspapers, and governments.

One labour body which had discussed the problem was the Scottish Trades Union Congress. In 1918, its delegates resolved that 'the government should bring a Bill into Parliament to take effect on demobilisation, in enactment of a 40 Hour Maximum Working Week, preferably so arranged as to make Saturday a holiday, the hours worked to be 8 per day for the first 5 days of the week, with a break each day of an hour for dinner.'[28] Opposition to this came not from conservatives but from radicals who believed that it did not go far enough, for instance the Glasgow Trades Council, who urged a 30-hour week instead of a 40-hour one.

In one industry, at least, some progress towards shortening working hours was being made. Immediately after the Armistice in November 1918, the craft unions in engineering and shipbuilding negotiated a reduction in the number of hours in the basic working week from 54 to 47, with a corresponding increase in the hourly rate. The agreement took effect with the new year, and the A.S.E. reflected proudly on its achievement: 'The concession of a 47-hour week without reduction of wages will rank as one of the greatest triumphs of British Trade Unionism.'[29] In most parts of the country, this settlement was welcomed by union members (the total vote on the proposal by members of all the unions affected favoured it by two to one). In the Glasgow area, however, the majority vote was hostile among members of the A.S.E. and other unions (notably the iron- and brass-moulders) whose local officials were urging a 40- or 30-hour week. Popular hostility to the 47-hour week was increased when it was put into operation. The previous working period had involved a 6 a.m. start and a breakfast break at 9.15; the new one required a 7.30 start and con- tinuous working through to 12.30. The psychological effect of this was that the men felt their work period was as onerous as before. They had to get up almost as early as ever, to eat their unaccustomedly early breakfast, and then had a long spell of continuous work to face before dinner. The arrange- ment aroused more resentment in Glasgow than elsewhere because of these long-established patterns of work, which in turn were made possible by the tradition of living in closely packed tenement blocks very near the workplace, and going home for meals.

There was nothing political in any of this, of course; it was the circumstances in which this occurred which made the Forty Hours' Strike so politically explosive. One relevant point was made by the local A.S.E. Executive when they referred to 'the rebound from the pressures of the war-period which had prevented the workers from using the power, which the abnormal conditions had put into their hands, to secure [their] demands'.[30] Wartime negotiations had vastly increased the power of shop stewards. Labour was in a sellers' market; munitions production had brought in its train complex bonus systems and overtime arrangements. So shop-floor bargainers had greatly increased their power in negotiations at the expense of permanent union officials. At the end of the war this situation affected different groups in different ways. Militant shop stewards again took up the theme of 'betrayal' on which they had played profitably in 1915 and 1916. In this case it was easy to argue that union officialdom had 'betrayed' its Glasgow membership, which was against the 47-hour proposal. Thus the C.W.C. was revived, initially under the name of the 'Ways and Means

Committee', to denounce the 47-hour system and to press for a 30-hour week. It is possible that, over and above their overt grievance, the militants suspected that their time was running out, that the end of the war would mean the end of their favourable negotiating position, and that union officials might be able to reassert their authority. This was certainly the view of many union leaderships, including that of the A.S.E., whose reaction to the Forty Hours' Strike was totally hostile: they suspended their Glasgow District Committee for supporting it. On the other hand, non-revolutionary trade unionists on Clydeside saw a constraint removed from their action. Men who had not been opposed to the war were unwilling to strike while it was in progress, for fear of being dubbed 'allies of the Huns' in the local press, or even of actually hindering the war effort. But once the war was over, many militant trade unionists who had previously been reluctant to show their strength thought the time had come for the workers to use their increased bargaining strength.

The result of this was that by January 1919 both moderates and extremists among local trade union leaders were in favour of a strike to pursue the 40-hour week demand. The involvement of the S.T.U.C. sprang initially from its commitment, dating from the 1918 Congress, to the principle of spreading the available work; in the first weeks of the new year, the Executive of the S.T.U.C. became more and more closely involved as it tried to keep the strike movement on course for 40 hours and away from the wholly impracticable 30-hours demand being made by the C.W.C. The terms on which the strike was called, for January 27th, represented a compromise between the two wings. It was for 40 hours, not 30; but the S.T.U.C. Executive, while asking its member unions to support the strike, called it 'hasty and unwise'[31] because its timing did not allow for proper preparations being made.

The organisers were reasonably satisfied by the numbers of men who came out on strike: 40,000 on the first day and 70,000 on the second.[32] But the strike had no sooner started than the moderates began to look for ways out of a position which had become acutely embarrassing because of the failure of national union executives to support the strike. The Ministry of Labour sent a chilly telegram to the S.T.U.C. executive in response to its appeal for intervention:

'I am directed by the Minister of Labour to call your attention to the fact that the matter is one which should form the subject of negotiations between the unions and employers' associations concerned . . . In the meantime the Minister trusts that the Parliamentary Committee[33] of the S.T.U.C. will use their influence to support the unions in advising a return to work.'[34]

It was in vain for the S.T.U.C. to protest that the 'Scottish movement for a 40 Hours' Week is general and cannot be dealt with by individual employers' associations'.[35] Neither the unions nor the government in London showed the slightest sympathy for their case: '. . . the General Secretaries in London were strongly opposed to government action, [and] had used all their influence to prevent such intervention'.[36]

Government action was certainly being contemplated, but it was very different from what the strike leaders had in mind. On January 28th the War Cabinet considered the strike, but decided that for the meantime there was nothing for it to do:

'Sir Robert Horne [Minister of Labour] said that . . . the position was rendered extremely difficult as the Government could not actively interfere in the settlement of these strikes over the heads of the Union Executives . . .

The War Cabinet requested the Minister of Labour to give to the Press at the latest on the following day the full facts regarding the present unrest, laying stress on the unauthorised character of the strikes'[37]

The Cabinet was sufficiently alarmed by the events of the next two days, however, to take a more active part. On the

29th, a delegation of the strikers met the Lord Provost of Glasgow with their demands, which he undertook to transmit to the Government for their reply. (For which he was furiously assailed by the *Glasgow Herald*, on the grounds that he was giving in to the strikers' threats. In fact, his motive was to alert the government to the seriousness of the situation, as he saw it. The intransigence of the strikers' demands did this job admirably.) The telegram ran, in part:

'It was further stated [by the delegation of strikers] that they had hitherto adopted constitutional methods in urging their demand, but that failing consideration being given to their request by the government they would adopt any other methods which they might consider would be likely to advance their cause. They have, however, agreed to delay taking any such action until Friday in order that I may communicate your reply. I have just learnt from the manager of the electricity department that all men in generating stations have been compelled today to join the strike.'[38]

The Cabinet's reply to the request for intervention was to reiterate its flat refusal. But the Lord Provost's conjunction of the strikers' threats with the news of the total shutdown of electricity generation in the city (which was, in fact, untrue, although the Lord Provost probably wrote in good faith) alerted the War Cabinet to the risk of a serious threat to public order. Bonar Law telephoned to Lloyd George, who was at Versailles, about the Glasgow situation. Lloyd George said that he was prepared to come to London, but that he did not want to undermine Sir Robert Horne's authority. The War Cabinet therefore soldiered on without him. Bonar Law was the first to propose the use of troops in Glasgow to protect the 'volunteers' who might be found to run the municipal utilities. 'It was certain that if the movement in Glasgow grew, it would spread all over the country.' Most of the Cabinet agreed (an exception, interestingly, being Churchill, who thought that 'the moment for the use [of troops] had not yet arrived,' and advocated the use of the

Defence of the Realm Acts against the strike leaders).[39] Accordingly, they turned to discussing the reliability of different forces of order for such an occasion. The spectre of police strikes and army mutinies clearly loomed large behind the discussion. The Secretary for Scotland argued for sending in 2,000 special constables, who, he thought, would be more reliable than soldiers. Sir William Robertson presented a gloomy picture of the troops available in Scotland: '. . . all sorts of men, old, young, convalescents, and men with wounds. As regards the officers, they were not very efficient.' Nevertheless, it was agreed to hold the military 'in readiness to give their services when requested by the civil authorities', and to send a senior Scottish Office official to Glasgow to provide liaison between the local authority and the government.

No sooner had this official arrived in Glasgow than he was plunged into further trouble. On Friday, January 31st, a large crowd had assembled in Glasgow and was waiting in George Square, outside the City Chambers, to hear Bonar Law's answer to the Lord Provost's telegram. In order to clear a way for the tramcars on one side of the square, the police mounted a baton charge on the strikers and spectators on that side. Next, they proceeded to clear other sides of the square

'with a vigour and determination that was a prelude to the extraordinary scenes which the Square was afterwards to witness, and to which the city, with all its acquaintance with labour troubles, can happily offer no parallel. A strong body of police . . . swept the crowd in front of them, raining a hurricane of blows which fell indiscriminately on those actually participating in the strike and on those who had been drawn to the scene merely through curiosity'.[40]

This account is from the *Glasgow Herald*, a paper vociferously hostile to the strikers. It leaves no room for serious doubt that the riot on 'Bloody Friday', as the affair came to be known, was initiated by the behaviour of the police, not the strikers. A further point, not noticed at the time, is that the alleged reason for the baton charge was to clear the tramlines for traffic – but that after the first charge the police proceeded to turn up the east side of the square, next to the City Chambers, and then up a steep minor street opposite, neither of which contained any tramlines. It would be charitable to describe this as panic on the part of senior police officers; less charitable to call it a police riot, or a deliberate attempt to intimidate the strikers.

William Gallacher, at this time a leading shop steward but not yet a Communist, reacted to the *mêlée* not with revolutionary enthusiasm but with horror. Like most of the strike leaders, he was a pacific man who made militant speeches, not a tough-minded revolutionary. He shouted to the crowd to get out of the way of the police, to disperse, and to meet again on Glasgow Green. ' "Now, keep order. Understand that it has been a very unfortunate occurrence. March, for God's sake. Are you going to do that much for us?". (Cries of "Yes".)'[41]

The War Cabinet met again that afternoon, and the Minister of Labour informed them that

'he had no details, but understood that foot and mounted police had charged the crowd in order to quell a riot, and casualties had resulted.

The Secretary for Scotland said that in his opinion it was more clear than ever that it was a misnomer to call the situation in Glasgow a strike – it was a Bolshevist rising'.[42]

As steps had already been taken to move in the military forces – up to 12,000 troops, 100 motor lorries, and six tanks – the Cabinet had no further decisions to take. The first troops arrived at 10 p.m. the same day, and the rest arrived in the course of the weekend. By Monday morning the six tanks were stationed in the cattle market in the East End of Glasgow.

The rest of the history of the Forty Hours' Strike is anti-climax. The strikers began to drift back to work from about February 4th, as the effects of over a week with neither wages nor strike pay began to make themselves felt. The leaders of the strike – Gallacher, Emanuel Shinwell (at the time chairman of the Glasgow Trades Council), David Kirkwood and Harry Hopkins (district secretary of the A.S.E.) – had all been arrested on Bloody Friday, and no new leaders had been found to take their places. The only promise of sympathetic action from anywhere else in the country came from the London electricians, and they called off their proposed strike at the last minute although not before causing further alarm in the War Cabinet, which set up an Industrial Unrest Committee to deal with the situation. The Forty Hours' Strike was finally called off on February 12th. Later, the four leaders and eight others were tried at the High Court in Edinburgh on charges of incitement to riot and rioting. Eight of the defendants, including Hopkins and Kirkwood, were acquitted altogether; three, including Gallacher, were sentenced to three months' imprisonment each, and Shinwell was given five months.

How serious a threat to public order did the strike and Bloody Friday actually represent? The local press, the Lord Advocate, most of the War Cabinet, and the Special Branch all took the strike with the utmost seriousness. At the time of the strike leaders' trial, the *Glasgow Herald* commented:

'The tiresome and confused nature of much of the evidence was in significant contrast to the sinister simplicity of the main purpose which the whole case revealed . . . For the lightness of their sentences, they [Shinwell and Gallacher] have to thank, in the first place, the phlegm or hesitancy of the mass of those they led, and, in the second place, and more especially, the admirable self-restraint displayed by the civic and legal authorities and by the police force.

The formation of the Joint Strike Committee was . . . the first step towards that squalid terrorism which the world now describes as Bolshevism'.[43]

In his speech to the jury, presenting the Crown case, the Lord Advocate had said dramatically:

'The incidents on January 31st in George Square constituted the gravest imaginable menace to public order and security. There were not, thank Heaven, many incidents like them recorded in our time, and as incidents of that sort were not only in the highest degree criminal in themselves, but involved a menace to the foundation of public peace and security, he asked the jury by their verdict to express the guilt of those who instigated them . . . Every act of revolution was in progress, and could be traced to the previous incitement'.[44]

The result of the trial itself cast some doubt on this view: neither judge nor jury was persuaded that Bloody Friday was the culmination of a violent and illegal conspiracy. But it was a view which undoubtedly had a part in persuading the War Cabinet to take the strong action it did, because the whole tenor of the official intelligence reaching it was excitable and alarmist. A so-called 'Fortnightly Report on Revolutionary Organisations in the United Kingdom, and Morale in Foreign Countries'[45] was submitted to the War Cabinet by Basil Thomson, head of the Special Branch. Thomson (whose own assessment of the seriousness of the Forty Hours' Strike is printed at the head of this chapter) was Assistant Commissioner of the Metropolitan Police at the outbreak of war, when the activities of the C.I.D. had been combined with those of the Special Branch, so that Thomson found himself in charge of civilian intelligence relating to extremist political movements. (The Special Branch had been founded in the 1880s to deal with Irish terrorists, but its brief had been widened to deal with all sorts of political extremism.) Halfway through the War, Thomson's bailiwick was extended by his takeover of the intelligence services the Ministry of Munitions had built up to deal with labour unrest affecting munitions production. The Ministry, Thomson wrote somewhat smugly, 'came to the conclusion that the work would be more efficiently and more cheaply done by professionals, and I was called upon to take over the service with my own trained men'.[46] But Thomson's background as a policeman and (earlier) a colonial governor gave him no special insight into the nature of political extremism, and the quality of the information he supplied to the War Cabinet was often disastrously bad. It sometimes differed from the 'Red scares' of the popular press only in being printed on paper headed 'This Document is the Property of His Britannic Majesty's Government'. Indeed, one reason for the government's worse miscalculation of the labour situation in 1919 than in 1916 may be precisely that Thomson had taken over part of the intelligence service from the Ministry of Munitions. One of his wilder flights of fancy, for instance, was the notion that George Lansbury was the helpless dupe of a Bolshevik conspiracy:

'The wirepullers behind him have not yet been disclosed, but the plan is, by holding a series of revolutionary meetings in what is regarded as a stronghold of the capitalist class, the *Royal*[47] Albert Hall, to test the strength of the revolutionary movement and fan the temper of the London workers with a view of [sic] preparing for action of a much more serious character. With this object Lansbury was primed with the scheme of turning the weekly *Herald* into a daily paper'.[48]

He also gave advice on how to handle anti-Bolshevik propaganda:

'*Bolshevism in England.*
The Ministry of Information and the War Aims Committee are now circulating information on the state of Russia under the Bolshevik regime. It is to be hoped that when they are giving details about the Terror they will not lay too much stress on outrages committed on the bourgeoisie, a matter about which the English extremists will feel unsympathetic, but will give ample details, especially in the Sunday newspapers, of what working men have to suffer.
    . . . An exact translation of the word "Bolshevik" is, I am told, "out-and-outer".'[49]

Thomson's verdict on Bloody Friday itself was:

'The plan of the revolutionary minority was to use the Clyde as the touchstone of a general strike and, if it proved to be successful, to bring out the engineers and the railways all over the country, to seize the food and to achieve a revolution. The scheme failed . . . It is now known that during the disorder on Friday, January 31st, the intention was to seize the Municipal Buildings in Glasgow, but the police were too strong for them'.[50]

In January 1919 revolution seemed to be looming all over Europe. The Spartacist revolt in Berlin against the social-democratic regime there had been bloodily suppressed: Bavaria was degenerating into anarchy as various sections of the socialist parties fought for control. A Communist regime in Hungary lay only two months in the future. Above all, the Bolshevik regime in Russia appeared to be a very special kind of threat. So it is small wonder that the Cabinet reacted with nervous alarm to reports like Thomson's rather than to the cooler counsels of (for instance) Tom Jones, Deputy Secretary to the Cabinet. Jones wrote in a memorandum to Lloyd George: 'Bolshevik propaganda in this country is only dangerous in so far as it can lodge itself in the soil of genuine grievances . . . A definite reiteration by yourself of the government's determination to push forward with an advanced social programme is the best antidote.'[51]

One of the points on which alarmist views like those of Thomson and the *Glasgow Herald* were most consistently wrong was the degree of revolutionary purpose behind the strike. The C.W.C. was only one of the patrons of the strike; others, such as the S.T.U.C., could not possibly be accused of revolutionary tendencies. And even the most militant strike leaders had no very clear idea of what they wanted to do. Gallacher, for instance, writing in 1936 as an orthodox Communist, is explicitly self-critical for his lack of revolutionary purpose in 1919:

'Had we been capable of planning beforehand, or had there been an experienced revolutionary leadership of these great and heroic masses, instead of a march to Glasgow Green there would have been a march to Maryhill Barracks . . . If we had gone there we could easily have persuaded the soldiers to come out, and Glasgow would have been in our hands'.[52]

As we have seen, Gallacher's actual reaction to the riot was more that of a shocked pacifist than that of a dedicated revolutionary. The one strike leader who perhaps had more robust ideas was Emanuel Shinwell, who had been much the most outspoken in his speeches to 'mass pickets' at factory gates. 'When the workers in the power station knew that the strikers insisted on their participation, he believed they would not be at work in the morning. At the same time he recommended the police to take a holiday.'[53] Shortly before Bloody Friday, according to Gallacher, 'Manny had made a suggestion of a pretty desperate nature'.[54] If the suggestion was, in fact, that the workers should seize the City Chambers, then the behaviour of Gallacher and the other principals on the Friday was extremely good dissembling. It is much more likely that it was a plan to sabotage the electricity supply because the workers at one power station had not struck. But, whatever it was, it was not done. And in any case Shinwell was no revolutionary. He was one of those who had fought for a 40-hours, not a 30-hours strike, and he was an outspoken opponent of revolutionary speakers on the Glasgow Trades Council. His intention was surely to provoke government intervention in the strikers' favour; the result was government intervention, but of a sort very different from what he had expected.

It is worth reviewing the fundamental weaknesses of the 40 Hours' Strike. In spite of the involvement of the S.T.U.C., hardly any union gave it official backing. Only the Electricians and two small moulders' unions were giving strike pay, and the A.S.E. was totally hostile—in sharp contrast with its connivance at the dilution strikes of 1916. No serious attempt was made to spread the strike outside Glasgow, and no sympathetic action followed elsewhere. Wartime resentments between skilled and unskilled men had by no means died down, and the unskilled men were suspicious at what seemed to them another craftsmen's strike. Two key 'unskilled' unions failed to join in: the Scottish Horse and Motormen's Association, and the Municipal Employees' Association, the union which organised the tramwaymen and the workers at the one power station which continued to work throughout the strike.

The strike movement of January 1919 was the final fling of the C.W.C., and it might be argued that its failure to reappear after the end of the Forty Hours' Strike justified the government's firm stand. But this would be to ignore the catalogue of structural weaknesses just cited. The strike would certainly have collapsed, and discredited unofficial action, without any help from the government. Indeed, the net effect of the tanks in the cattle market was probably the same as that of the police misbehaviour in George Square: it gave the strike a romantic history which concealed, more or less successfully, an otherwise ignominious failure.

The Forty Hours' Strike ushered in a period of extreme government concern about industrial unrest, which lasted until the breakdown of the Triple Alliance of miners, railwaymen, and transport workers in April 1921. The most vivid account of ministers' anxieties at this time shows that they were continually obsessed with the problem and turning to unlikely remedies. In February 1920, for instance, Lloyd George raised with Sir Hugh Trenchard (the Chief of Air Staff) the question of the availability of the R.A.F. to deal with labour unrest. 'Trenchard replied that . . . the pilots had no weapons for ground fighting. The P.M. presumed they could use machine guns and drop bombs.' At the same meeting, 'Bonar Law so often referred to the stockbrokers as a loyal and fighting class until [sic] one felt that potential battalions of stockbrokers were to be found in every town.'[55] A similar concern about a possible breakdown in public order was paramount in Ministers' minds during the weeks leading up to the threatened Triple Alliance strike in April 1921.[56] One tangible result of this concern was the innocuously named Supply and Transport Committee. In February 1919 the War Cabinet set up an Industrial Unrest Committee which, after two changes of name, became the Supply and Transport Committee. This was reduced to a skeleton organisation after the failure of the railwaymen and the transport workers to join the striking miners on 15th April, 1921, which led to the collapse of the Triple Alliance. But it was never entirely disbanded, even by the 1924 Labour Government, and it had its day in 1926, when it was the government's means of organising supplies during the General Strike.

The Committee was at its most alarmist right at the beginning, in the shadow of the Forty Hours' Strike. On 17th February, 1919, it was reported that 40,000 lorries and 100,000 motor cars had been earmarked for use in the event of a strike. In March, the Committee drafted a Strikes (Exceptional Measures) Bill which would have empowered the government, *inter alia*, to arrest trade union leaders and to prevent unions from drawing on their strike funds by declaring a bank holiday. The proposal was too much even for the Cabinet of 1919, which turned it down.[57]

The Committee also turned its hand to political propaganda. During the 1921 crisis, for instance:

'Briefs for the use of speakers and writers, but bearing no indication of their official origin, were issued two or three times a week during the critical period, and were distributed to about 1200 people through the good offices of the following Organisations: the Central Unionist Association, the Coalition Liberal Organisation, the British Commonwealth Union, the National Political League, the Middle Classes Union, and the Women's Guild of Empire'.[58]

Admiral Sir Reginald Hall, the recently retired Director of Naval Intelligence, had earlier been helping the Committee by distributing propaganda through an unofficial (and secret) body called National Propaganda.[59] Like others mentioned in this account, Hall saw nothing improper in the identification of the national interest with the interests of the government of the day – provided that it was not a Labour one. His (probable) behaviour in the Zinoviev letter affair in 1924 presents an instructive contrast with his eagerness to help the Supply and Transport Committee in 1920.[60]

When the Committee's arrangements were reviewed by the first Labour Government, in 1924, the minister responsible (Josiah Wedgwood) commented: 'There has been an almost melodramatic air of secrecy about the whole business, as though a revolution were being combated, rather than a straightforward effort made to keep the essential services going'.[61] If the Labour Government had seen their predecessors' Cabinet papers, they would have been impressed by the extent to which members of the Committee did think they were trying to combat a revolution. However, the MacDonald government continued the pruning of the Committee's powers which had been begun under Bonar Law and Baldwin, and left as its central feature the power to appoint a Chief Civil Commissioner (a Cabinet minister) and his eleven regional deputies (who were to be junior ministers). These officials were to be responsible for the maintenance of essential services in an emergency.

When the prospect of a general strike began to loom in 1925, the Baldwin government had only to put this machinery into action. The Committee's attitude was much cooler and less feverish than in 1921, even though it was chaired by Sir William Joynson-Hicks,[62] and its machinery went smoothly into operation on 2nd May, 1926. It was a far cry from Sir Basil Thomson, and still further from Red Clydeside. Nonetheless, Red Clydeside played its part in the foundation of the Supply and Transport Committee. If the Forty Hours' Strike has had an enduring impact on history, it is as one of the catalysts of that committee, not as the harbinger of revolution.

Notes

1. (Sir) Basil Thomson, *Queer People* (London, 1922), p. 276.
2. W. Gallacher, *Revolt of the Clyde* (London, 1936), p. 234. Emphasis in original.
3. *History of the Ministry of Munitions* (London, n.d.), vol. IV; J. Hinton, 'The Clyde Workers' Committee and the Dilution Struggle', in *Essays in Labour History, 1886–1923*, edited by A. Briggs and J. Saville (London, 1971); I. S. McLean, 'The Ministry of Munitions, the Clyde Workers' Committee, and the suppression of the *Forward:* An Alternative View', *Scottish Labour History Society Journal*, no. 6, December 1972.
4. Ministry of Munitions papers at the Public Record Office, MUN 5/73. Report by J. Paterson, Chief Labour Officer, Ministry of Munitions, Glasgow, 18th December, 1915, in file marked 'Material supplied to the Minister before Tyne and Clyde visits'.
5. MUN 5/73. Commission on Dilution of Labour on the Clyde. Memorandum on the Progress of the Commission by Mr Lynden Macassey, 5th February, 1916.
6. Quoted in, for example, W. R. Scott and J. Cunnison, *The Industries of the Clyde Valley during the War* (Oxford, 1924), p. 210.
7. MUN 5/73. Causes of unrest among munition workers on the Clyde and Tyne, by Lynden Macassey, 18th December, 1915.
8. For further details of which see T. Brotherstone, 'The Suppression of the *Forward*', *Scottish Labour History Society Journal*, no. 1, May 1969; McLean, *op. cit.*
9. MUN 5/73. The Industrial Situation on the Clyde. Memorandum (incomplete) by Lynden Macassey, 9th February, 1916.
10. Beveridge Collection on Munitions, British Library of Political and Economic Science, vol. III, ff. 355–8. I. H. Mitchell to Sir H. Llewellyn Smith, 21st February, 1916.
11. Manifesto from the Parkhead Forge Engineers to their Fellow-workers. Highton Collection, Glasgow University Department of Economic History. Also in Scott and Cunnison, *op. cit.*, pp. 215–6.
12. C. Addison, *Politics from Within*, 2 vols (London, 1924), vol. I, p. 191.
13. See, for example, *History of the Ministry of Munitions*, 12 vols. in parts (London, n.d.), vol. IV part iv, p. 130; (Sir) Lynden Macassey, *Labour Policy, False and True* (London, 1922), p. 79.
14. Addison, *loc. cit.*
15. From Lord Crewe's letter to the King reporting the meeting. Public Record Office, CAB 37/144. Reproduced from the original in the Royal Archives.
16. See, for example, Crewe to Lloyd George, 3rd April, 1916. Lloyd George Papers, Beaverbrook Library, London. D/16/9.
17. Labour Party, *Report . . . [on] the Deportation . . . of David Kirkwood and other workmen employed in Munitions Factories in the Clyde District* (London, 1918).
18. Labour Party, *op. cit.*, para. 31.
19. CAB 23/3. War Cabinet 207 of 8th August, 1917. Cf. also CAB 24/22, OT 1625 of 6th August, 1917: Memorandum of Robert Munro (Secretary for Scotland) on the Proposed Prohibition of a Meeting at Glasgow.

20. Extracts from the Minutes of the Glasgow Trades Council, 15th August, 1917. Mitchell Library, Glasgow.
21. CAB 24/44. J. S. Ewart to Secretary, War Office, enclosed as appendix to GT 3838 of 7th March, 1918: 'Revolutionary Agitation in Glasgow and Clydeside with special reference to the cases of John Maclean and others'.
22. CAB 23/5. War Cabinet no. 364, 12th March, 1918.
23. CAB 23/42. Imperial War Cabinet 39 of 28th November, 1918; cf. also CAB 24/70. GT 6379 of 26th November, 1918.
24. Daily Record and Mail (Glasgow), 4th December, 1918.
25. W. F. H. Kendall, The Revolutionary Movement in Britain, 1900–1921 (London, 1969), p. 132.
26. Newbold was a Quaker turned Communist who became, briefly, Communist M.P. for Motherwell (1923–4).
27. Autobiographical TS material (unsorted) in Walton Newbold MSS, Manchester University Library.
28. S.T.U.C. Annual Report, 1918, p. 37.
29. A.S.E. Monthly Journal and Report, December 1918, p. 18.
30. A.S.E. Statement by suspended Glasgow District Committee, February 1919, with request for reinstatement. Highton Papers, Glasgow University Department of Economic History.
31. S.T.U.C. Annual Report 1919, p. 44.
32. Glasgow Herald, 28th January, 1919, p. 5; 29th January, 1919, p. 7.
33. (i.e. Executive).
34. Quoted in S.T.U.C. Minutes of the Parliamentary Committee, 27th January, 1919.
35. Ibid.
36. Ibid. 8th January, 1919.
37. CAB 23/9. War Cabinet no. 521, 28th January, 1919.
38. CAB 23/9. War Cabinet no. 522, 30th January, 1919.
39. All quotations in this paragraph are from CAB 23/9: War Cabinet 522 of 30th January, 1919. It may seem surprising that Churchill, 'the man who sent troops to Tonypandy', the scourge of the workers, the future editor of the British Gazette, should have been counselling moderation, but Churchill seems to have been consistently less agitated about the home front at this time than were most of his colleagues. Cf. Sir Maurice Hankey to Tom Jones, 17th January, 1920: 'The ministers . . . seem to have the "wind-up" to the most extraordinary extent about the industrial situation. C.I.G.S. also is positively in a state of dreadful nerves on the subject. Churchill is the only one who is sane on this subject, and on the subject of Denekin he is a nuisance.' T. Jones, Whitehall Diary, vol. I (ed. Middlemas, London, 1969), p. 97.
40. Glasgow Herald, 1st February, 1919.
41. Daily Record, 1st February, 1919.
42. CAB 23/9. War Cabinet 523. 31st January, 1919.
43. Glasgow Herald, 19th April, 1919.
44. Ibid., 18th April, 1919.
45. Originally 'Fortnightly Report on Pacifism and Revolutionary Organisations in the United Kingdom'. They were not quite fortnightly (sometimes more frequent, sometimes less); not all of them appear to have reached the GT series of Cabinet papers in CAB 24.

46. Thomson, *op. cit.*, p. 269.
47. Emphasis in original.
48. *Fortnightly Report* . . . 2nd December, 1918. GT 6425. CAB 24/71.
49. *Ibid.*, 21st October, 1918. GT 6079. CAB 24/67.
50. *Ibid.*, 10th February, 1919. GT 6816. CAB 24/75.
51. Jones to Lloyd George, 8th February, 1919. Jones, *op. cit.*, pp. 73–4.
52. Gallacher, *op. cit.*, pp. 233–4.
53. *Daily Record and Mail*, 30th January, 1919.
54. W. Gallacher, *Last Memoirs* (London, 1966), pp. 123–4. Earlier accounts of the same meeting are more reticent: neither T. Bell, *Pioneering Days* (London, 1941), nor Gallacher's *Revolt on the Clyde* names Shinwell in this context, although both refer to him.
55. Jones, *op. cit.*, pp. 99–101. Lloyd George's comment may have been sarcastic: Jones thought that 'the P.M. did a lot of unsuspected leg-pulling as he does not believe in the imminence of the revolution' (p. 103). But Bonar Law, Long, the Geddes brothers, and other ministers were in deadly earnest.
56. Jones, *op. cit.*, pp. 131–50.
57. Industrial Unrest Committee, 14th March, 1919: CAB 27/59. War Cabinet, 19th March, 1919: CAB 23/15. The Cabinet discussion was recorded in the separate 'A' series of secret minutes, which were duplicated instead of being printed because of fears as to the loyalty of the printers.
58. CAB 27/75. Meeting of the Supply and Transport Committee, 23rd July, 1921 (but reporting on activities during April 1921).
59. CAB 27/84. Supply and Transport Committee: Propaganda Sub-Committee, 9th March, 1920.
60. L. Chester, S. Fay and H. Young, *The Zinoviev Letter* (London, 1967), Ch. 8 present strong circumstantial evidence that Hall tipped off the *Daily Mail* about the value of the Zinoviev letter as a stick with which to beat the outgoing Labour Government during the 1924 election campaign. Although an ex-intelligence man, Hall did not consider, or was prepared to ignore, the likelihood of the letter's being a forgery.
61. CAB 27/259. Supply and Transport Organisation: Emergency Committee, February–March 1924.
62 'Jix', as Home Secretary from 1924 to 1929, was responsible for the prosecution of leading Communists under the Incitement to Mutiny Act, 1797, in October 1925, and for the raid on the Soviet trading company in London, Arcos, in 1927 in an abortive search for subversive documents.

For Product Safety Concerns and Information please contact our EU
representative GPSR@taylorandfrancis.com
Taylor & Francis Verlag GmbH, Kaufingerstraße 24, 80331 München, Germany

www.ingramcontent.com/pod-product-compliance
Lightning Source LLC
Chambersburg PA
CBHW070404270326
41926CB00014B/2692

9 781032 033594